# AVENGERS

## SOLO AVENGERS CLASSIC

SOLO AVENGERS CLASSIC VOL. 1

**WRITERS:**
TOM DEFALCO, ROGER STERN, DENNIS MALLONEE, DAN MISHKIN, BOB LAYTON, JACKSON GUICE, MIKE W. BARR, J.M. DEMATTEIS, D.G. CHICHESTER & MARGARET CLARK

**PENCILERS:**
MARK BRIGHT, JIM LEE, KIERON DWYER, BOB HALL, RON LIM, PAUL RYAN, JOHN RIDGWAY, TOM GRINDBERG, JACKSON GUICE, LARRY ALEXANDER, JUNE BRIGMAN & LEE WEEKS

**INKERS:**
JOSEF RUBINSTEIN, AL WILLIAMSON, BOB MCLEOD, STAN DRAKE, BOB LAYTON, JOHN RIDGWAY, JOSÉ MARZAN JR. & LEE WEEKS

**COLORISTS:**
KEN FEDUNIEWICZ, PAUL BECTON, GREGORY WRIGHT, JANET JACKSON & STEVE BUCCELLATO

**LETTERERS:**
JACK MORELLI & BILL OAKLEY

**EDITOR:**
MARK GRUENWALD

**FRONT COVER ARTISTS:**
JACKSON GUICE, BOB LAYTON & TOM CHU

**BACK COVER ARTISTS:**
MARK BRIGHT, JOE RUBINSTEIN & TOM SMITH

**COLLECTION EDITOR:**
NELSON RIBEIRO

**ASSISTANT EDITOR:**
ALEX STARBUCK

**EDITORS, SPECIAL PROJECTS:**
MARK D. BEAZLEY
& JENNIFER GRÜNWALD

**SENIOR EDITOR, SPECIAL PROJECTS:**
JEFF YOUNGQUIST

**RESEARCH & LAYOUT:**
JACOB ROUGEMONT & JEPH YORK

**SENIOR VICE PRESIDENT OF SALES:**
DAVID GABRIEL

**SVP OF BRAND PLANNING & COMMUNICATIONS:**
MICHAEL PASCIULLO

**EDITOR IN CHIEF:**
AXEL ALONSO

**CHIEF CREATIVE OFFICER:**
JOE QUESADA

**PUBLISHER:**
DAN BUCKLEY

**EXECUTIVE PRODUCER:**
ALAN FINE

**AVENGERS: SOLO AVENGERS CLASSIC VOL. 1.** Contains material originally published in magazine form as SOLO AVENGERS #1-10. First printing 2012. ISBN# 978-0-7851-5903-2. Published by MARVEL WORLDWIDE, INC., a subsidiary of MARVEL ENTERTAINMENT, LLC. OFFICE OF PUBLICATION: 135 West 50th Street, New York, NY 10020.  **Printed in the U.S.A.** ALAN FINE, EVP - Office of the President, Marvel Worldwide, Inc. and EVP & CMO Marvel Characters B.V.; DAN BUCKLEY, Publisher & President - Print, Animation & Digital Divisions; JOE QUESADA, Chief Creative Officer; DAVID BOGART, SVP of Business Affairs & Talent Management; TOM BREVOORT, SVP of Publishing; C.B. CEBULSKI, SVP of Creator & Content Development; DAVID GABRIEL, SVP of Publishing Sales & Circulation; MICHAEL PASCIULLO, SVP of Brand Planning & Communications; JIM O'KEEFE, VP of Operations & Logistics; DAN CARR, Executive Director of Publishing Technology; SUSAN CRESPI, Editorial Operations Manager; ALEX MORALES, Publishing Operations Manager; STAN LEE, Chairman Emeritus. For information regarding advertising in Marvel Comics or on Marvel.com, please contact John Dokes, SVP Integrated Sales and Marketing, at jdokes@marvel.com. For Marvel subscription inquiries, please call 800-217-9158. **Manufactured between 12/14/2011 and 1/9/2012 by R.R. DONNELLEY, INC., SALEM, VA, USA.**

10 9 8 7 6 5 4 3 2 1

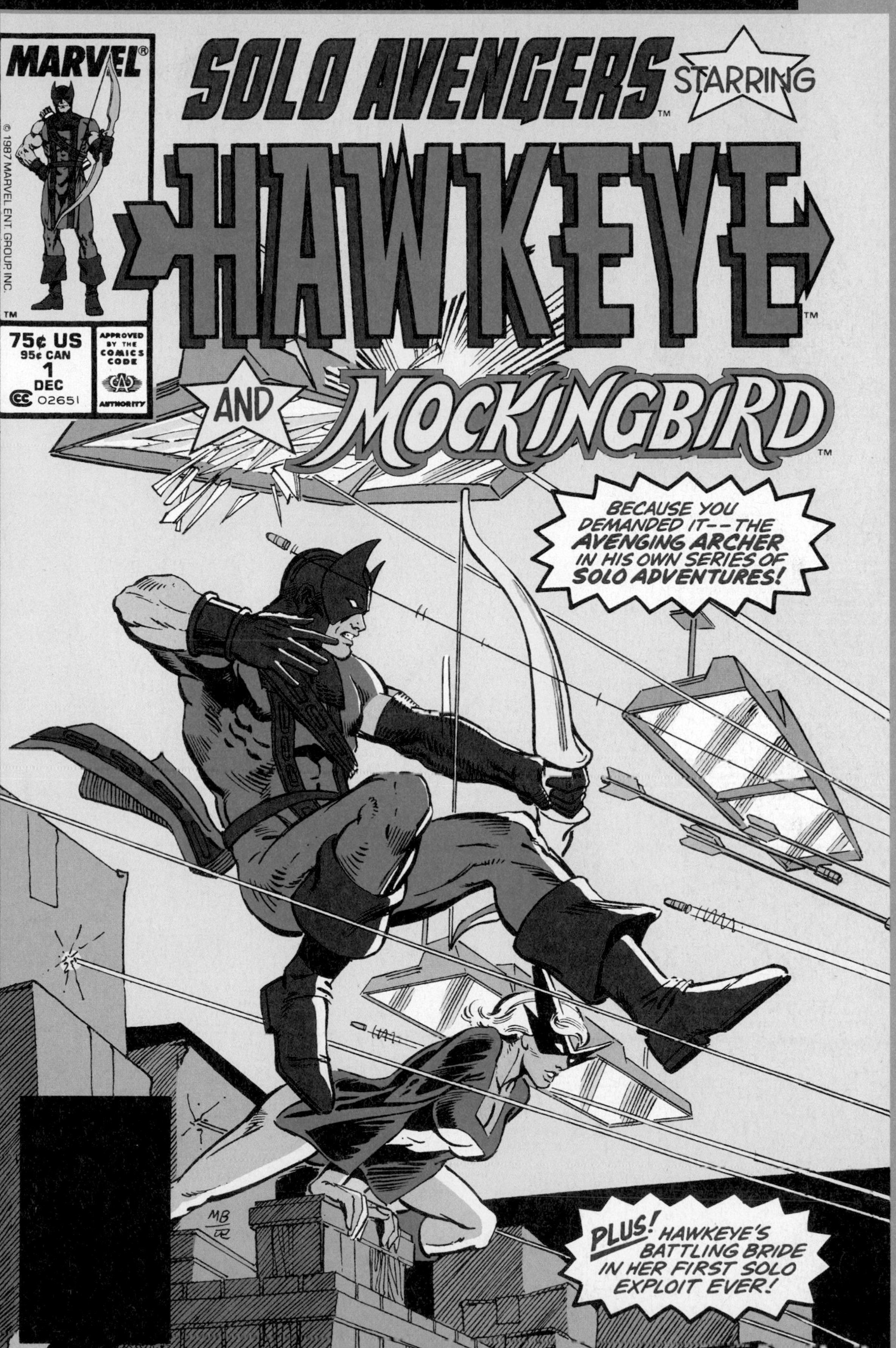
MARVEL®
SOLO AVENGERS™ STARRING
HAWKEYE™
AND
MOCKINGBIRD™
© 1987 MARVEL ENT. GROUP INC.
75¢ US
95¢ CAN
1
DEC
02651
APPROVED BY THE COMICS CODE AUTHORITY
BECAUSE YOU DEMANDED IT--THE AVENGING ARCHER IN HIS OWN SERIES OF SOLO ADVENTURES!
PLUS! HAWKEYE'S BATTLING BRIDE IN HER FIRST SOLO EXPLOIT EVER!

STAN LEE PRESENTS:
HERE COMES HAWKEYE
YOU CLOWNS DON'T STAND A CHANCE AGAINST ME!
AT LAST! THE MOST POPULAR WEST COAST AVENGER IN HIS VERY OWN ACTION-PACKED SERIES!!
I'VE BEATEN YOU BEFORE-- AND I'LL DO IT AGAIN!
THEY DON'T CALL ME THE WORLD'S GREATEST ARCHER FOR NOTHING!
CAUTION:
THRILLS LIKE THESE COULD BECOME HABIT-FORMING!

TOM DeFALCO WRITER · MARK BRIGHT PENCILER · JOE RUBINSTEIN FINISHED ART · JACK MORELLI LETTERER · KEN FEDUNIEWICZ COLORIST · MARK GRUENWALD EDITOR · TOM DeFALCO KAHUNA

GO AHEAD, JUMP AROUND ALL YOU LIKE!
KEEP TRYING TO DISTRACT ME!
ANY BETS I STILL NAIL THREE FOR THREE?

H-HE DID IT, AGAIN! THREE BULLSEYES!
THE GUY'S UNBELIEVABLE!
C'MON! WE'VE STILL GOT ONE MORE ROUTINE TO PRACTICE!

THIS IS GOING TO BE SOME SHOW, MOCKINGBIRD! I WISH I COULD SEE THE REAL THING TONIGHT!
AT LEAST YOU MADE THE DRESS REHEARSAL, WONDER MAN!

WHERE DOES YOUR GUY FIND THE TIME TO VOLUNTEER FOR THESE SPECIAL BENEFIT PERFORMANCES? YOU'D THINK HE'D HAVE HIS HANDS FULL RUNNING THE WEST COAST AVENGERS!

WELL, THE PROCEEDS FROM THIS PARTICULAR EXHIBITION WILL BE DONATED TO A LOCAL ORPHANAGE--

"--AND HAWKEYE STILL REMEMBERS THE DAYS WHEN HE AND HIS BROTHER BARNEY WERE STUCK IN ONE!
"AS YOU KNOW, THEY EVENTUALLY RAN AWAY--

"--AND ENDED UP AT A TRAVELING CARNIVAL!
"THAT'S WHERE HE FIRST MET THE SWORDSMAN--

"--WHO TOOK HAWK UNDER HIS WING, GAVE HIM HIS FIRST BOW--
"--AND RELENTLESSLY TRAINED HIM TO BECOME THE GREATEST TRICK-SHOOTER OF ALL!"

I'VE HEARD THAT STORY BEFORE... AND ONE THING HAS ALWAYS PUZZLED ME!
WHY DID THE SWORDSMAN TEACH HAWK ARCHERY!?
YO, MOCK!

WE'RE OUT OF HERE, LADY!
I'M FREE UNTIL SHOW TIME!
SEE YOU TONIGHT, HAWKEYE!

MOMENTS LATER...
YOU'RE GOING TO KNOCK 'EM DEAD TONIGHT, HAWKEYE!
BREAK A LEG!
THANKS... I THINK!
WE'LL MEET YOU BACK AT THE AVENGERS COMPOUND!

TOO BAD NONE OF THE OTHER AVENGERS CAN CATCH MY SHOW TONIGHT!
THEY DON'T KNOW WHAT THEY'RE MISSING!
SIMMER DOWN, SUPERSTAR. I'VE GOT A QUESTION ABOUT THE SWORDSMAN! WHY DID HE--

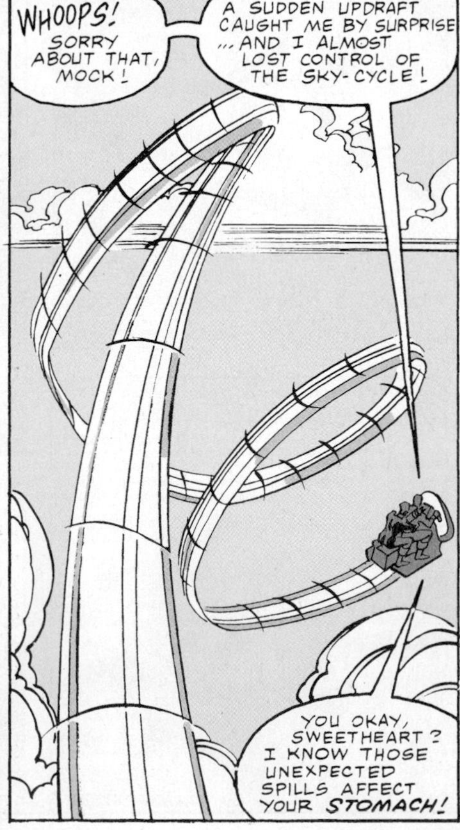
WHOOPS! SORRY ABOUT THAT, MOCK!
A SUDDEN UPDRAFT CAUGHT ME BY SURPRISE ...AND I ALMOST LOST CONTROL OF THE SKY-CYCLE!
YOU OKAY, SWEETHEART? I KNOW THOSE UNEXPECTED SPILLS AFFECT YOUR STOMACH!

I... I'M J-JUST D-DUCKY!
THERE THEY GO! GUESS IT'S TIME FOR ME TO CHECK IN WITH THE BOSS MAN!

SOMETIME LATER...

INCOMING--!
LOOK ALIVE, YOU LUNKHEADS! THOSE ARROWS ARE RAZOR-SHARP!

BIG DEAL! THEY CAN'T PENETRATE OUR STEEL ARM PROTECTORS!
ME AN' ARNIE GOT OPEN SHOTS AT THE TARGET!
WELL, TAKE 'EM, AND DON'T MISS!

SCRATCH ONE CEMENT STATUE!
AW, SHOOT! THE BOSS WASN'T EVEN LOOKIN'!!

I WENT TO THE LOS ANGELES COLISEUM AS YOU ORDERED!
THE ARCHER WAS THERE-- AND HE'S DEFINITELY PLANNING TO BE TONIGHT'S FEATURED ATTRACTION.
GOOD! MY ASSASSINS ARE ALL TRAINED AND READY FOR A REAL BATTLE! TREAT THE RUBES TO A SHOW THEY'LL NEVER FORGET!

I AM ANXIOUS TO SEE HOW GOOD HAWKEYE HAS BECOME OVER THE YEARS! IT'S BEEN A LONG--A VERY LONG TIME SINCE I LAST SAW HIM!
HE OWES ME A DEBT WHICH CAN ONLY BE PAID IN BLOOD!!

A FEW HOURS LATER...
LOS ANGEL
MEMORIAL
COLISEUM

HEY, YOU GUYS SHOULD SEE THE CROWD OUT THERE!
WE'RE TALKING FULL HOUSE!
CLOSE THE DOOR, MANNY--AND GIVE THE REST OF US A CHANCE TO GET DRESSED!

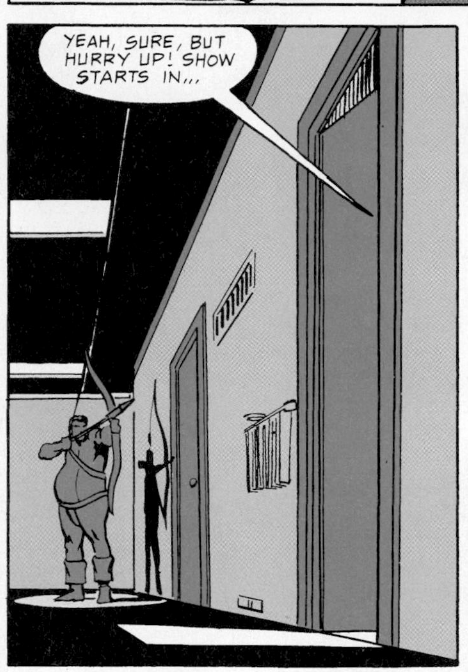
YEAH, SURE, BUT HURRY UP! SHOW STARTS IN...

...FIFTEEN MINUTES...
WHAT THE HECK IS--

--THATTTT--
UHN

LADIES AND GENTLEMEN! CHILDREN OF ALL AGES! THE MANAGEMENT OF THE LOS ANGELES VETERANS MEMORIAL COLISEUM IS PROUD TO PRESENT--
HAWKEYE THE AVENGING ARCHER!!

YAHOO! WAY TO GO, AVENGER!
C'MON, GUYS, LET'S SHOW THESE PEOPLE A LITTLE ACTION!
HEY! GET IN POSITION! YOU'RE NOT ANYWHERE NEAR THE TARGETS!

WRONG, PALLY! THE ONLY TARGET AROUND HERE -- IS YOU!
ICE HIM, ELMO!

HEY!!
WHAT'S WITH THE BAZOOKA?!
KA-BWAM!

THROWN FROM HIS HORSE, HAWKEYE INSTINCTIVELY NOTCHES TWO ARROWS AS HE ROLLS TO SAFETY, AND THEN--
COOL IT, FELLAS! I DON'T MIND A FEW AD LIBS -- BUT LET'S NOT GET RIDICULOUS!!

YOU'RE GOING TO HAVE TO DO BETTER THAN *THAT*, AVENGER!
*YEAH!* WE KNOW ALL OF YOUR TRICKS! ALL YOUR DEFENSES!

YEOW!
THEY'RE USING *LACROSSE*-LIKE GIZMOS TO HURL IVORY BALLS AT ME! I CAN'T AVOID THEM OUT HERE!

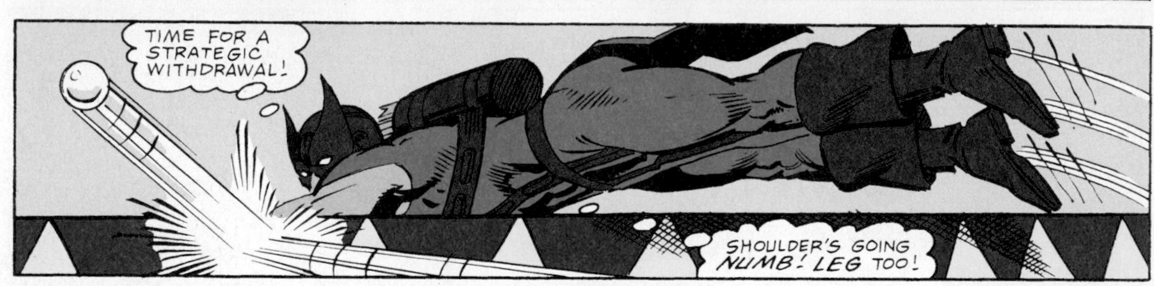
TIME FOR A STRATEGIC WITHDRAWAL!
SHOULDER'S GOING *NUMB!* *LEG* TOO!

SOMETHING'S GONE WRONG! *REAL WRONG!* THESE JOKERS ARE FIGHTING *FOR REAL!* AND THEY'RE MAKING ME LOOK BAD IN FRONT OF MY ADORING PUBLIC!
WELL, *NO MORE!*

EAT SOME ARROW, WISE GUYS!
FWIP
YOU'RE ABOUT TO LEARN *FIRSTHAND* THE REASONS WHY THEY CALL ME AN AVENGER!
PAY ATTENTION NOW! THERE WILL BE A QUIZ LATER!

HA! YA AIN'T AS GOOD AS YER REP, ARCHER!
THWOOP

YA MISSED US!!

DID I?
BWAK
BOING!

TWHIIIP

COUGH!
CHOKE!
PWOMP

FWOKK

PWAMM

ELSEWHERE AT THAT VERY MOMENT...
IT TOOK ME A LOT LONGER TO GET HERE THAN I PLANNED! I'M CERTAIN I'VE MISSED THE FIRST ACT BY NOW!
REST ROOMS
DRESSING ROOMS
MAY AS WELL MEET HAWK IN HIS DRESSING--

--ROOM?!
THOSE ARE THE MEN HAWK'S SUPPOSED TO BE SPARRING WITH! THEY'VE OBVIOUSLY BEEN DRUGGED!
WHAT'S THAT ON THE FLOOR?

A GAS ARROW! I DON'T RECOGNIZE THE DESIGN! IT CAN'T BELONG TO HAWK!
WHAT'S GOING ON?

MEANWHILE!
WAHOO! WHAT A SHOW!
THE WAY THEY'RE GOING AT IT, YOU'D BELIEVE IT'S A REAL FIGHT!
LOOKS LIKE WE'RE COMING DOWN TO THE GRAND FINALE!

IT'S ALL OVER, AVENGER! THERE'S NOWHERE TO RUN! NOWHERE TO HIDE!
WE CAN PICK YOU OFF AT OUR LEISURE NOW!
UNG! MY LEFT SHOULDER AND LEG ARE KILLING ME! BUT I CAN'T LET THEM KNOW IT!

YOU DID WELL IN THE EARLY ROUNDS, BUT IT WAS ONLY A MATTER OF TIME!
OUR SUPERIOR NUMBERS AND SKILL OVERWHELMED YOU!
YOU'RE TOTALLY DEFENSELESS WITHOUT YOUR BOW!

I'VE GOT A FLASH FOR YOU, MISTER!
A TRAINED FIGHTING MAN IS NEVER DEFENSLESS!
HE ALWAYS HAS WITS AND HIS REFLEXES TO FALL BACK ON!

MY SPECIALTY IS HURLING PROJECTILES! I USUALLY USE A BOW TO DO SO--

--BUT THAT DOESN'T MEAN I'M ANY LESS ACCURATE, OR DEADLY, BY HAND!

'NUFF SAID?

WISH I KNEW WHAT THIS ATTACK WAS ALL ABOUT!
THE CROWD'S GOING WILD! THEY THINK THIS IS JUST THE WAY WE REHEARSED IT!
WHAT DO I DO FOR AN ENCORE?!

HAWKEYE!
SOMEONE BEHIND ME!
YOU!!

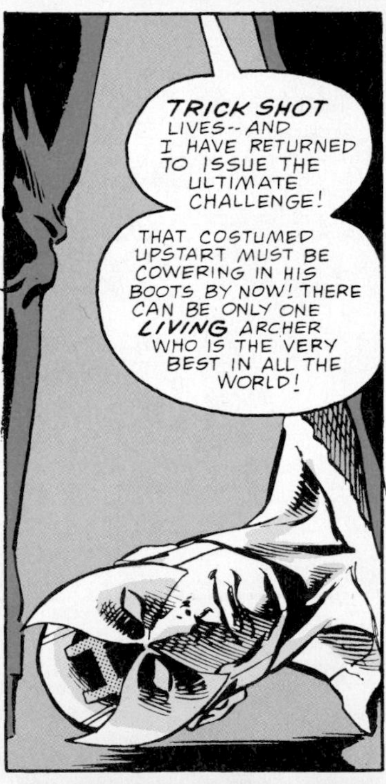

NEXT THE REAL ORIGIN OF HAWKEYE

LISTEN TO THE MOCKINGBIRD
TOM DeFALCO WRITER
JIM LEE PENCILS
AL WILLIAMSON INKS
JACK MORELLI LETTERS
KEN FEDUNIEWICZ COLORS
HAWKEYE'S GOING TO FREAK OUT! I'M LATE, LATE, LATE FOR HIS BIG SHOW AT THE LOS ANGELES COLISEUM!
IT'S NOT MY FAULT! I NEVER EXPECTED TO RUN INTO A TRAFFIC JAM AT THIS TIME OF DAY!
WAIT'LL I TELL THE WIFE! I'VE HAD FARES RUN OUT ON ME BEFORE -- BUT NEVER QUITE LIKE THIS!
OHMIGOSH! IT'S THAT AVENGERS LADY!
WHATSHERNAME! THE ONE MARRIED TO THE GUY WITH THE ARROWS!
OFF TAXI DUTY

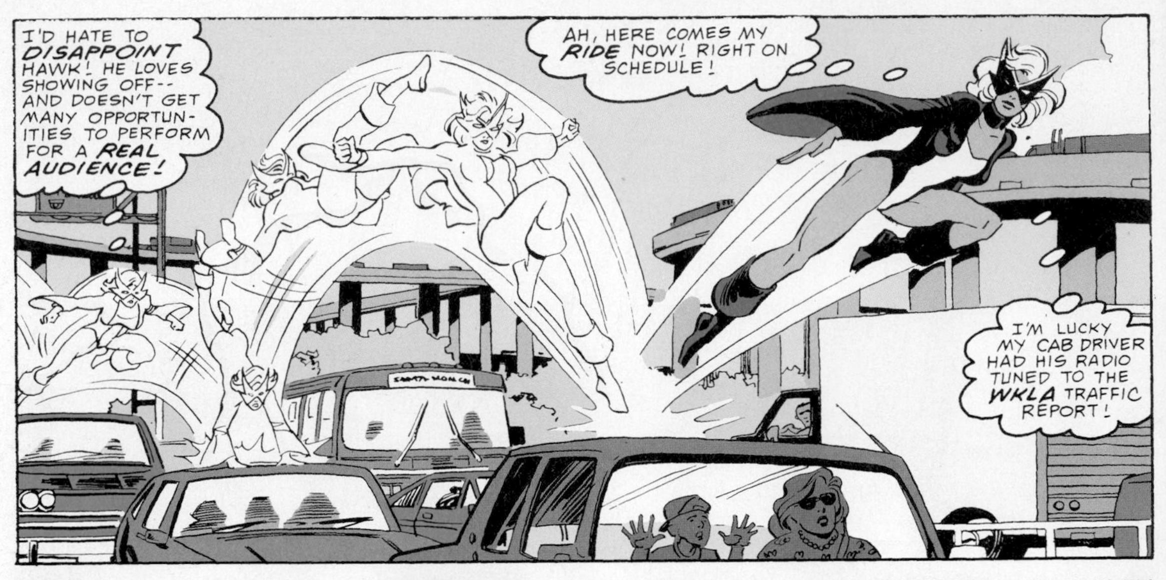
I'D HATE TO DISAPPOINT HAWK! HE LOVES SHOWING OFF-- AND DOESN'T GET MANY OPPORTUNITIES TO PERFORM FOR A REAL AUDIENCE!
AH, HERE COMES MY RIDE NOW! RIGHT ON SCHEDULE!
I'M LUCKY MY CAB DRIVER HAD HIS RADIO TUNED TO THE WKLA TRAFFIC REPORT!

IT TOOK SOME FANCY TALKING, BUT I FINALLY MANAGED TO CONVINCE MY DRIVER TO GET HIS DISPATCHER TO PATCH ME INTO THE STATION'S MANAGER--
--SO THAT I COULD WANGLE MYSELF A LIFT WITH THEIR TRAFFIC HELICOPTER!

THE PILOT'S SPOTTED ME!
HE'S LOOKING FOR A PLACE TO LAND!
I CAN SAVE HIM THE TROUBLE IF ONLY I CAN USE THAT EXIT SIGN TO GIVE ME SUFFICIENT MOMENTUM TO--

MADE IT!
THE PILOT SAW ME COMING, AND COMPENSATED FOR MY ADDITIONAL WEIGHT!

WELCOME ABOARD, LADY!
HANG TIGHT! WE'LL GET YOU TO THE COLISEUM IN NOTHING FLAT!

WHAT A VIEW!
I NEVER WOULD'VE IMAGINED THAT A SIMPLE GIRL FROM SAN DIEGO WOULD EVER EXPERIENCE A WILD RIDE LIKE THIS?!

"IT'S HARD TO BELIEVE THAT JUST A FEW YEARS AGO I WAS JUST PLAIN OLD BARBARA MORSE, AN A+ STUDENT AT GEORGIA TECH.
"WHEN MY FAVORITE PROF. TOOK A SABBATICAL TO WORK ON A GOVERNMENT PROJECT, I WENT WITH HER.

"S.H.I.E.L.D. WAS ONE OF ITS MAJOR SPONSORS --AND THE IDEA OF BECOMING MATA HARI APPEALED TO ME--
SHIELD COMBAT SEOUL
"--SO I ENROLLED IN SPY SCHOOL!

"I BECAME A FIELD AGENT FOR A WHILE! WHEN THAT DIDN'T WORK OUT, I DECIDED TO GO SOLO...

LOS ANGELES VETERANS MEMORIAL COLISEUM
...UNTIL I MET HAWKEYE! HE MAY NOT BE MR. PERFECT, BUT NO MAN HAS EVER GOTTEN TO ME THE WAY HE DID --AND STILL DOES!
HE'S SOME PIECE OF WORK! EVEN THOUGH HE'S LEADER OF THE WEST COAST AVENGERS, HE STILL MANAGES TO FIND THE TIME TO PUT ON THESE OCCASIONAL BENEFITS FOR CHARITY!

A FEW MINUTES LATER, INSIDE THE COLISEUM...
I'M CERTAIN I'VE ALREADY MISSED THE FIRST ACT BY NOW! MAY AS WELL MEET HAWK IN HIS DRESSING--

--ROOM!
THESE ARE THE MEN HAWK'S SUPPOSED TO BE SPARRING WITH IN HIS EXHIBITION! THEY'VE OBVIOUSLY BEEN DRUGGED!
WHAT'S THAT ON THE FLOOR?

A GAS ARROW!

YOU SHOULDN'T BE STICKING YOUR NOSE WHERE IT DOESN'T BELONG, MISSY!
HAVEN'T YOU HEARD THAT CURIOSITY KILLED THE CAT!
YES, BUT--

--I'M THE MOCKINGBIRD AND YOU'RE THE CLUMSY CAT!
BWAKK

NOT BAD, LADY! YOU MADE MY FRIEND HARRY LOOK LIKE A REAL JERK!
YOU MUST BE FEELING PRETTY PROUD OF YOURSELF!

WELL, I CAN CHANGE THAT!!
HE'S USING THAT CONTRAPTION TO HURL THREE BALLS AT ME!

UNG! BARELY MANAGED TO BLOCK 'EM WITH MY BATTLE-STAVE!
HAVE YOU EVER CONSIDERED THERAPY, BUSTER?
PWOK
PWOK
PWOK
THE SYMBOLISM BEHIND YOUR CHOICE OF WEAPON IS PAINFULLY OBVIOUS!

OF COURSE I'M THE ONE WITH THE BATTLE-STAVE WHICH TELESCOPES TO TWICE ITS LENGTH!

I HOPE THIS KIND OF TALK ISN'T MAKING YOU UNCOMFORTABLE OR ANYTHING!
LOOK OUT! SHE'S SPRINGING FORWARD!
UNGH!
LET ME AT HER!

MY STEEL-PLATED FIST WILL FINISH HER OFF!
DREAM ON!

A WEAPON IS ONLY AS DEADLY AS THE PERSON BEHIND IT--
BOK

--AND YOU'RE A CREAMPUFF!
SHUT UP! YOU'RE MAKING ME CRAZY!
I CAN'T TAKE ALL THE THE CREDIT!

I'VE GOT YOU NOW!
DO YOU?

I'M BETTING THAT THE REST OF YOU ISN'T AS WELL-ARMORED AS YOUR FIST!
UFFF
WHAT DO YOU KNOW? I WAS RIGHT!
I'M NOT TAKING ANY CHANCES WITH THIS BROAD! SHE'S CRAZY!

BAD MOVE, RAMBO! MY COSTUME IS MADE OF A SPECIAL BLEND OF MATERIAL WHICH IS IMPERVIOUS TO SMALL ARMS FIRE!

THE PERFECT ACTION WEAR--
--FOR THE CONTEMPORARY GAL ON THE GO!
SPWAT!
ARRGH!

CAN'T STOP HER! SHE FIGHTS LIKE A WILD-CAT!
MOVE IT! WE'VE ALREADY WASTED ENOUGH TIME HERE!
THE OTHERS MUST'VE FINISHED OFF THE ARCHER BY NOW!
WHAT?! THEY'RE TALKING ABOUT MY HAWK! WHO ARE THESE GUYS? WHAT DO THEY WANT?
OH, NO! THAT WOMAN!
EXIT

STAY BACK, OR WE'LL KILL HER!
DON'T FOLLOW US! WE'RE WARNING YOU!

I HAD NO INTENTION OF FOLLOWING THEM... UNTIL NOW!

"I WANTED TO FIND MY HUSBAND!

"I KNOW THAT HE'S IN REAL TROUBLE!

"I CAN SENSE HE NEEDS ME--"

--BUT HE'LL JUST HAVE TO TAKE CARE OF HIMSELF FOR NOW!

AND SO, A FEW MOMENTS LATER...
OH, NO! THEY'RE TAKING THE HOSTAGE WITH THEM!

THERE'S NO WAY I CAN OUT-RACE THAT VAN!
BUT I CAN CUT IT OFF-- IF ONLY I CAN SNAP MY BATTLE-STAVES TOGETHER IN TIME!
VROOM

I DID IT! NOW, I HAVE TO TIME THIS JUST RIGHT--!
PERFECT!
BUT THIS IS NO TIME TO CONGRATULATE MYSELF! HAVE TO MOVE--

BDAM BDAM BDAM
--FAST!!

DUMB BROAD MUSTA THOUGHT WE COULDN'T HEAR HER UP THERE!
SHE'S HISTORY NOW!

WANNA BET?!
HIYA, FELLAS!
MIND IF I JOIN THE FUN?

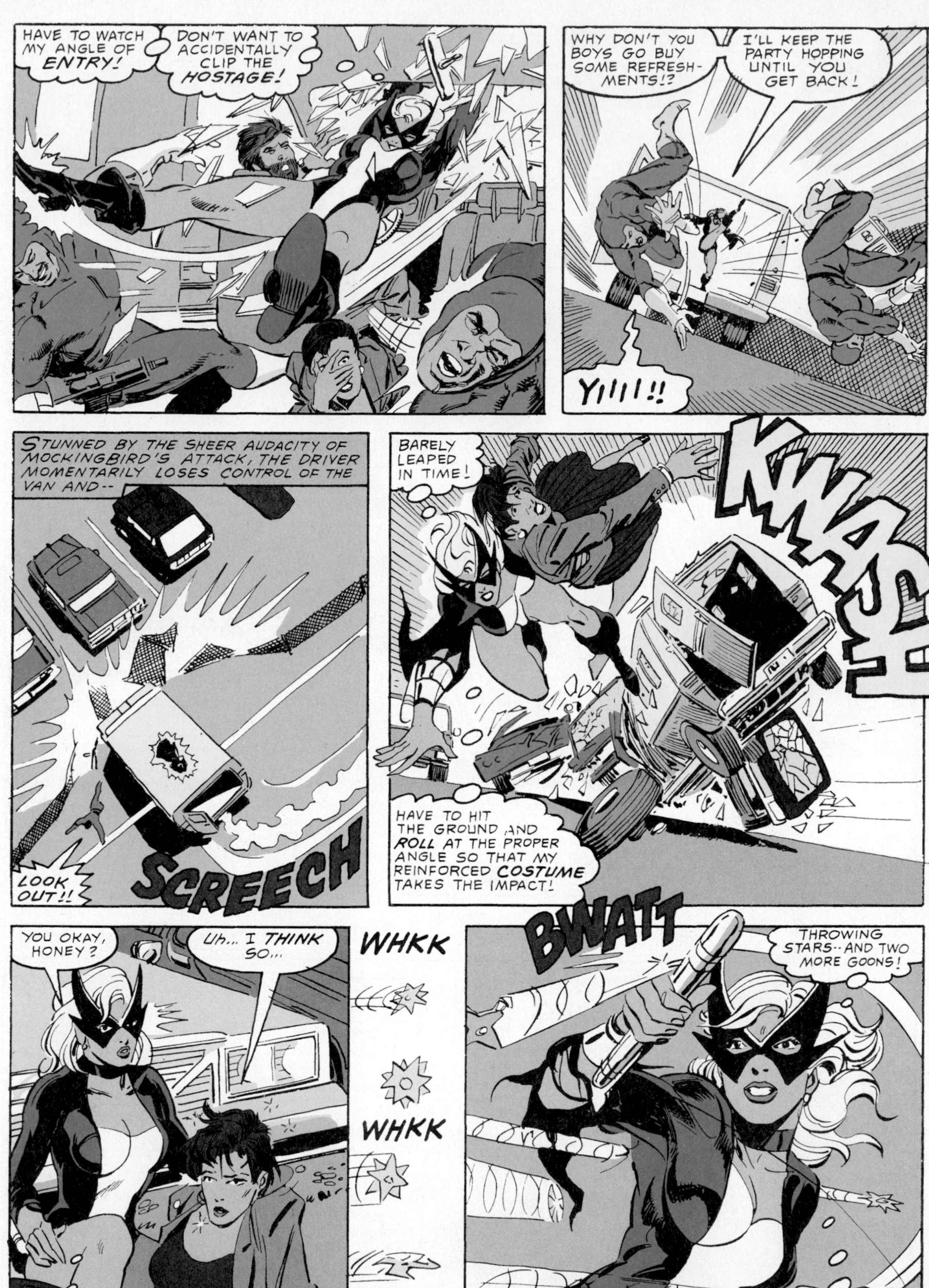
HAVE TO WATCH MY ANGLE OF ENTRY!
DON'T WANT TO ACCIDENTALLY CLIP THE HOSTAGE!
WHY DON'T YOU BOYS GO BUY SOME REFRESH- MENTS!?
I'LL KEEP THE PARTY HOPPING UNTIL YOU GET BACK!
YIIII!!
STUNNED BY THE SHEER AUDACITY OF MOCKINGBIRD'S ATTACK, THE DRIVER MOMENTARILY LOSES CONTROL OF THE VAN AND--
SCREECH
LOOK OUT!!
BARELY LEAPED IN TIME!
KWASH
HAVE TO HIT THE GROUND AND ROLL AT THE PROPER ANGLE SO THAT MY REINFORCED COSTUME TAKES THE IMPACT!
YOU OKAY, HONEY?
Uh... I THINK SO...
THAT SOUND!
WHKK
WHKK
WHKK
BWATT
THROWING STARS-- AND TWO MORE GOONS!
I'M REAL GLAD S.H.I.E.L.D. TRAINED ME TO REACT INSTINCTIVELY TO ANY ATTACK!

I'VE REALLY GOT TO HAND IT TO YOU BOYS! YOU CERTAINLY CAME PREPARED FOR A SERIOUS FIGHT!
UNG!
WHO ARE YOU WORKING FOR?

I'D LIKE TO PERSONALLY COMPLIMENT HIM ON HIS TRAINING PROCEDURES!
SUCH PROFESSIONAL WORK SHOULDN'T GO UNREWARDED!
UUF!

WHAT A MAGNIFICENT CREATURE!
I CAN EASILY SEE WHY MY FORMER STUDENT IS SO ATTRACTED TO HER!

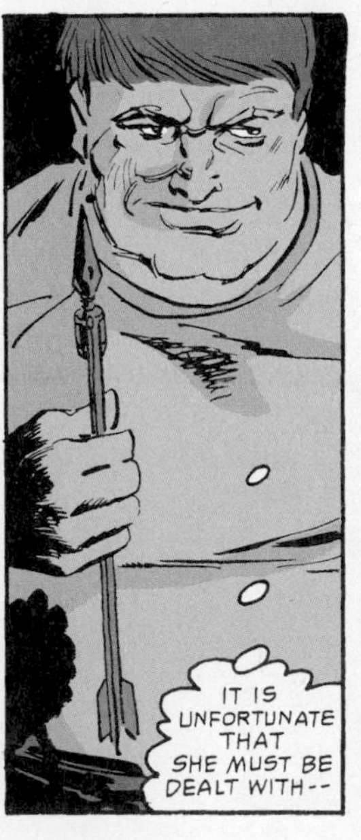
IT IS UNFORTUNATE THAT SHE MUST BE DEALT WITH--

"--QUITE UNFORTUNATE!
MOCKING-BIRD! RUN!!
RUN!
A FLAMING ARROW!

IF IT SHOULD IGNITE ANY OF THESE RUPTURED GAS TANKS--!
NO! I CAN'T LET THAT HAPPEN!

THIS HAS GOT TO BE THE CRAZIEST STUNT I'VE EVER ATTEMPTED!
OH, WELL, IF I WANTED SANITY I SHOULDN'T HAVE JOINED THE AVENGERS!
I'VE ONLY GOT ONE CHANCE AT THAT ARROW! HAVE TO MAKE IT COUNT!

YA-HOO!

UH-OH! I'M CERTAIN THE ARROW CAME FROM THAT FLEEING LIMO, BUT I CAN'T WORRY ABOUT THAT NOW!
I'VE GOT TO FIND OUT WHAT HAPPENED TO--

"-HAWKEYE!"
LOOKS LIKE I'VE ALREADY MISSED THE GRAND FINALE!

MAYBE HAWK CAN CLUE ME IN ON THE CURVED ARROW! I'M GLAD I STOPPED TO RETRIEVE IT FROM HIS DRESSING ROOM!
HAWKEYE!
YOU--?!

OF COURSE IT'S ME!
ARE YOU ALL RIGHT?
YEAH, I'M FINE-- BUT WHAT HAPPENED TO YOU? YOUR COSTUME'S IN SHREDS!

NEVER MIND THAT NOW! I HAVE SOMETHING IMPORTANT TO ASK YOU!
HAVE YOU EVER SEEN AN ARROW LIKE THIS BEFORE?
OH, NO!
WHAT IS IT? WHAT'S WRONG, HAWK?

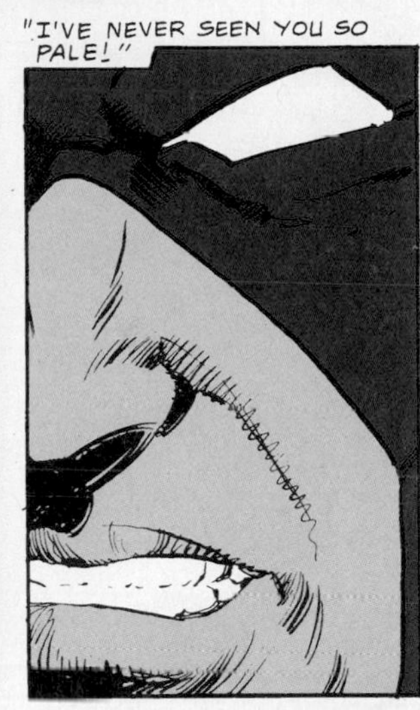

"I'VE NEVER SEEN YOU SO PALE!"

I-IT BELONGS TO THE MAN WHO REALLY TRAINED ME!
I PRAYED I'D NEVER HAVE TO FACE HIM AGAIN!
YOU WON'T... IF I HAVE ANYTHING TO SAY ABOUT IT!

THIS MAN IS OBVIOUSLY A TOP PROFESSIONAL! A KILLER!
PROMISE ME YOU WON'T GO UP AGAINST HIM ALONE!
PROMISE ME!
YEAH, SURE...

I PROMISE.

TO BE CONTINUED...

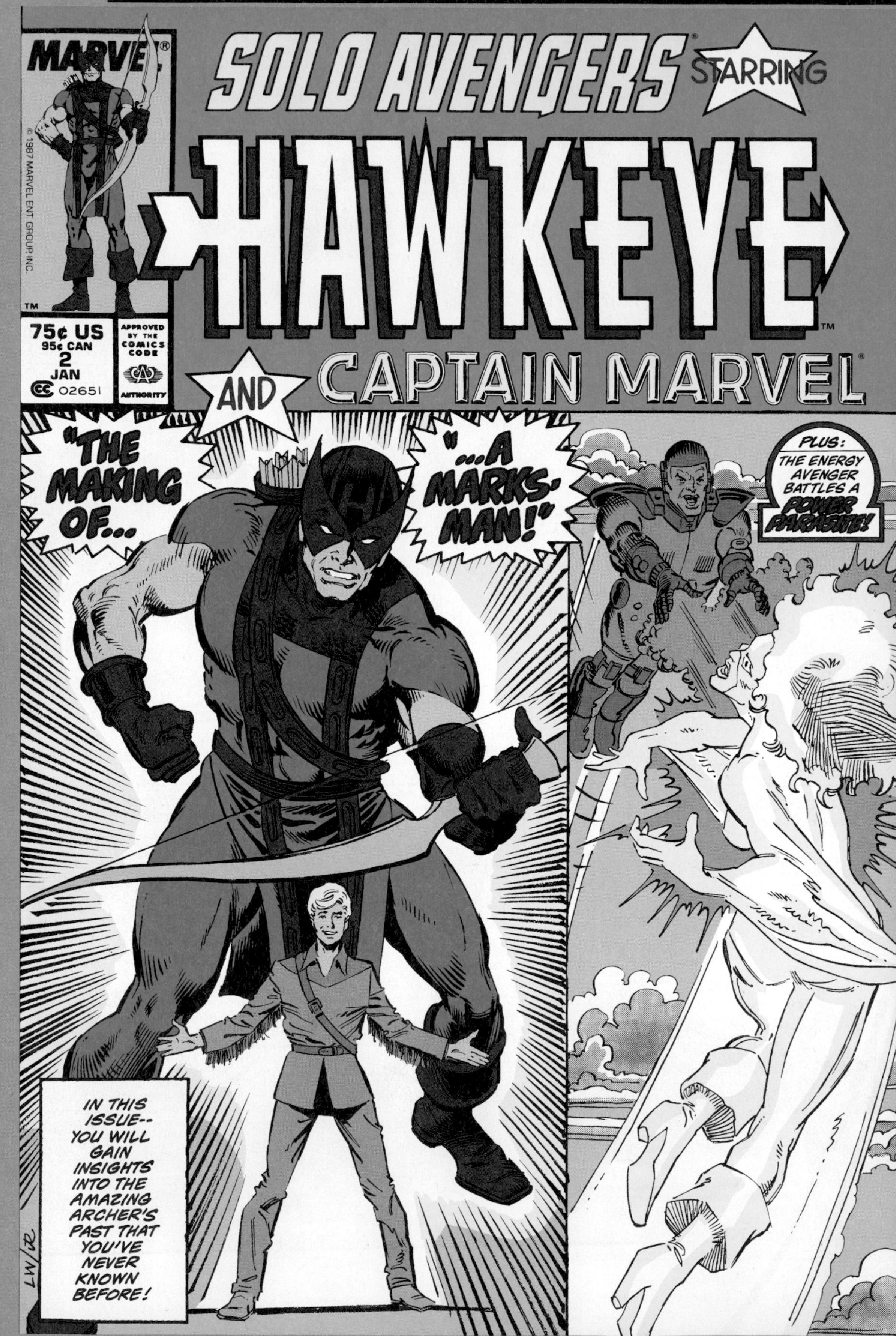
MARVEL
SOLO AVENGERS STARRING
HAWKEYE
AND
CAPTAIN MARVEL
75¢ US
95¢ CAN
2
JAN
02651
APPROVED BY THE COMICS CODE AUTHORITY
© 1987 MARVEL ENT GROUP INC.
"THE MAKING OF...
"...A MARKS-MAN!"
PLUS: THE ENERGY AVENGER BATTLES A POWER PARASITE!
IN THIS ISSUE-- YOU WILL GAIN INSIGHTS INTO THE AMAZING ARCHER'S PAST THAT YOU'VE NEVER KNOWN BEFORE!

THE STORY THAT COULDN'T BE TOLD! BY THE GUYS WHO ALMOST DIDN'T TELL IT!

TOM DeFALCO WRITER · MARK BRIGHT PENCILS · JOE RUBINSTEIN FINISHER · JACK MORELLI LETTERS · PAUL BECTON COLORS · MARK GRUENWALD EDITOR

GOTTA TIME THIS JUST RIGHT!
I WON'T GET A SECOND CHANCE!
PA-TANG

PWOOSH


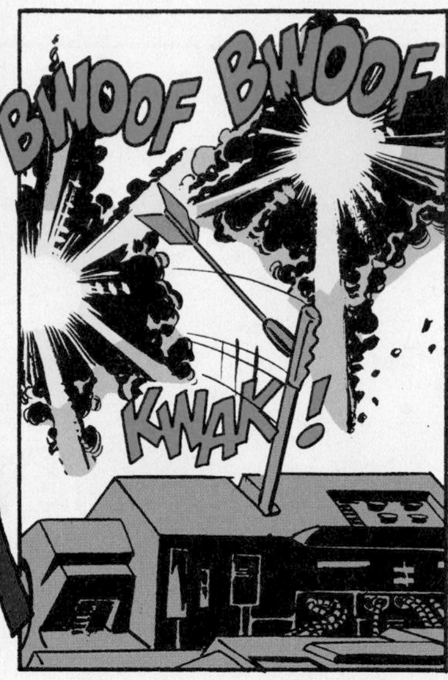

BWOOF BWOOF
KWAK!

THAT WAS FANTASTIC, HON! YOU CROSSED THE TRAINING GAUNTLET IN RECORD TIME -- AND SNAGGED BOTH MISSILES AND THE CUT-OFF SWITCH WITH A SINGLE SHOT

I SHOULD'VE BEEN FASTER!
MY TIMING WAS OFF A FULL THREE SECONDS!

WHAT'S BOTHERING YOU, HAWK? YOU'VE BEEN PUSHING SO HARD LATELY!

YOU STILL WORRIED ABOUT THOSE GOONS WHO TRIED TO ACE US LAST WEEK?*
TALK TO ME, HAWK! TELL ME WHAT'S WRONG!
YEAH... I GUESS I JUST DON'T KNOW WHERE TO...
*LAST ISSUE!

"MAYBE I SHOULD START WITH MY PARENTS. DID I EVER TELL YOU MY FATHER WAS A BUTCHER BY TRADE?
BUTCHER SHOP
BUTCHER
"HE OWNED A SMALL SHOP IN WAVERLY, THE ARMPIT OF IOWA, AND MY OLD HOME TOWN.

"MAN, THE HOURS WE USED TO PUT IN AT THAT STORE! MOM AT THE CASH REGISTER! POP BEHIND THE COUNTER! MY BIG BROTHER BARNEY AND ME HELPING OUT AFTER SCHOOL!

"POP WAS A REAL WORKHORSE! POPULAR WITH HIS CUSTOMERS, TOO! BUT HE COULDN'T CONTROL HIS LIQUOR... OR HIS TEMPER!
I'M GONNA KILL THAT SMART-MOUTH BRAT!
HAROLD! NO!!
"MOM DID HER BEST TO PROTECT BARNEY AND ME, BUT SHE WASN'T ALWAYS SUCCESSFUL!

"WHEN HE WAS DRINKING, THERE WAS JUST NO LIVING WITH HIM!
YOU OKAY, BARNEY?
I'LL BE BIGGER THAN HIM SOMEDAY!
THEN I'LL SHOW HIM!
I'LL SHOW THEM ALL!

"I USED TO THINK THAT IF I COULD JUST WORK HARDER-- AND BE A BETTER SON--POP WOULD JUST NATURALLY BECOME A BETTER FATHER.
"NO SUCH LUCK!

"EVENTUALLY, DAD'S DRINKING GOT THE BEST OF HIM AND MOM!
"POOR MOM! SHE HAD TRIED SO HARD TO MAKE THINGS WORK OUT... SO VERY HARD!

"BARNEY AND I DIDN'T HAVE ANY OTHER CLOSE RELATIVES, SO WE GOT STUCK IN THE ORPHANAGE!

"I GUESS IT REALLY WASN'T SUCH A BAD PLACE... AS FAR AS THOSE THINGS GO... BUT WE WERE TOO OLD TO BE CONSIDERED BY MOST OF THE YOUNG COUPLES WHO WERE LOOKING TO ADOPT!

"BARNEY USED TO TAKE HIS FRUSTRATIONS OUT ON ME! I TRIED TO WIN HIM OVER BY BEING A BETTER BROTHER AND DOING ALL HIS CHORES!
"BUT THAT TRICK NEVER WORKED!

"ONE NIGHT, WHEN I WAS ABOUT THIRTEEN OR SO, BARNEY FINALLY HAD HIS FILL -- AND DECIDED TO RUN AWAY FROM THE ORPHANAGE!
"I DIDN'T WANT TO GO--BUT HE WAS MY ONLY FAMILY --SO I JUST COULDN'T LET HIM LEAVE ALONE!

"WE HAD A FEW ROUGH--AND HUNGRY--DAYS ON THE ROAD, BUT WE EVENTUALLY WOUND UP AT THIS TRAVELING CARNIVAL THAT HAD JUST COME TO TOWN!

"BARNEY WAS ALWAYS A FAST-TALKER! SOMEHOW HE MANAGED TO GET THE OWNER TO HIRE US ON!
"WE BUSTED OUR BACKS DOING ALL SORTS OF ODD JOBS--

"--BUT WE LOVED IT, AND WE JUST TAGGED ALONG WHEN THE CARNIVAL MOVED ON!

"WE WERE LIVING HIGH! THE CARNEY PEOPLE MADE US FEEL RIGHT AT HOME--AS IF WE WERE PART OF A LARGE FAMILY--AND WE GOT TO SEE ALL THE ACTS FOR FREE!
"BUT OUR FAVORITE ALWAYS WAS--

"--THE SWORDSMAN!!
"MAN, HE HAD THIS CRAZY ACT WHERE HE'D WRAP HIS ASSISTANT IN RIBBONS FROM HEAD TO TOE--

"--THEN, HE'D JUST HACK AWAY AT HER, HIS SWORD FLASHING FASTER THEN THE HUMAN EYE COULD FOLLOW, UNTIL SHE WAS COMPLETELY FREE!

"UNTIL ONE DAY HE CUT A LITTLE TOO CLOSE AND--"
HEY! MY HAIR!!

THAT DOES IT! I'VE HAD ENOUGH!
GO! YOU ARE EASILY REPLACED!
I NEED AN ASSISTANT WITH COURAGE!

WOULD ONE OF YOU BOYS LIKE TO BE A STAR?
NO WAY, IVANHOE!
SURE! I'D LIKE TO GIVE IT A TRY!

I LIKE YOU, KID! YOU'VE GOT GUTS!

JUST RELAX, KID! LEAVE EVERYTHING TO ME!
DON'T MOVE! DON'T EVEN FLINCH... NO MATTER HOW CLOSE THE SWORD GETS!

YOU HAVE NOTHING TO FEAR... AS LONG AS YOU DO WHAT I SAY!

YOU DID ALL RIGHT, KID! I'M CERTAIN I CAN USE YOU!
IF YOU HAVE A GOOD EYE AND SHARP REFLEXES I MIGHT EVEN BE ABLE TO TEACH YOU HOW TO THROW KNIVES SO THAT YOU CAN REALLY CONTRIBUTE TO THE ACT.

"AND, IN THE DAYS THAT FOLLOWED HE BEGAN TRAINING ME! TALK ABOUT DISCIPLINE! HE WOULD PLUNK ME DOWN IN FRONT OF A TARGET, AND MAKE ME PRACTICE A FULL EIGHT HOURS EVERY DAY!

"BUT I DID IT EAGERLY! I WANTED TO SUCCEED, TO IMPRESS THE SWORDSMAN! HE HAD ALMOST BECOME LIKE A REAL FATHER TO ME!
NOT BAD, KID! NOT BAD AT ALL!
"I WORSHIPPED HIM, AND DESPERATELY SOUGHT HIS APPROVAL!

"BUT, ONE DAY--
THUNK
THUNK
THUNK
THUNK
THUNK
"--OUR PRACTICE SESSION WAS RUDELY INTERRUPTED!"

SORRY, PAL! BURRP I NEVER COULD RESIST SHOWING OFF!

THE KID AIN'T HALF BAD, SWORDSMAN!
'BOUT TIME YOU SPRUCED UP YOUR ACT!

BUT TRICK SHOT IS THE NEW STAR OF THIS SHOW, AND DON'T YOU FORGET IT!

"A NEW ATTRACTION TO THE CARNEY, TRICK SHOT, SOON BECAME THE FEATURED ATTRACTION -- STEALING THE TOP SPOT FROM THE SWORDSMAN!
NOW STARRING TRICK SHOT
WORLD'S GREATEST ARCHER

"BUT, THE SWORDSMAN HAD A PLAN TO GET EVEN, AND ONE NIGHT...
THAT WAS A NASTY RUN OF BAD LUCK, TRICKY OL' BOY! YOU OWE ME A WHOLE WEEK'S PAY!
BUT I'M WILLING TO FORGET IT...

...IF YOU TEACH THE KID ARCHERY!
WHY? WHAT'S WRONG WITH HIM THROWING KNIVES?
IT ISN'T AS POPULAR WITH THE RUBES--
--AND I WANT TO EXPLOIT HIM TO HIS FULLEST!

"AND SO...
YOU MUST LEARN TO USE YOUR BOW GENTLY, NATURALLY, INSTINCTIVELY! SUCH IS THE WAY OF THE ARROW!

"WITHIN A FEW MONTHS I WAS PRETTY GOOD!
THUNK
TRICK SHOT SAYS I HAVE A NATURAL FLAIR FOR ARCHERY!

SOMEDAY I'LL BE AS GOOD WITH MY BOW AS YOU ARE WITH YOUR SWORD! YOU'LL SEE!
DON'T TRY IT, BOY... DON'T EVER TRY IT!

I'M WARNING YOU... IT WOULDN'T BE HEALTHY!
DON'T EVER FORGET...

...WHICH ONE OF US IS THE MASTER!

DON'T TAKE IT SO PERSONAL!
THE GUY'S ONLY USING YOU! HE'S ON A POWER TRIP!
DO ME A FAVOR, BARNEY ... SHUT UP!

"AT THE TIME, I DIDN'T REALIZE THE KIND OF PRESSURE THE SWORDSMAN MUST HAVE BEEN UNDER! I JUST KNEW HE ALWAYS SEEMED TENSE, IRRITABLE, MOODY-- BUT I DIDN'T KNOW WHY!

"HE HAD ALWAYS BEEN A BIT OF A GAMBLER... BUT HIS LUCK HAD RECENTLY TURNED SOUR... AND HE COULDN'T PAY HIS DEBTS!
SWORDSMAN, PAY UP, PAL, OR WE'LL HAVE TO BREAK SOMETHING LUV'N KISSES MARKO

"I GUESS THAT'S WHAT FINALLY PUSHED HIM OVER THE EDGE!
HEY, SWORDSMAN! DID YOU HEAR THAT SOMEONE STRUCK THE PAYMASTER FROM BEHIND... AND ROBBED THE ENTIRE--

WHA--? WHERE'D YOU GET ALL THAT MONEY??
YOU LITTLE PUNK! I WARNED YOU NEVER TO COME IN HERE WITHOUT ASKING FIRST!

NOW THAT YOU KNOW, YOU'RE IN WITH ME!
NOBODY WILL EVER CATCH US--WITH YOUR BOW AND MY SWORD!
FORGET IT! I'M GETTING OUT OF HERE!

SO! YOU'RE TURNING YOUR BACK ON ME, ARE YOU?!
"THE AREA WAS COMPLETELY DESERTED! EVERYONE ELSE MUST HAVE BEEN AT THE PAYMASTER'S WAGON... AT THE OPPOSITE END OF THE LOT!

"I PANICKED-- RAN INTO THE MAIN TENT-- AND CLIMBED THE HIGH-WIRE--
"--THINKING THAT HE WOULDN'T DARE FOLLOW!

"I WAS WRONG!
IGNORANT PUP! WITH ONE SIMPLE THRUST, I'LL END YOUR CAREER ... AND YOUR LIFE!!

"I WAS BEATEN! HELPLESS! BUT, BEFORE THE SWORDSMAN COULD FINISH ME OFF...
GET AWAY FROM THAT KID!

HEY, BARNEY, THE SWORDSMAN IS GETTING AWAY!
FINE BY ME! I AIN'T LOOKING TO TANGLE WITH HIM!
I JUST WANNA KNOW WHY HE ATTACKED MY BROTHER!

"I'LL NEVER FORGET THE LOOK ON BARNEY'S FACE-- OR THE WAY HE REACTED--WHEN I TOLD HIM WHAT HAD HAPPENED!
HE WAS WILLING TO SPLIT THE RECEIPTS WITH YOU--AND YOU TURNED HIM DOWN?
WE COULD HAVE BEEN ON EASY STREET... BUT YOU MUFFED IT!

"BARNEY VANISHED LATER THAT NIGHT, AND I AWOKE IN THE HOSPITAL TO DISCOVER COMPOUND FRACTURES IN BOTH LEGS...
TRICK SHOT ?!
I GOT A PROPOSITION FOR YOU, KID!

WITH YOUR NATURAL ABILITY, I FIGURE I CAN TRAIN YOU TO BE ONE HOTSHOT ARCHER ... FOR A PRICE!
WHAT KIND OF PRICE?
DOES IT REALLY MATTER?

"IT DIDN'T... BECAUSE I HAD NOWHERE ELSE TO GO!
"TRICK SHOT WAS AN EXCELLENT TEACHER. HE MADE ME THE ARCHER I AM TODAY.

"HE EVEN INTRODUCED ME TO THE CONCEPT OF THE GIMMICK ARROW... AN ARROW CUSTOM-MADE FOR A SINGLE, SPECIFIC PURPOSE!

THWAK
"TRICK SHOT REALLY ENJOYED KILLING AND INFLICTING PAIN!

"HE MADE ME SICK... BUT I DESPERATELY WANTED THE KNOWLEDGE THAT WAS HIS TO GIVE... SO I STAYED!

"EVERY NOW AND THEN HE'D TAKE OFF FOR A FEW DAYS--
"BUT I DIDN'T THINK MUCH OF IT AT THE TIME!

"AFTER MY EXPERIENCE WITH THE SWORDSMAN, I KNEW BETTER THAN TO STICK MY NOSE INTO OTHER PEOPLE'S BUSINESS!
"I JUST CONTINUED TO PRACTICE--

"--AND PRACTICE!
NICE! FOUR MIRRORS AND A BULLSEYE ON A SINGLE ARROW!

YOU'RE GETTING THERE, KID! YOU SHOULD BE READY SOON!
FOR WHAT?
I'LL LET YOU KNOW WHEN IT HAPPENS!

"ONCE MY LEGS WERE FULLY HEALED, I BECAME ANXIOUS TO REJOIN THE CARNIVAL, BUT--
NOT YET, KID! WE GOT US A SPECIAL JOB TO DO FIRST!
LET'S SEE WHAT THE EASTER BUNNY LEFT ON MY WINDSHIELD!

HEY, I KNOW THAT GUY! HE USED TO PLAY CARDS WITH THE SWORDSMAN! HIS NAME'S MARKO!
KID, IT'S TIME YOU STARTED EARNING YOUR KEEP!

"I DIDN'T KNOW WHAT HE MEANT UNTIL LATER THAT NIGHT...
WHAT ARE WE DOING HERE, TRICK? WHAT'S GOING ON?
QUIET!

JUST FOLLOW ME!

STAY HERE... AND SING OUT IF ANY-ONE COMES!
B-BUT, TRICK--!
NOT NOW, KID!

EVENING, MARKO! THAT THE MONEY YOU'VE BEEN SKIMMING FROM THE BIG BOYS?!
TRICK SHOT!?

DUMB! GOING FOR YOUR GUN WAS A REAL DUMB MOVE, MARKO! WE MIGHT HAVE COME TO AN ARRANGEMENT IF YOU HADN'T BEEN SO TRIGGER HAPPY!
THUNK
ARRGH!

"I HEARD THE SCREAM... BUT I HAD MY OWN PROBLEMS!
LOOK! IT'S ROBIN HOOD!
BWAM
BWAM
WASTE HIM!

I'M GLAD YOUR WIFE HEARD YOUR SCREAM, MARKO.
IT'S SO UNTIDY TO LEAVE A WIDOW BEHIND!

"I HAD MANAGED TO PIN THE TWO GUNMEN TO A WALL... BUT, BEFORE I COULD MOVE, MAKE ANOTHER A SPOTLIGHT HIT ME...
YOU'RE DEAD, PUNK!

"INSTINCTIVELY, I WHIRLED AND FIRED IN THE DIRECTION OF THE VOICE--
BWAM
"EVEN AS MY SIDE EXPLODED IN AGONY!

"I WAS HURT, BLEEDING, AND IN SHOCK-- BUT I STILL MANAGED TO STUMBLE FORWARD...
P-PLEASE DON'T LET HIM BE DEAD!
I DIDN'T MEAN TO KILL ANYONE!

"BUT THEN I SAW HIS FACE-- AND THE WHOLE WORLD CAME CRASHING IN ON ME!"
BARNEY!

FORGET HIM, KID!
WE'VE GOT TO MAKE TRACKS BEFORE MORE GUNS ARRIVE!
HE'S MY BROTHER, TRICK! AND HE NEEDS HELP!

I SAID WE'RE LEAVING!
NO! I'M TAKING MY BROTHER TO A HOSPITAL AND YOU'RE NOT GOING TO STOP ME!

ONE LAST TIME, KID... WE'RE GOING!
I'M WARNING YOU TRICK, I'LL SHOOT!
THEN DO IT! DO IT!

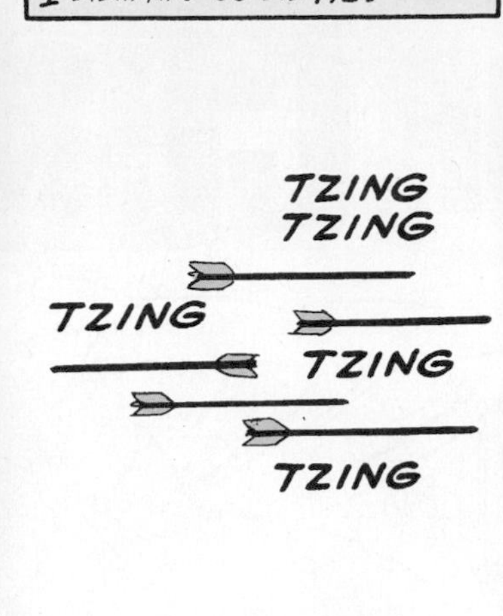
"I DID... AND SO DID HE!
TZING
TZING
TZING
TZING
TZING
TZING
"I NEVER HAD A CHANCE!"

I COULD HAVE KILLED YOU JUST NOW, SONNY-BOY... BUT I ONLY KILL FOR MONEY... AND MY OWN PLEASURE!

YOU OWE ME, KID! OWE ME BIG FOR ALL THE KNOWLEDGE I'VE GIVEN YOU!
THE PRICE IS YOUR LIFE!

BUT YOU'RE NOT QUITE RIPE ENOUGH! YOU NEED MORE EXPERIENCE! MORE SEASONING!
I'M GOING TO WAIT UNTIL YOU'VE MADE SOMETHING OF YOURSELF! UNTIL YOU HAVE SOMETHING WORTH LOSING!

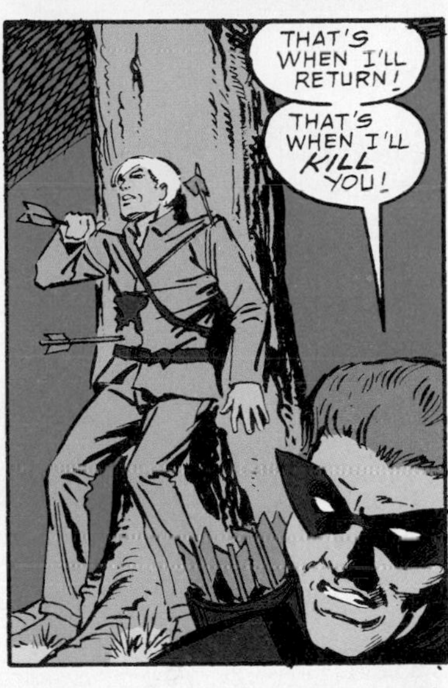
THAT'S WHEN I'LL RETURN!
THAT'S WHEN I'LL KILL YOU!

SOMEHOW I MANAGED TO GET BARNEY AND ME TO A HOSPITAL, BUT I LEFT BEFORE HE REGAINED CONSCIOUSNESS! I COULDN'T FACE HIM!
OH, HAWK, WHY ARE YOU TELLING ME ALL OF THIS NOW?!

BECAUSE I'VE MADE QUITE A SUCCESS OF MY LIFE! I'M CHAIRMAN OF THE WEST COAST AVENGERS AND I'M MARRIED TO A VERY BEAUTIFUL WOMAN!
I COULDN'T HAVE BEEN HAPPIER... UNTIL I RECEIVED THIS!
WHAT IS IT?

A ONE-WAY TICKET TO PARIS!
IT'S FROM TRICK-SHOT... HIS DEATH CHALLENGE!!
ATLANTIC AIR LINES
NEXT
AN AMERICAN ARCHER IN PARIS!

OUT OF CONTROL
SHE STREAKS ACROSS THE BORDELAISE REGION OF FRANCE AT MANY TIMES THE SPEED OF SOUND, YET THERE IS NO THUNDERING RUMBLE TO SIGNAL HER PASSING.
BY THE TIME THESE VINEYARD WORKERS NOTICE THE GLOW OF HER AMAZING LIVING ENERGY, SHE IS ALREADY MILES AWAY.
‹THAT LIGHT... IT MOVES AS IF ALIVE!›
‹IT... SHE... IS ALIVE! I HAVE SEEN PICTURES OF HER... SHE CAN ONLY BE THE AVENGER ...THE ONE THE AMERICANS CALL CAPTAIN MARVEL!›
STAN LEE PRESENTS:
CAPTAIN MARVEL
created by
ROGER STERN & JOHN ROMITA, JR.
ROGER STERN - WRITER
KIERON DWYER - PENCILER
BOB McLEOD - INKER
BILL OAKLEY - LETTERER
GREGORY WRIGHT - COLORIST

PROFESSOR LeCLARE'S TELEGRAM WAS SO ODD... BUT IF HE THINKS THERE'S CAUSE FOR ALARM, I WANT TO KNOW MORE!
IF NOT FOR THE PRO-FESSOR, I MIGHT STILL BE WITH THE NEW ORLEANS HARBOR PATROL... I'D CER-TAINLY NEVER HAVE BECOME CAPTAIN MARVEL!
"WHEN I FIRST SET OUT TO HELP LeCLARE INVESTIGATE DR. PICARO, HIS FORMER ASSISTANT, I DIDN'T BE-LIEVE HIS TALK OF ENERGY WEAPONS... I THOUGHT I WAS JUST HUMORING ONE OF GRANDPA'S OLD WAR BUDDIES.
"I WASN'T REALLY CONVINCED UNTIL I MADE CONTACT WITH PICARO'S ENERGY GRID! THAT SHOULD HAVE KILLED ME--BUT INSTEAD, IT CHANGED ME...

...ENABLING ME TO TRANSFORM MY BODY INTO ANY KIND OF ENERGY I CHOOSE! IT FELT WEIRD AT FIRST, BUT I'VE GOTTEN TO LIKING IT!
LeCLARE'S MESSAGE MEN-TIONED SOME NEW CALCULATIONS HE'D MADE CONCERNING MY POWERS. HE WANTED ME TO COME SEE HIM, BUT HE ALSO WANTED ME TO STICK TO SUB-LIGHT SPEEDS. THAT DOESN'T BODE WELL.

SOME MILES AWAY...
AH! AT LAST I HAVE FOUND THE LOVELY AVENGER!
JUST A LITTLE CLOSER... CLOSER...
...AND SHE IS MINE!

PAIN!!
ERUPTING INTO A BURST OF LIGHTNING, THE GOLDEN AVENGER ARCS FROM THE SKY-- HER UNLEASHED ENERGY INSTANTLY SEEKING OUT THE NEAREST PATH TO THE GROUND.
KRAKOOM
WHAT... HAPPENED? FELT LIKE MY HEAD WAS SPLITTING OPEN!
WHERE AM I? LOOKS LIKE... OH, NO! THAT SWISS RESORT I WAS PASSING OVER!
WAS ANYONE HURT? I...
FIRE?!?
GOT TO GET OUT OF HERE!!
IT... IT'S BECAUSE OF ME! MY ENERGIES... ARE SHIFTING FROM LIGHT TO HEAT! I-I-I CAN'T STOP IT!

GOOD LORD! ONE BOLT OF LIGHTNING DID THAT?

LIGHTNING? I THOUGHT IT WAS AN EXPLOSION!
WHAT ARE YOU TALKING ABOUT? DIDN'T YOU SEE HER?
HER?!
CAPTAIN MARVEL! I'M SURE IT WAS HER!
MA'AM, I'M NOT SURE WHAT I SAW. BUT IF SOMEONE'S RUNNING WILD WITH POWER LIKE THAT... HEAVEN HELP US ALL!

AT THAT MOMENT, NEARLY 1000 MILES OVERHEAD...
WHAT IS HAPPENING TO ME?

I'VE NEVER FELT SUCH PAIN WHILE IN ENERGY FORM. OF COURSE, I'VE NEVER LOST CONTROL BEFORE, EITHER!
COULD THIS BE WHAT PROFESSOR LeCLARE WAS WARNING ME ABOUT? IS MY POWER STARTING TO RUN OUT OF CONTROL?
I FEEL ALL RIGHT NOW, BUT WILL IT LAST? IF MY ENERGY SUDDENLY TURNED TO MICROWAVES OR GAMMA RADIATION WHILE I WAS NEAR OTHER PEOPLE... IT COULD BE LETHAL!

I DON'T DARE GO NEAR ANYONE UNTIL I KNOW FOR SURE. I MUST LEARN MORE--!
CAREFULLY SHIFTING A TINY PORTION OF HER ENERGY INTO THE RADIO SPECTRUM, MARVEL BEAMS A SIGNAL EARTHWARD--

--TO THE ALPINE FACILITY OF THE BERN INSTITUTE OF SCIENCE.
CAPTAIN MARVEL CALLING PROFESSOR ANDRE LeCLARE... PLEASE RESPOND AT FREQUENCY DELTA-FIVE-FIVE. CAPTAIN MARVEL CALLING...

LeCLARE HERE, MON CAPITAINE. I... ANTICIPATED YOUR CALL. WE ALREADY RECEIVED A REPORT OF YOUR MISFORTUNE OVER THE WESTERN FOOTHILLS.
I THINK IT BEST THAT YOU COME HERE AND LET OUR RESEARCH STAFF TEST YOU THOROUGHLY.

NOT TO KNOCK YOUR INSTITUTE, PROFESSOR... BUT I DON'T THINK YOU HAVE ANYTHING STRONG ENOUGH TO SHIELD YOU, SHOULD I GO TOTALLY HAYWIRE.
I'LL HAVE THE AVENGERS DEVISE SOME SORT OF CONTAINMENT CHAMBER ON HYDROBASE... YOU CAN COME CHECK ME OUT THERE!

REASSURE HER! SHE MUST COME HERE!
PROFESSOR?
I-I HEARD YOU, MON CAPITAINE. BUT YOU NEED NOT BE CONCERNED. YOU SEE...

...THERE IS NOTHING WRONG WITH YOU! NOTHING AT ALL! IT IS ALL A TRICK!

STAY AWAY OR...
PROFESSOR!
IDIOTA!
WOK!
WHUNNGH!

WITH A THOUGHT, CAPTAIN MARVEL SHOOTS EARTHWARD--ACCELERATING TO 186,000 MILES PER SECOND, EVEN AS SHE WILLS HER ENERGY TOTALLY INTO RADIO WAVES.

AND, A FRACTION OF A SECOND LATER...

WRAKAK

COME NO FURTHER, CAPTAIN!

PICARO?!?

ARE YOU SO **SURPRISED,** MY DEAR? DID YOU THINK FELIPE PICARO WOULD REMAIN INCARCERATED FOREVER?

I WARN YOU ...MAKE A SINGLE FALSE MOVE--

ALL RIGHT, PICARO... SATISFIED?
FOR NOW. OH, DO NOT TRY TO DECEIVE ME BY BECOMING A HOLOGRAM... THE INSTRUMENTS IN MY EXO-SUIT WOULD NOT BE FOOLED!
YOU SHOULD BE FLATTERED, CAPTAIN... EVERY WAKING HOUR I SPENT BEHIND BARS WAS DEDICATED TOWARDS DEVISING YOUR DOWNFALL!

THE COUNTER-PHASE WEAPONRY WHICH MADE YOU LOSE CONTROL WAS A SIMPLE ADAPTATION OF MY ENERGY DISRUPTOR ... AS IS THE CIRCUITRY IN MY EXO-SUIT--
--WHICH, OF COURSE, HAS BEEN DESIGNED SPECIFICALLY TO SAFELY TRANSFER YOUR POWERS TO ME!

WHAT?! YOU THINK I'D LET A SLEAZE LIKE YOU HAVE THIS KIND OF POWER?
YOU ACQUIRED THE POWER BY ACCIDENT THROUGH MY EQUIPMENT! IF ANYONE HAS THE RIGHT TO SUCH POWER, IT IS I! I HAVE ALREADY SIPHONED OFF A MEAGER PORTION OF YOUR ENERGIES--
--EITHER YOU WILLINGLY ALLOW ME TO DRAIN THE REST... IN WHICH CASE I SHALL SPARE YOUR LIFE AND THOSE OF THESE SCIENTISTS ...OR I WILL ROB YOU OF ALL CONTROL!

DO YOU THINK THAT LeCLARE AND HIS FRIENDS WOULD SURVIVE THE SECOND CHOICE?
NO... THEY WOULDN'T.

LOOKS LIKE YOU WIN.

MON CAPITAINE--NON! YOU CANNOT... YOU MUST NOT--!
SHE HAS NO CHOICE, IDIOTA!

WRONG!
WRAAK

MUH... MY... NOSE!
YOU'RE LUCKY I ONLY USED MY FIST!
CHOOM
PROFESSOR-- GET YOUR FRIENDS OUT OF HERE! HURRY!

ESTUPIDO--! YOU ARE NOT THE ONLY ONE WITH POWER!

HAH! YOU DIDN'T BELIEVE ME WHEN I SAID THAT PART OF YOUR POWER WAS ALREADY MINE!
Y-YOU WON'T GET ANY MORE!
FEEL'S LIKE I'M ON FIRE, BUT I HAVE TO DRAW HIS ATTENTION AWAY FROM THE OTHERS!
YOU'LL NEVER ESCAPE ME NOW!

THAT'S IT, PICARO...
...TRY TO FOLLOW ME! LET'S SEE WHAT YOU'VE REALLY GOT!

KROOM

BUENO, CAPITAN... MUY BUENO!
THE MORE ENERGY YOU EXPEND, THE MORE MY EXO-SUIT LEECHES AWAY!
HE'S RIGHT, BLAST IT! I CAN'T SEEM TO GET UP TO SPEED... AND HE'S GAINING! I HAVE TO SHAKE HIM FAST!

YOU CANNOT LOSE ME, MARVEL!
SOON YOUR ENERGY WILL ALL BE MINE!

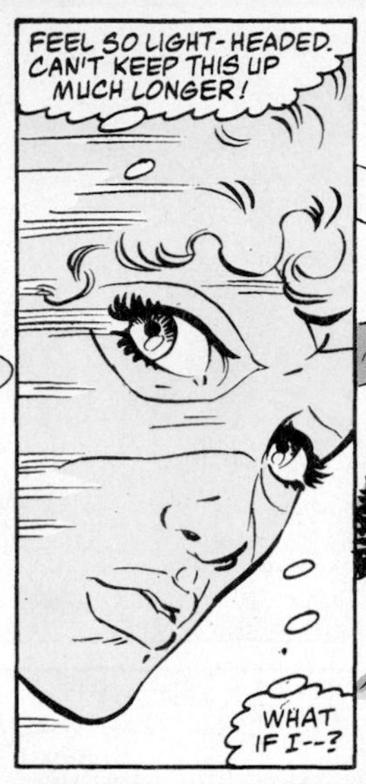
FEEL SO LIGHT-HEADED. CAN'T KEEP THIS UP MUCH LONGER!
WHAT IF I--?

HAH-HA-HA!
YOU CANNOT SAVE YOUR DWINDLING POWER BY SHUTTING IT OFF!

IT IS FAR TOO LATE FOR THAT! ALREADY MY CIRCUITRY HAS ENERGY ENOUGH TO BEGIN POWER TRANSFERAL! ANOTHER MOMENT, AND I SHALL DRAIN YOU DRY!

YOU WANT POWER SO MUCH, PICARO? OKAY, HERE!
QUE--?

NO! MY CIRCUITS CAN'T CONTAIN ALL THIS ENERGY AT ONCE! IT WILL OVER-LOAD! YOU'LL KILL US BOTH!
I'LL TAKE... THAT CHANCE! WILL YOU?

MILES AWAY...
ANDRE! ANDRE, LOOK!
MON DIEU! THAT PEAK IS LIT UP LIKE...

...HIROSHIMA.
EVERYONE ...DOWN!

BABOOM

M-MON CAPITAINE!

LATER...
NO RESIDUAL HARD RADIATION HERE. BACKGROUND EMISSIONS... ALL WELL WITHIN SAFE LEVELS.
ULTRAVIOLET SHIFT CHECKS. VISIBLE LIGHT... I'M READING FULL SPECTRUM, NO DEVIATION. ALL CLEAR ON INFRARED... AND BELOW.
I WOULD JUDGE THAT YOUR POWERS ARE PERFECTLY UNDER CONTROL, CAPITAINE. YOU MAY RETURN TO HUMAN FORM, IF YOU SO WISH!

ANDRE, AREN'T YOU BEING PREMATURE? A MOUNTAINTOP WAS JUST VAPORIZED!
THERE IS NO FURTHER DANGER.
I'M GLAD TO HEAR THAT!

I JUST WISH... THIS HADN'T BEEN NECESSARY.
CAPITAINE, HAD YOU NOT AT THE LAST INSTANT RE-ABSORBED THE ENERGY HE HAD STOLEN, PICARO WOULD HAVE SUFFERED THE SAME FATE AS THIS ROCK! YOU SAVED HIS LIFE...
...A FACT WHICH WILL GALL HIM, SHOULD HE REGAIN CONSCIOUSNESS.
WELL, I HATE TO RUN, BUT THERE'S A RESORT IN NEED OF REPAIRS! AU REVOIR!

ALL THAT POWER UNDER THE CONTROL OF ONE HUMAN BEING... FRIGHTENING! PERHAPS IT WOULD HAVE BEEN BETTER IF SHE'D LOST THAT POWER--!
YOU MIGHT AS WELL WISH THAT WE HAD NEVER DIS-COVERED NUCLEAR POWER! IT IS TOO LATE... IT IS FACT!

WE SHOULD COUNT OURSELVES LUCKY THAT THE FATES PLACED THAT POWER UNDER THE CONTROL OF SUCH A WOMAN AS CAPITAINE MARVEL!
IF HUMANITY COULD BUT LEARN TO USE ITS POWER AS WELL AS SHE HAS HERS... AH, MY FRIENDS, THERE IS A WISH WORTH WISHING!
END

MARVEL®
SOLO AVENGERS™ STARRING
HAWKEYE™
AND MOON KNIGHT®
© 1987 MARVEL COMICS GROUP
75¢ US
95¢ CAN
3
FEB
APPROVED BY THE COMICS CODE AUTHORITY
02651
THE ACE ARCHER VS.
BATROC™
THE LEAPER!
THE CRESCENT CRUSADER VS.
SHROUD™
MASTER OF DARKNESS!
BOB HALL
&STAN DRAKE

STAN LEE PROUDLY PRESENTS THE CONTINUING SAGA OF THE WORLD'S GREATEST ARCHER--
HAWKEYE
BLAST! I'VE BEEN ON THE DEFENSIVE EVER SINCE THIS BATTLE BEGAN... AND THINGS ARE GOING FROM BAD TO WORSE!
I'VE BEEN SHOOTING MY ARROWS FASTER THAN I CAN AIM JUST TO KEEP THESE GUYS OFF MY--
WRITTEN WITH STYLE BY: TOM DeFALCO
PENCILED WITH DRAMA BY: MARK D. BRIGHT
INKED WITH PRECISION BY: JOSEF RUBINSTEIN
LETTERED WITH LOVE BY: JACK MORELLI
COLORED WITH CARE BY: KEN FEDUNIEWICZ
EDITED WITH A TWO BY FOUR BY: MARK GRUENWALD

--YIKES!!
YOU ARE SLOWING DOWN, MON AMI! BURNING OUT!
YOU BARELY MANAGED TO DODGE THOSE *SAIS*, AND YOU CERTAINLY WON'T AVOID--

--ME?!
WANNA *BET*, PALLY? I HEARD YOU COMING A MILE OFF-- AND CAN EASILY ROLL BENEATH YOUR CLUMSY ATTACK!
ARCHERY MAY BE MY SPECIALTY BUT I ALSO TOOK COMBAT LESSONS FROM *CAPTAIN AMERICA* HIMSELF!

*WHEW* WISH I WAS HALF AS *CONFIDENT* AS I SOUND! TRUTH IS, I REALLY *AM* STARTING TO *TIRE*!
I'VE GOTTA PUT THE SKIDS TO THIS BUM BEFORE HE CAN--
WHAT THE--?!
HE'S... GONE!
NOT *GONE*, MON *AMI*!
WOK
I WAS MERELY PLACING MYSELF INTO THE PROPER POSITION TO DELIVER YOUR *DEATH BLOW*, AND BRING A DRAMATIC CLOSE TO THE ADVENTURES OF--

# AN AMERICAN ARCHER IN PARIS

WHOOPS!

BARELY TWENTY-FOUR HOURS AGO, HE WAS STILL IN LOS ANGELES AT WEST COAST AVENGERS HEADQUARTERS, WHEN...
YOU RECEIVED A ONE WAY TICKET TO PARIS FROM TRICK SHOT, YOUR FORMER MENTOR?

HAWK, THAT MAN VOWED TO KILL YOU! THIS IS OBVIOUSLY SOME KIND OF DEATH CHALLENGE!
OBVIOUSLY.
KLIK
YOU CAN'T POSSIBLY ACCEPT!

NO WAY! BUT I CAN CASH IN THE TICKET AND TAKE MY BEAUTIFUL WIFE TO DINNER WITH THE PROCEEDS!
PROMISE!?
I PROMISE ALREADY!

I'M SORRY, HONEY. IT'S NOT BECAUSE I DON'T TRUST YOU...
SHH! I KNOW, SWEETHEART... I KNOW! LISTEN, MOCKINGBIRD, I LOVE YOU! I REALLY DO!
KNOW SOMETHING, HAWK?

YOU'RE A LYING TWO-FACED CHEAT!
I HEARD YOU SLIP THAT GAS ARROWHEAD OUT OF YOUR TUNIC!
WHOMP

YOU DON'T UNDERSTAND, BABE!
OF COURSE I DO! I KNOW JUST HOW YOUR DEVIOUS MIND WORKS!

MACHO PRIDE IS FORCING YOU TO ACCEPT THAT RIDICULOUS CHALLENGE!
USED A FEW BAD THROWS TO DISTRACT HER SO THAT I COULD--

"-- EASILY CATCH HER ON THE WAY DOWN!"
PWUFF
UNG!

THOSE ARROWHEADS ARE FILLED WITH A FAST-ACTING SLEEP GAS! SHE WON'T BE HURT... UNTIL SHE WAKES AND FINDS I'VE GONE!

I FEEL LIKE SUCH A HEEL!
THE UNEVENTFUL TRIP TOOK A TOTAL OF TWENTY-TWO HOURS, INCLUDING A ONE HOUR LAYOVER IN CHICAGO AND THE NINE HOUR TIME DIFFERENCE BETWEEN LOS ANGELES AND PARIS.

LUCK WAS WITH HAWKEYE ON THE CUSTOMS LINE.
ONLY A FEW PEOPLE WERE ASKED TO UNPACK THEIR LUGGAGE, AND HE WASN'T ONE OF THEM.
AND, HE MANAGED TO SPOT TWO GENTLEMEN OBVIOUSLY SENT TO TAIL HIM!

NO SOONER DID HE CHECK INTO HIS HOTEL ROOM, THAN...
SOMEONE JUST SLIPPED AN ENVELOPE UNDER MY DOOR!
IT CONTAINED A SINGLE PICTURE--

--OF THE CATHEDRAL OF NOTRE DAME!
GOTTA HAND IT TO TRICK SHOT!

HE CERTAINLY DOESN'T BELIEVE IN WASTING TIME!
I KNOW HE'S AROUND HERE SOME-WHERE!
BUT INSTEAD OF HIS FORMER MENTOR, HAWKEYE FOUND--

--THREE OTHER ASSASSINS!
MONSIEUR TRICK SHOT SENDS HIS REGRETS!
SNAP
HE COULDN'T BE HERE... SO HE SENT US!
I RECOGNIZE THESE THREE... AND I WISH I DIDN'T! BATROC THE LEAPER-- ZARAN THE WEAPONS MASTER-- AND MACHETE THE KING OF KNIVES!

BUT WHERE'S TRICK SHOT? IT'S NOT LIKE HIM TO USE HIRED HELP ON A PERSONAL VENDETTA?
OH, WELL... GUESS I CAN'T WORRY ABOUT THAT NOW!

THE AMERICAN APPEARS TO BE IN A HOPELESS POSITION. SHOULD WE MOVE IN?
NO! I HAVE HEARD THAT HE IS VERY RESOURCEFUL...

"LET US SEE IF HE IS WORTHY OF HIS ILLUSTRIOUS REPUTATION!"

CAN YOU SEE HIM, MACHETE?
WHAT IS THE BLOODY FOOL DOING NOW?
HE IS CRAZY, ZARAN! MUY LOCO!

HE'S USING HIS REMAINING ARROW LINE TO SWING TO THAT NEARBY ROOFTOP!
LOGIC SAYS I SHOULD KEEP RUNNING--BUT NO ONE'S EVER CONFUSED ME WITH MR. SPOCK!
I JUST CAN'T LEAVE PARIS UNTIL I'VE FOUND TRICK AND FINALLY SETTLED THINGS BETWEEN US!

HURRY, MES AMIS!
WE MUST FOLLOW!

OUR CLIENT WILL BE LESS THAN PLEASED IF WE FAIL HIM!
WHERE IS TRICK SHOT?!
WHY'D HE HIRE YOU, BATROC?

MODESTY AND PROFESSIONAL ETHICS DEMAND THAT I KEEP SILENT, HAWKEYE!
MISSED HIM!
I'VE GOT A FLASH FOR YOU, PAL! YOUR LEAP WAS WAY OFF TARGET!

IT WAS MEANT TO BE!
I WAS MERELY CUTTING OFF YOUR ESCAPE ROUTE!
WHO'S ESCAPING?
I WAS JUST TRYING TO GET IN A LITTLE SIGHTSEEING BEFORE I FLATTEN YOU!

PWUFF
AND YOUR HEAVY-FOOTED FRIENDS!

WELL DONE, ARCHER! YOU MANAGED TO STUN MACHETE WITH A LUCKY SHOT!
IT'S A PITY THAT I HAVE MOVED IN MUCH TOO CLOSE FOR YOUR BOW AND ARROWS TO BE OF ANY USE NOW!

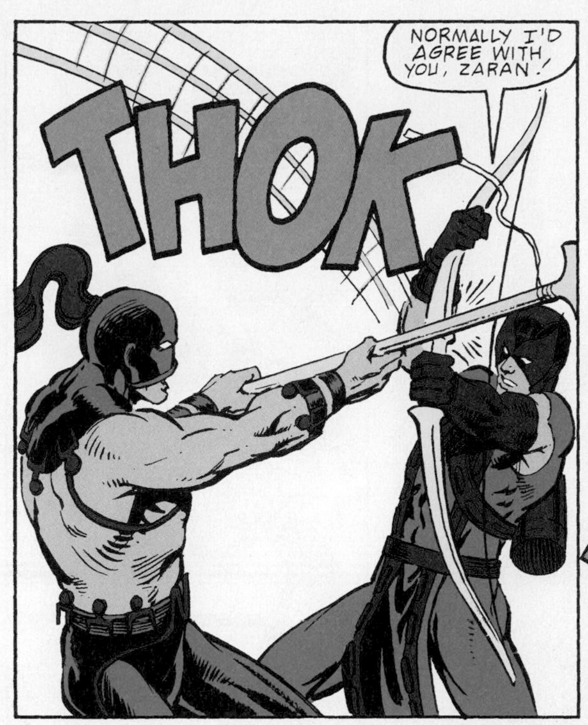
THOK
NORMALLY I'D AGREE WITH YOU, ZARAN!

THIS BOW IS A FINELY TUNED INSTRUMENT.
A WORK OF ART WHICH SHOULD NEVER BE USED LIKE A COMMON BASEBALL BAT!
THOUGH I GUESS IT'LL DO IN A PINCH!
WHUD

I AM IMPRESSED, AVENGER! YOU SEEM MORE THAN A MATCH FOR MY TWO BUMBLING ASSOCIATES!
BUT WHAT DO YOU INTEND TO DO ABOUT ME?
WELL, I COULD BUY A POGO STICK TO KEEP UP WITH YOU!

OR I COULD JUST SETTLE ON USING THIS HANDY LITTLE MANUEVER WHICH CAPTAIN AMERICA TAUGHT ME!
IT'S CRUDE, BUT VERY EFFECTIVE!

ENOUGH!
WE HAVE SUFFERED ENOUGH PAIN AND HUMILIATION AT YOUR HANDS!
KEEP IT DOWN, WILL YA?
I'D HATE TO BE ACCUSED OF ASSASSIN ABUSE!

THIS IS STARTING TO GET WAY OUT OF HAND!
PERHAPS WE SHOULD INTERFERE NOW!

NO! LET THEM FINISH!!

WHAT'S WITH YOU GUYS? DON'T YOU KNOW YOU'RE SUPPOSED TO BE UN-CONSCIOUS AFTER A HERO CLOBBERS YOU?
IT'S IN YOUR UNION CONTRACT!
AND ZARAN... YOUR BAD KNIFE-THROWING IS REALLY STARTING TO BUG ME!

WHERE'S YOUR PRIDE, MAN?!
MAYBE A LITTLE QUICK-DRYING ADHESIVE WILL GIVE YOU TIME TO CONSIDER YOUR APPALLING LACK OF PROFESSIONALISM!
SPOIT

BUT THEN, BEFORE HAWKEYE CAN DRAW ANOTHER ARROW, BATROC STRIKES WITH THE SPEED OF AN ENRAGED COBRA!
YOU HAVE GONE TOO FAR, ARCHER! YOU MUST BE TAUGHT TO RESPECT YOUR BETTERS!
KRASH

LOOK! THEY CRASHED INTO THE RESTAURANT BELOW--AND HAWKEYE LOST HIS BOW!
DON'T WORRY! HE IS AN AVENGER--

"--AND WON'T ALLOW ANY INNOCENTS TO BE HARMED!"
I SHALL SOON SKEWER YOU LIKE THE PIG YOU ARE!
MIND IF I GET A LITTLE NIBBLE FROM THAT SHISH-KABOB FIRST? I'M FAMISHED!
IF YOU'RE GONNA EAT WITH YOUR FINGERS--

--I INSIST YOU USE A NAPKIN!
FWAPP

STOP IT! STOP TRYING TO MAKE A FOOL OF ME!
WHY? WOULD YOU RATHER DO IT YOURSELF?!

IT'S OBVIOUS THESE FRENCH-MEN HAVEN'T SEEN MANY COSTUMED CLOWNS MIX IT UP!
THEY DON'T KNOW ENOUGH TO CLEAR OUT!

GUESS I'M JUST GONNA HAVE TO TAKE A FEW BAD KICKS
UGNN
SO I CAN DIRECT THE FIGHT OUT-SIDE!
WAKT
WUNK

YOU THOUGHT TO ESCAPE ME, MON AMI?
NOPE! JUST WANTED TO GET AWAY FROM ALL THAT FANCY FOOD-- BEFORE I WAS TEMPTED TO GO OFF MY DIET!
HOPE YOU DON'T MIND THAT I CHOSE A QUIET CORNER-- THAT'S A LITTLE TO CRAMPED FOR YOU TO BOUNCE AROUND-- AND USE YOUR SAVATE AGAINST ME!

YOU INSOLENT SWINE! SAVATE IS AN ARTISTIC FORM OF FOOT-BOXING RESERVED FOR GENTLEMEN!
I DO NOT NEED IT AGAINST ONE SUCH AS YOU!
THWAK
UNN!
YOU'RE EXHAUSTED! DEAD ON YOUR FEET!
YOU CAN'T EVEN AVOID THIS OBVIOUS HEAD-BUTT!
BWAK
NO! NO! DON'T FALL DOWN YET, HAWKEYE! I HAVEN'T FINISHED PUNISHING YOU! YOU CAN TAKE ONE MORE SHOT, CAN'T YOU?
CAN'T YOU?!
PWOOM
SURE,
CAN YOU?!

STAN LEE PRESENTS
MOON KNIGHT!
WHAT WAS IT SHAKESPEARE WROTE: "ALL THE WORLD'S A STAGE"? YEAH... "AND ONE MAN IN HIS TIME PLAYS MANY PARTS". OLD WILLIE WAS ON THE MONEY THERE.
IN MY TIME I'VE BEEN A BOXER, A MERCENARY, AND A MILLIONAIRE. I'VE DRIVEN CABS AND I'VE DEALT IN FINE ART. WHO'D HAVE THOUGHT I'D END UP PLAYING HERO.
I'VE USED A LOT OF NAMES IN MY LIFE. THE ONE I ANSWER TO MOST IS THE ONE MY FATHER GAVE ME... MARC SPECTOR... 'CEPT WHEN I'M DUDED UP IN MY SKIN-TIGHTS AND CAPE. THEN I CALL MYSELF... MOON KNIGHT!
FUNNY, THE THINGS THAT RUN THROUGH YOUR MIND WHEN YOU'RE THOUSANDS OF FEET IN THE AIR.
JUST DAYS BEFORE, I'D JOINED THE AVENGERS, ARGUABLY THE WORLD'S FOREMOST GROUP OF HEROES. SO WHY WAS I DOING MY LONE RANGER NUMBER AGAIN? BECAUSE OF A FELLOW NAMED CORNELIUS VAN LUNT.
TOWER OF SHADOWS
ROGER STERN SCRIPTER
BOB HALL PENCILER
STAN DRAKE INKER
JACK MORELLI LETTERER
PAUL BECTON COLORIST
NOTE: THIS STORY TAKES PLACE BEFORE EVENTS SHOWN IN WEST COAST AVENGERS #29!

VAN LUNT WAS A WOULD-BE CRIMINAL MASTERMIND WHO'D GIVEN MY NEW PARTNERS PLENTY OF GRIEF. HE WAS STILL AT LARGE, AND I WAS LOOKING FOR INFORMATION ON HIS WHEREABOUTS.
PROBLEM WAS, THE ONLY REAL CONTACT I HAD HERE IN CALIFORNIA WAS JACK RUSSELL AND HE WAS A WEREWOLF!
BUT ASIDE FROM THE FACT THAT HE GOT A LITTLE WILD UNDER A FULL MOON, RUSSELL WAS AN OKAY GUY... I FELT I COULD TRUST HIM.

AT HIS SUGGESTION, I'D COME TO THIS ISOLATED ESTATE IN THE SANTA MONICA MOUNTAINS. SEEMS THAT IT WAS RUMORED TO BELONG TO A RENEGADE L.A. GANGSTER...
...AND RUSSELL SAID THAT IF ANYONE KNEW WHERE VAN LUNT WAS, THE MAN INSIDE WOULD. I HOPED JACK WAS RIGHT.
I ALSO HOPED I COULD PERSUADE THIS CRIME BOSS TO TALK... HIS KIND ARE NOTORIOUSLY UNCOOPERATIVE AROUND PEOPLE IN MY LINE OF WORK. LUCKILY I WASN'T THAT WELL KNOWN ON THE WEST COAST--

--AND IF "MR. KNOW-IT-ALL" HADN'T HEARD ABOUT MY NEW GROUP AFFILIATION, MAYBE I COULD CONVINCE HIM WE WORK THE SAME SIDE OF THE STREET.
MAYBE I COULD SPOOK HIM BY SNEAKING UP ON HIM UNANNOUNCED.

THEN AGAIN, MAYBE I COULDN'T. WHOEVER LIVED IN THIS PLACE HAD TO BE PRETTY MUCH SPOOK-PROOF... OR AN OLD SPOOK HIMSELF.
FROM SOMEWHERE OUTSIDE CAME A SOUND.. I COULD HAVE SWORN IT WAS A CROSS BETWEEN A BELLY LAUGH AND THE HOWL OF A WOLF. IT MADE ME WONDER JUST WHERE RUSSELL WAS TONIGHT...
...AND IF I WAS WRONG TO TRUST HIM SO SOON BEFORE A FULL MOON.

I KNOW I SHOULDN'T LET THESE THINGS GET TO ME. AFTER ALL, I'M AS MUCH A CREATURE OF THE NIGHT AS RUSSELL IS. STILL, THERE WAS SOME-THING ABOUT THIS PLACE THAT SET MY NERVES ON EDGE.

KLIK
GOOD THING, REALLY...
THAT BOOBY TRAP COULD HAVE BEEN TRIGGERED AUTOMATICALLY, BUT I'VE GOT THE SINKING FEELING IT WASN'T.

MY FEELINGS WEREN'T ALL THAT WERE SINKING.
THE FLOOR OF THE TOWER STILL LAY SEVERAL STORIES BENEATH ME, AND WHILE I COULD PROBABLY SURVIVE THE FALL WITHOUT INJURY...

...I SAW NO NEED TO TAKE FURTHER CHANCES... NOT WHEN THESE GARGOYLES PROVIDED SUCH AN EASILY ACCESSIBLE PERCH.
TOO EASILY ACCESSIBLE, AS IT TURNED OUT.

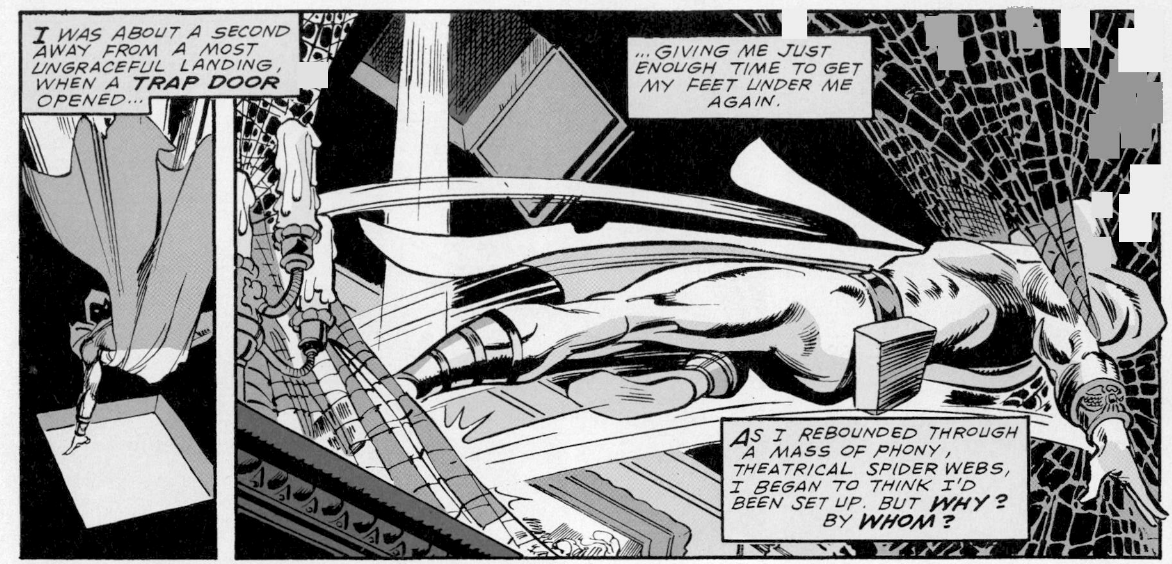
I WAS ABOUT A SECOND AWAY FROM A MOST UNGRACEFUL LANDING, WHEN A TRAP DOOR OPENED...
...GIVING ME JUST ENOUGH TIME TO GET MY FEET UNDER ME AGAIN.
AS I REBOUNDED THROUGH A MASS OF PHONY, THEATRICAL SPIDER WEBS, I BEGAN TO THINK I'D BEEN SET UP. BUT WHY? BY WHOM?

AND WHAT WERE THEY GOING TO THROW MY WAY NEXT?

THEY DIDN'T LEAVE ME WONDERING FOR LONG!
FFT
FFT
FFT

I CAUGHT A GLIMPSE OF LIQUID ON THE TIPS OF THE DARTS AS THEY FLASHED BY...
...COULD HAVE BEEN AN ANESTHETIC DRUG, OR A HALLUCINOGEN...OR SOMETHING MORE LETHAL.

WHATEVER IT WAS, I WANTED NO PART OF IT!

AH, BUT THE MAN BEHIND ALL THIS? HIM, I DEFINITELY WANTED A PART OF... SEVERAL PARTS PREFERABLY!
BY NOW I WAS CERTAIN THAT SOMEONE WAS DIRECTLY RUNNING THIS CHILLER-THEATER OBSTACLE COURSE.
IF THERE HAD BEEN ANY INFRARED BEAMS OR TRIP-WIRES, I WOULD'VE SPOTTED THEM. BUT NO... THERE WEREN'T EVEN ANY TELLTALE SIGNS OF HIDDEN CAMERAS.
WHICH MEANT THAT THE RESIDENT MASTERMIND WAS WATCHING FROM SOMEWHERE CLOSE BY!
THAT DOES IT!!
I'VE HAD ENOUGH! SHOW YOURSELF!
FACE ME LIKE A MAN!
SURE, IT WAS A STUPID, MACHO CHALLENGE. I JUST HOPED MY OPPONENT WAS STUPID AND MACHO ENOUGH TO FALL FOR IT!

THE ECHOES OF MY CHALLENGE HAD JUST DIED OUT WHEN SOMETHING ACROSS THE ROOM BEGAN TO MOVE...
I'D HAVE SWORN HE WASN'T THERE A MOMENT BEFORE, HE JUST MELTED OUT OF THE SHADOWS!
YOU HAVE ENTERED MY TOWER OF SHADOWS UNBIDDEN! AND SO YOU MUST FACE MY JUDGMENT--

--THE JUDGMENT OF THE SHROUD!
FACE THIS!

I'D MEANT TO PIN HIS CAPE TO THE WALL, BUT...
YOU ONLY THINK YOU KNOW THE DARK, MOON KNIGHT... BUT I AM ITS MASTER!

I COULDN'T HAVE TAKEN MORE THAN A SECOND TO REACT, BUT IN THAT TIME HE WAS GONE AGAIN!

WAK
YOU ARE WASTING YOUR TIME... AND MINE. YOU CAN NOT BEAT THE SHROUD!

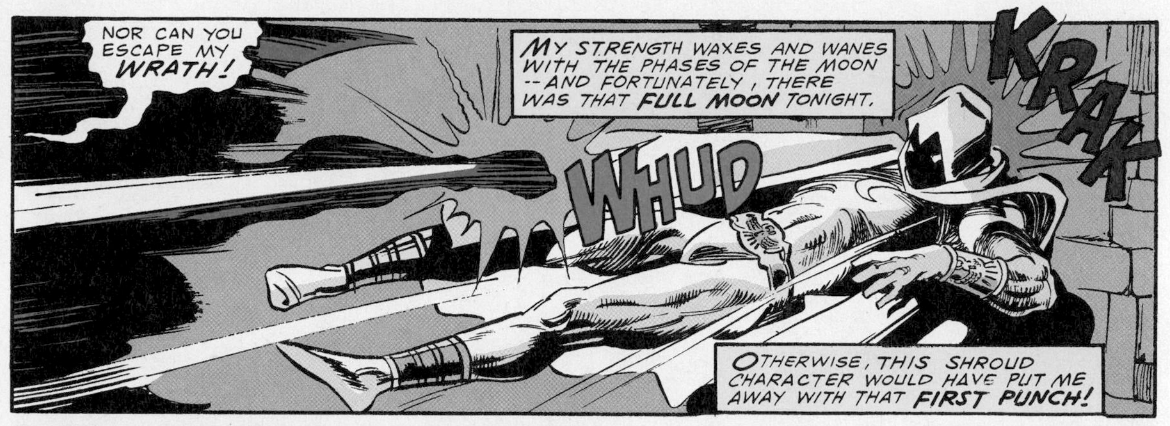
NOR CAN YOU ESCAPE MY WRATH!
MY STRENGTH WAXES AND WANES WITH THE PHASES OF THE MOON --AND FORTUNATELY, THERE WAS THAT FULL MOON TONIGHT.
KRAK
WHUD
OTHERWISE, THIS SHROUD CHARACTER WOULD HAVE PUT ME AWAY WITH THAT FIRST PUNCH!

HE SEEMED TO BE EVERYWHERE, AND I COULDN'T LAY A HAND ON HIM. I COULD BARELY SEE HIM!
SWAKT

HE HAD ME AT A DISADVANTAGE IN THE DARK, BUT I HAD A LITTLE SOMETHING IN MY WEAPONS POUCH TO TURN THAT AROUND...

...A SELF-IGNITING MAGNESIUM FLARE THAT HAWKEYE ADDED TO MY PERSONAL ARSENAL!
I FIGURED THE GLARE WOULD SHOW ME WHERE THE SHROUD WAS, AND BLIND HIM ENOUGH TO MAKE HIM AN EASY COLLAR.

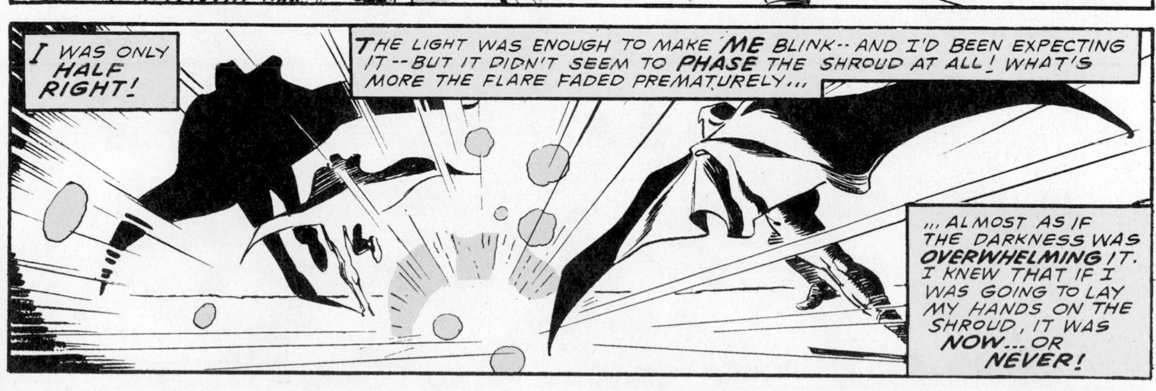
I WAS ONLY HALF RIGHT!
THE LIGHT WAS ENOUGH TO MAKE ME BLINK-- AND I'D BEEN EXPECTING IT--BUT IT DIDN'T SEEM TO PHASE THE SHROUD AT ALL! WHAT'S MORE THE FLARE FADED PREMATURELY...
...ALMOST AS IF THE DARKNESS WAS OVERWHELMING IT. I KNEW THAT IF I WAS GOING TO LAY MY HANDS ON THE SHROUD, IT WAS NOW...OR NEVER!

IT WAS NOW!
DON'T GO SLIPPING BACK INTO THE SHADOWS JUST YET, SHROUD.
YOU AND I--
--HAVE THINGS TO DISCUSS!
SLAM
YOU KNEW MY NAME... EVEN THOUGH IT'S NOT EXACTLY A HOUSEHOLD WORD IN THESE PARTS!
DID RUSSELL SET ME UP? DID HE?!
YOU'RE A PERSISTENT MAN, MOON KNIGHT...

--BUT IT TAKES MORE THAN PERSISTENCE TO WIN THE DAY!
I'D NEVER SEEN ANYONE SLIP OUT OF A CHOKE HOLD LIKE THAT. HE WAS OUT AND IN CONTROL OF THE SITUATION BEFORE I COULD STOP HIM.
THE SHROUD HAD MOVES I HADN'T SEEN ANYWHERE THIS SIDE OF THE ORIENT-- AND HE KNEW HOW TO USE THEM.
KRASH
I WILL TEACH YOU TO RESPECT THE HAND OF DARKNESS!
WAKT!
SORRY, I'M A SLOW LEARNER.
THAP
THE SHROUD ROLLED AWAY FROM MY KICK SO FAST, YOU'D THINK HE KNEW THE BLOW WAS COMING BEFORE I DID.
KRAK
BUT I'D RATTLED HIM... AND WE BOTH KNEW IT.
HE STRUCK BACK WITH THE FIRST THING HE COULD LAY HIS HANDS ON...

... NOT THAT IT DID HIM MUCH GOOD.
A CANDLE... YOU HIT ME WITH A CANDLE?

THAT'S WHEN I REALLY LOST MY TEMPER...
I'M TIRED OF THIS NONSENSE, SHROUD-- IT'S OVER!

DON'T TRY SLIPPING OUT OF THIS... UNLESS YOU WANT ME TO CUT YOUR WIND OFF COMPLETELY!
I WAS SURE I HAD THE UPPER HAND THIS TIME...

... BUT THEN THE ROOM TURNED BLACK AS PITCH...!

EVEN IN MY STRANGLE HOLD, THE SHROUD STILL CONTROLLED THE DARKNESS. I HAD TO BREAK HIS CONTROL SOMEHOW!
WUNK
THAT DID IT. THE DARK MELTED AWAY...
...AND I FOUND MYSELF FACING THE WEIRDEST BUNCH I'VE EVER SEEN!
MOON KNIGHT... MEET THE NIGHT SHIFT!!

NIGHT SHIFT WAS A GOOD NAME FOR THIS CREW... THEY LOOKED LIKE THEY'D STEPPED OUT OF SOME-BODY'S NIGHTMARE.
AND RUSSELL -- "MY BUDDY" THE WEREWOLF -- WAS AT THE HEAD OF THE PACK!
I BEGAN TO REGRET COMING HERE ON MY OWN.
BUT THEN...
THE MOON KNIGHT HAS ACCOUNTED FOR HIMSELF VERY WELL, MY FRIENDS.
THERE IS NO NEED FOR ANY FURTHER TESTING ON OUR PART, YOU MAY GO!
I DON'T BELIEVE IT! THERE'S A FULL MOON... RUSSELL SHOULD BE WILDER THAN A BAG OF BOBCATS!
HE'S UNDER THE CONTROL OF THE LADY WITH THE SWIRLING SASHES. HER DANCE CAN BE QUITE ENTRANCING.
YOU'RE SAYING RUSSELL IS YOUR PUPPET? THEN YOU USED HIM TO LURE ME HERE.
NOT AT ALL. THE WEREWOLF JOINED MY BAND OF HIS OWN FREE WILL. HE'S QUITE GRATEFUL THAT WE CAN HELP KEEP HIS CURSE IN CHECK.
AS A MATTER OF FACT, IT WAS ON HIS SUGGESTION THAT I DECIDED TO HOLD THIS INITIATION RITE. HE WAS RIGHT. YOU'D MAKE AN EXCELLENT ADDITION TO THE NIGHT SHIFT!
THE OBSTACLE COURSE-- OUR BATTLE-- IT WAS ALL A TEST!?
AS I STOOD THERE DUMBFOUNDED, THE SHROUD TOLD ME HOW HIS ROLE AS A CRIME-LORD WAS AN ELABOR-ATE CHARADE HE'D DEVISED TO ATTACK THE UNDERWORLD FROM WITHIN.

IT WAS THE CRAZIEST STORY I'D EVER HEARD, BUT AS THE SHROUD LAID IT OUT FOR ME... HIS SEPULCHRAL TONE FADED... HIS VOICE WENT UP HALF AN OCTAVE. HE WAS SO EARNEST.
YOU'RE SERIOUS ABOUT THIS. YOU REALLY WANT ME TO JOIN!
BUT I JUST JOINED THE AVENGERS...

HAWKEYE'S WEST COAST SQUAD... YES, I KNOW. THEY OFFERED ME MEMBERSHIP ONCE* --BUT I TURNED THEM DOWN.
WE'RE NIGHT PEOPLE, YOU AND I... BEING AN AVENGER IS A DAY JOB. YOU'RE OUT OF YOUR ELEMENT THERE.
*IN ISSUE #1 OF THE WEST COAST AVENGERS LTD SERIES.

I... I COULDN'T BACK OUT ON THE AVENGERS NOW. BESIDES, YOUR GROUP IS LARGER THAN THE AVENGERS. YOU DON'T NEED ME.
I WAS LOOKING FOR SOMEONE TO TAKE MY PLACE AS LEADER.
HA! NO THANKS! NOW, I DID HAVE A PURPOSE IN COMING HERE...
I KNOW... VAN LUNT. I'VE ALREADY PUT THE WORD OUT THROUGH MY PEOPLE!
IF HE'S ANYWHERE IN THE VALLEY, I'LL FIND HIM WITHIN 24 HOURS. ONCE I HAVE A FIX ON HIM, YOU'LL BE THE FIRST TO KNOW.
YOU HAVE THE WORD OF THE SHROUD!
UH... THANKS!
S'OKAY. YOU OWE ME ONE FOR TONIGHT.

AS I ACTIVATED MY 'COPTER'S AUTOPILOT TO TAKE ME OUT OF THERE, I MADE A MENTAL NOTE TO CHECK THE AVENGERS FILES FOR EVERYTHING THEY HELD ON THE SHROUD.
WHY? MAYBE I DIDN'T BUY HIS STORY 100 PERCENT. MAYBE I'M TOO OLD AND CYNICAL TO BELIEVE ANYONE COULD BE THAT BIG A BOY SCOUT.
AND MAYBE I JUST DIDN'T TRUST SOMEONE WHO'S EVEN MORE A "CREATURE OF THE NIGHT" THAN I AM!
THE END

MARVEL®

75¢ US
95¢ CAN
4
MAR
02651

APPROVED BY THE COMICS CODE AUTHORITY

# SOLO AVENGERS™

STARRING

# HAWKEYE™

AND BLACK KNIGHT™

WEAPONLESS AGAINST THE
WILD PACK!™
PLUS:
RAGE OF THE
LAST KNIGHT!™

Stan Lee presents
HAWKEYE
THE GREAT ESCAPE!
RECEIVING A DEATH CHALLENGE FROM HIS FORMER MENTOR--TRICK SHOT--HAWKEYE JOURNEYS TO PARIS!
BUT, EVEN BEFORE HE CAN FIND THE MAN WHO TAUGHT HIM ARCHERY, HAWKEYE GETS ARRESTED FOR MURDER.
I APOLOGIZE FOR THE ACCOMMODATIONS. THEY WERE THE BEST I COULD ARRANGE ON SUCH SHORT NOTICE.
AFTER ALL, ONE DOESN'T USUALLY ARREST A GENTLEMAN OF YOUR STATURE -- THE CHAIRMAN OF THE WEST COAST AVENGERS -- FOR MURDER! THE MURDER OF TRICK SHOT!
I DIDN'T KILL ANYBODY, LADY! THE CHARGES AGAINST ME ARE RIDICULOUS!
BE A GOOD LITTLE GIRL -- AND RELEASE ME! C'MON, LADY, YOU KNOW THAT I'M INNOCENT!
GLORIOUSLY WRITTEN BY TOM DeFALCO
GRANDLY PENCILED BY RON LIM
GALLANTLY INKED BY JOSEF RUBINSTEIN
GRACEFULLY LETTERED BY JACK MORELLI
GORGEOUSLY COLORED BY JANET JACKSON
GRUDGINGLY EDITED BY MARK GRUENWALD

STOP CALLING ME LADY!
MY NAME IS SILVER SABLE--AND I AM NO LADY IN ANY SENSE OF THE WAY YOU MEAN THAT WORD!
THE FRENCH GOVERNMENT AUTHORIZED ME TO CAPTURE A MURDERER--AND I HAVE DONE SO!
SAYS YOU!
HOWSABOUT A LAWYER?

ALL IN GOOD TIME, FRIEND.
THE AMERICAN EMBASSY WILL EVENTUALLY PROVIDE YOU WITH ONE. UNTIL THEN...

...PLEASE ENJOY YOUR STAY. LUNCHEON WILL BE SERVED WITHIN THE HOUR.
SLAM

YEAH... SURE, LADY.

MADAM SABLE, I FEAR I MUST PROTEST YOUR HANDLING OF THIS MOST DELICATE SITUATION!
IF THAT MAN SHOULD CONTACT THE OTHER AVENGERS--!

HE WON'T, MINISTER. TRUST ME.
HOW CAN YOU BE SO CERTAIN?
I KNOW MEN.
I HATE THESE DAILY WORKOUTS! HATE THEM ALL!

HAWKEYE IS MUCH TOO STUBBORN AND EGOTISTICAL TO CALL FOR HELP AT THE FIRST SIGN OF TROUBLE!
B-BUT YOU HAVE NO LEGAL RIGHT TO DETAIN HIM.
WHAM
KRAK
I KNOW THAT--
"--BUT HE DOES NOT!"
WAK
MINISTER, YOUR GOVERN-MENT HIRED MY ORGANIZATION --SILVER SABLE INTERNATIONAL --TO APPREHEND A DANGEROUS CRIMINAL--
--A CONTRACT KILLER KNOWN AS TRICK SHOT!
SNAP
RRIIIIP
THROUGH VARIOUS SOURCES, I HAVE LEARNED THAT HE AND HAWKEYE HAVE A PRIOR RELATIONSHIP--AND WERE TO MEET IN PARIS-- AND BATTLE TO THE DEATH!
WAP
SNAP

SINCE YOUR PEOPLE WANT TRICK SHOT TO STAND TRAIL FOR HIS MANY CRIMES, I ARRANGED FOR HAWKEYE'S FALSE ARREST.
THWAK

KRAK
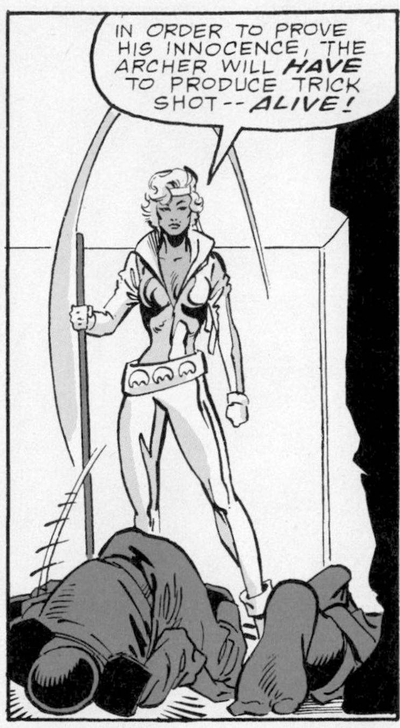
IN ORDER TO PROVE HIS INNOCENCE, THE ARCHER WILL HAVE TO PRODUCE TRICK SHOT--ALIVE!

"QUITE A SIMPLE PLAN... NO?"

BUT HOW DO YOU EXPECT HAWKEYE TO CAPTURE TRICK SHOT IF YOU ARE HOLDING HIM PRISONER?
SILLY BOY!

THE MAN'S AN AVENGER, ISN'T HE?
BY THE WAY, GENTLEMEN, NICE WORKOUT...

"...BUT LET'S TRY TO PICK UP THE PACE A BIT NEXT TIME!"
LUNCH TIME, ARCHER!
WE DO HOPE YOU'RE PARTIAL TO PHEASANT UNDER GLASS...

AFTER ALL, IT'S A SPECIALTY OF THE HOUSE!
TOO BAD! I HAD A REAL HANKERING FOR A BIG MAC!
SWAP
SO I'LL JUST HAVE TO GIVE YOU GUYS THE BIRD--
--AND GO OUT AND FIND THE BEEF MYSELF!
WHAT'S THE MATTER, PAL? FAST FOOD NOT YOUR STYLE?
NO PROBLEM.
IF YOU REALLY HAVE AN ITCH FOR SOMETHING OF THE VEGETARIAN PERSUASION, YOU COULD ALWAYS--
THAK
--EAT WOOD, JERK!
OKAY, SUNSHINE, THE MAIN COURSE IS OVER! NOW IT'S TIME FOR DESSERT!
I WANT MY BOW AND ARROWS! NOW!!

MADAM SABLE! THE AVENGER HAS ESCAPED!
RELAX, MINISTER...
WHA--?!

"--EVERYTHING IS PROCEEDING ACCORDING TO PLAN!
AND, A CASTLE IS A WEIRD PLACE TO HOLD A MURDER SUSPECT!
RECOVERING MY STUFF WAS EASY! ALMOST TOO EASY!
WHAT GAME IS SABLE PLAYING?
UH-OH! CAN'T WORRY ABOUT THAT NOW! SOMEONE'S COMING!

PLOOSH
TAGGED HIM WITH AN ADHESIVE ARROW --BUT NOW I HEAR A WHOLE CROWD HEADED MY WAY!

SOMETHING TELLS ME I NEED AN ARROWHEAD WITH A BIT MORE STOPPING POWER!
CLIK
SNAP

AN EXPLOSIVE TIP ARROW SHOULD THROW A REAL SCARE INTO THESE COSTUMED CLOWNS -- AND CONVINCE 'EM THAT I MEAN BUSINESS!

GOTTA AIM LOW AND OUTSIDE! DON'T WANT TO ACCIDENTALLY HURT 'EM!
BLAM
HEY! HE MISSED US!
GET HIM! SILVER WILL PROBABLY GIVE US A BIG BONUS FOR HIS RECAPTURE!
WHOOPS!

WOW! THOSE GUYS ARE A LOT TOUGHER THAN THEY LOOK! BUT I CAN'T PULL THE STOPS!
FOR ALL I KNOW THEY MIGHT REALLY WORK FOR THE FRENCH GOVERNMENT!
AFTER HIM! WE MUST STOP HIM BEFORE HE REACHES THE END OF THE PARAPET!

LOOKS LIKE THERE'S NO MORE RUNNING ROOM!
GLAD I CAME PREPARED WITH A CABLE ARROW!

TA-TA, GENTLEMEN! I REALLY WOULD LIKE TO STAY AND FIGHT IT OUT WITH YOU GUYS--
SLAM
--BUT THERE JUST AREN'T ENOUGH OF YOU TO GIVE ME A DECENT WORKOUT!

UH-OH! OUT OF THE FRYING PAN--AND INTO THE MICROWAVE!
ZZZZZ
FREEZE, AVENGER--OR WE FLASH-FRY YOUR FACE!
REALLY?

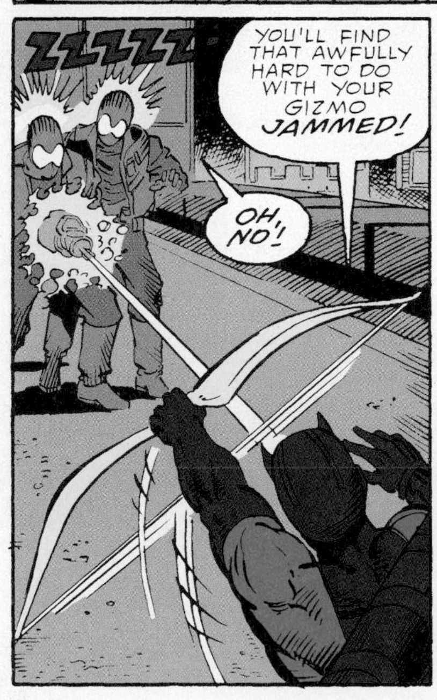
ZZZZZ
YOU'LL FIND THAT AWFULLY HARD TO DO WITH YOUR GIZMO JAMMED!
OH, NO!

BOOM
YOU'VE BEEN LUCKY, ARCHER! REAL LUCKY!

BUT THAT WAS BEFORE YOU MET ME!
KWAK
YEOW!

MY ELECTRO-WHIP WILL FLAY YOU ALIVE!

NO MATTER HOW FAST YOU ARE, YOU CAN'T DODGE ME FOREVER!

I DON'T HAVE TO--NOT WHEN AN OLD FASHIONED SOCK ON THE JAW CAN PUT YOU OUT OF MY MISERY!
PWOK

A WORD TO THE WISE, SUNSHINE. A MAN SHOULDN'T RELY ON HIS WEAPONS TO FIGHT HIS BATTLES FOR HIM!
THWAK
WEAPONS CAN MALFUNCTION OR BE TAKEN AWAY!
YOU'VE GOT TO BE ABLE TO DEPEND ON YOURSELF--ON YOUR OWN NATURAL ABILITIES!

WELL SAID--
--FROM A MAN WHO'S ENTIRE REPUTATION IS BUILT ON A BUNCH OF TRICK ARROWS!
SURE, I USE MY SHARE OF GIMMICKS, BUT I BACK THEM UP WITH A LOT OF SKILL AND SMARTS!

OBSERVE HOW I USE THIS NET ARROW..

--TO HELP POSITION MYSELF TO STRIKE AT YOUR MOST VULNER-ABLE AREA!
'NUFF SAID!

OH, SWELL! HERE COME FRESH TROOPS!
MAYBE I SHOULD'VE EATEN THAT PHEASANT WHEN I HAD THE CHANCE!
ALL THIS EXERCISE IS MAKING ME HUNGRY!
GUESS I CAN ALWAYS STOP FOR SOMETHING AFTER I'M THROUGH HERE!
THIS BATTLE SHOULDN'T LAST MUCH LONGER ANYWAY!
LOOK OUT!
TEAR GAS!!
CAN'T COFF! BREATHE!
ONCE I GET TO THE TOP OF THESE STAIRS, I'M HOME FREE!
BZAP
BZAP
WHOA!
JUST WHAT I NEED -- SOME JERK WITH A LASER PISTOL!
OH WELL, I GUESS HE HAS THE RIGHT TO EARN A LIVING TOO!
SAY, I WONDER IF SILVER SABLE IS PAYING HER PEOPLE EXTRA FOR ALL THIS?
SNAK

I'D BE REAL INSULTED IF I EVER LEARNED THAT SHE CONSIDERS TUSSLING WITH ME TO BE A NORMAL DAYS WORK!
TWAP

IMPRESSIVE. MOST IMPRESSIVE!
MY MEN ARE TOP PROFESSIONALS--THE VERY BEST MERCENARIES MONEY CAN BUY!

I ASSUMED HAWKEYE WAS GOOD, BUT I NEVER IMAGINED ANYONE COULD BE THIS GOOD!
I WONDER IF I COULD ENTICE HIM INTO ACCEPTING A RETAINER--

"--AND WORKING FOR ME ON A JOB BY JOB BASIS?"
I COULD MAKE A SHOT LIKE THIS WITH MY EYES CLOSED!

JUST HAVE TO CLEAR THE MOAT AND I'M OUTTA HERE!
SAYONARA, SILVER! I HAVEN'T HAD FUN LIKE THIS SINCE MY LAST ROOT CANAL!

NOW I JUST HAVE TO FIND TRICK SHOT... AND MY PROBLEMS ARE OVER!
WRONG, PUNK!
HUH?
THWAKT!
THEY'RE JUST BEGINNING!
YOU DONE YOUR OLD TEACHER PROUD, KID! IT BARELY TOOK YOU AN HOUR TO ESCAPE SILVER SABLE'S STRONGHOLD!
TOO BAD YOU COULDN'T KEEP YOUR WINNING STREAK GOING!
YOU CHOKED WHEN IT CAME TO YOUR FINAL EXAM!
TO BE CONCLUDED NEXT ISSUE...
"WHEN ARROWS FAIL!"

Stan Lee Presents:

# BLACK KNIGHT

# KNIGHT'S ERRANT

DEEP WITHIN THE LABORATORIES OF THE AVENGERS' HYDROBASE OUTPOST, DR. ANTHONY DRUID FINDS ONE OF HIS TEAMMATES ENGROSSED IN A MAZE OF ELECTRONICS...
DANE, WHAT THE DEUCE ARE YOU DOING?
JUST RUNNING A FEW TESTS, DOC... OR TRYING TO! MY EBONY BLADE PRETTY MUCH DEFIES SCIENTIFIC ANALYSIS!
BUT I'M NOT LICKED YET! IF THERE'S ANY WAY ON EARTH, I'M GOING TO KNOW THIS SWORD RIGHT DOWN TO ITS MOLECULAR STRUCTURE!
ROGER STERN STORY • PAUL RYAN BREAKDOWNS • BOB LAYTON FINISHED ART
PAUL BECTON COLORS • JACK MORELLI LETTERS

A MOST WORTHY GOAL, TO BE CERTAIN!
I MUST CONFESS, I MYSELF AM INTRIGUED BY YOUR SWORD... IT IS, AFTER ALL, THE ONLY KNOWN ARTIFACT OF LOST CAMELOT.
HAVE YOU LEARNED ANYTHING OF ITS CONSTRUCTION?
NOT MUCH MORE THAN I KNEW ALREADY. IT WAS CREATED IN THE SIXTH CENTURY FOR SIR PERCIVAL OF SCANDIA, THE FIRST BLACK KNIGHT. THE WIZARD MERLIN FORGED THE SWORD FROM A METEORITE--
--AND WORKED ALL MANNER OF ENCHANTMENT ON THE METAL, MAKING IT INDESTRUCTIBLE, CREATING A BOND BETWEEN IT AND PERCIVAL. AS I AM PERCIVAL'S DESCENDANT, THAT BOND HAS PASSED ON TO ME!

IF I'M SEPARATED FROM THE SWORD, I CAN WILL IT BACK TO MY HAND -- THROUGH A SORT OF MENTAL TELE-PORTATION. IN MY HAND IT FEELS LIGHT AS A RAPIER...
...BUT IT ACTUALLY WEIGHS A GOOD FIFTY POUNDS!
WATCH THIS! I HAVE ONLY TO REST THE SWORD POINT DOWN ON THIS GRANITE BLOCK--


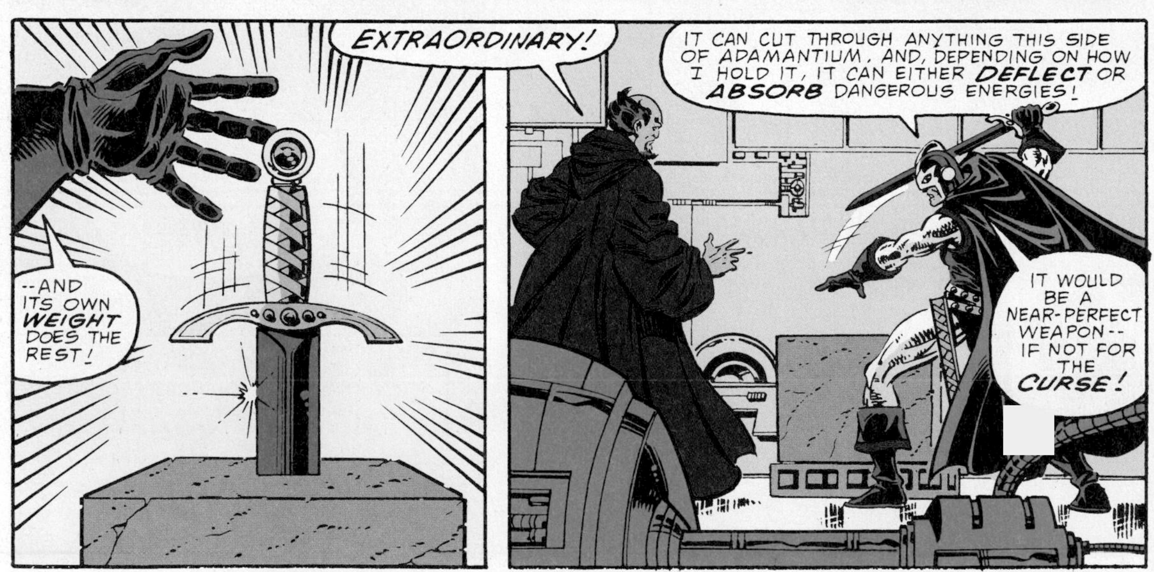

--AND ITS OWN WEIGHT DOES THE REST!
EXTRAORDINARY!
IT CAN CUT THROUGH ANYTHING THIS SIDE OF ADAMANTIUM, AND, DEPENDING ON HOW I HOLD IT, IT CAN EITHER DEFLECT OR ABSORB DANGEROUS ENERGIES!
IT WOULD BE A NEAR-PERFECT WEAPON -- IF NOT FOR THE CURSE!

CURSE?
YEAH... A SIDE-EFFECT OF THE ENCHANTMENTS. IF THE SWORD TASTES HUMAN BLOOD--
--IT WOULD START TO CONTROL ME, FORCING ME TO DRAW MORE BLOOD... EVEN TO KILL.

I USE THE FLAT OF THE SWORD WHEN I MUST FIGHT ONE-ON-ONE, BUT IF THE BLADE SHOULD SLIP--! EVEN A DROP OF BLOOD WOULD BE TOO MUCH!
THAT'S WHY I CONTINUE TO STUDY THE SWORD. THE BLACK KNIGHT MUST NEVER BECOME A DANGER!
PERHAPS I CAN HELP, DANE!

I HAVE, IN TIMES PAST, BEEN ABLE TO DISCERN CLUES OF MYSTIC ORIGIN THROUGH SUSTAINED MENTAL CONCENTRATION.
Ahhhh... YES... I CAN FEEL...
...CONSIDERABLE POWER... BOUND UP IN THIS METAL. ITS ENCHANTMENTS HAVE NOT DIMINISHED WITH THE PASSAGE OF TIME. TIME? ODD...
WHAT IS IT, DOC?
I CAN HEAR A VOICE... FAINTLY ... CALLING OUT, AS IF FROM ACROSS TIME. I CAN ALMOST FEEL THE PRESENCE!

YAAAHHHGH!!
NO! GET BACK!
WHAT'S WRONG?!
THE PRESENCE... IS HERE! MY PSYCHIC PROBE ... FORMED A CONDUIT...
--C-CAN'T HOLD IT BACK! TOO POWERFUL... TOO... POWERFUL!

DOC! WHAT'S HAPPENING?
DOC? WHY DO YOU CALL ME THAT?

YOU DO NOT RECOGNIZE ME? NO, OF COURSE NOT... THIS TIME MUST BE CENTURIES BEFORE MY BIRTHING!
YOU KNOW, PRIMITIVE, THAT BEFORE YOU NOW STANDS ERNST WYYTHIM... THE LAST KNIGHT!
SINCE THE SECOND MILLENNIA OF THE LEGENDARY EBONY SWORD, I HAVE BEEN ITS PRIME WIELDER. NOTHING CAN SEPARATE IT FROM ME... NOT EVEN DEATH!
HOW... HOW IN BLAZES DID YOU GET HERE? AND WHAT HAVE YOU DONE TO DOCTOR DRUID!?
WHO ARE YOU TO DEMAND... EH? THE SWORD!
WHAT ARE YOU DOING WITH MY SWORD?!
YOUR SWORD? THIS IS MY SWORD! I'M THE BLACK KNIGHT!
THEN YOU ARE MY ANCESTOR! TELL ME -- QUICKLY -- HAVE YOU YET SIRED ANY PROGENY?

HAVE I HAD ANY KIDS? NO, BUT WHAT DOES THAT--?
THE ENCHANTMENT WORKED! I MAY YET END THE CURSE!!
HEY!! WHAT'S THE BIG IDEA?!

THE IDEA IS MY SALVATION THROUGH YOUR DEATH!
WHANK
WHAT ARE YOU, NUTS?!

IF I'M YOUR ANCESTOR, WHY DO YOU WANT TO KILL ME?!
YOU MUST DIE... YOUR LINE MUST BE ENDED...

...SO THAT I WILL NEVER BE BORN!!
HE IS CRAZY! HE MUST BE!

WOK
HE HAS ABSOLUTELY NO INHIBITIONS ABOUT USING THE BLADE! GOT TO GET IT AWAY FROM HIM!

WAS THAT MEANT TO INCAPACITATE ME?
WELL, I HAD HOPED...
YOU STILL DO NOT REALIZE WHAT YOU FACE!
MY BODY ARMOR IS THE PRODUCT OF A TECHNOLOGY SOME 600 YEARS MORE ADVANCED THAN YOUR OWN! I MYSELF AM THE VICTOR OF THOUSANDS OF BATTLES!
AND YOUR EGO'S AS BIG AS ALL OUTDOORS! JUST KEEP TALKING!

I WOULD HAVE MADE YOUR DEATH A FAST, MERCIFUL ONE! WHY WILL YOU NOT ACCEPT YOUR FATE?
KLANK
I'VE FALLEN INTO THE HABIT OF STAYING ALIVE OVER THE PAST THIRTY YEARS!

ADMITTEDLY NOT AN EASY HABIT FOR SOMEONE IN MY LINE OF WORK! BACK OFF! LET'S TALK THIS THING OVER SENSIBLY!
YOU MENTIONED ENDING THE SWORD'S CURSE... I'D HOPED TO BEAT THAT!

MAYHAP YOU DID, BUT I COULD NOT! WHEN THE SWORD FELL TO ME, I SOUGHT TO USE ITS POWER IN THE CAUSE OF JUSTICE!
BUT EVENTUALLY MY BLADE TASTED BLOOD AND I WAS COMPELLED TO GIVE IT MORE! OVER TEN THOUSAND SOULS DIED AT MY HANDS... BEFORE I TOOK MY OWN LIFE!

TOOK YOUR OWN--?!
HAH! THE TRUTH CAN BE DISTRACTING, CAN IT NOT?

I HAVE ONLY YOUR WORD AS TO THE "TRUTH"... I'D LIKE A SECOND OPINION!
OWW! BLAST IT!!
WHU--!

NEARLY BUSTED MY KNEE TRYING TO KNOCK THE WIND OUT OF HIM AND IT HARDLY SLOWED HIM DOWN! HE'S JUST TOO WELL PADDED!

WHATEVER THIS GUY IS, HE MUST HAVE TOLD THE TRUTH ABOUT BEING MY DESCENDANT! I'VE BEEN CONCENTRATING ON THE SWORD, TRYING TO ZAP IT BACK TO ME...
...AND GETTING NOWHERE! HIS LINK TO THE SWORD IS AT LEAST AS STRONG AS MINE!

LOOKS LIKE THERE'S JUST ONE THING LEFT FOR ME TO DO, ERNIE!
DIE!!
FSSS
NOPE! FIGHT DIRTY!

EMERGENCY BACKUP SYSTEMS WILL SHUT DOWN THAT GAS LINE IN SECONDS-- BUT A FEW SECONDS IS ALL I NEED!
KOFF KAFF KAFF

ALL RIGHT, NOW LET'S GO BACK TO SQUARE ONE... HOW DID YOU GET HERE, AND WHERE'S DOCTOR DRUID ?!
I CAME HITHER VIA THE SWORD'S MYSTIC BOND. I TURNED THE EBONY BLADE UPON MYSELF... SPILLING MY OWN BLOOD TO SEND MY MIND BACK THROUGH TIME... SEEKING OUT A RECEPTIVE MIND TO DISPLACE!
THIS DOCTOR YOU SPEAK OF MUST HAVE PROVIDED THAT MIND!

YOU'RE NOT KIDDING... YOU REALLY DID COME BACK TO KILL OFF YOUR FAMILY LINE? BUT THAT'S IMPOSSIBLE... YOU CAN'T WIPE OUT YOUR OWN EXISTENCE!
FROM WHAT I UNDERSTAND OF TIME, THE MOST YOU'D ACCOMPLISH BY KILLING ME IS CAUSE AN ALTERNATE REALITY... ONE WITHOUT OUR FAMILY TREE... THAT'S ALL!

THEN THAT MUST SUFFICE! AS LONG AS THERE IS ONE FUTURE DENIED THE CURSE OF THE SWORD, I WILL NOT HAVE DIED IN VAIN!

MY SACRED MISSION MUST BE COMPLETED!
LET'S SWING OUR SWORD, ANCESTOR! WE SHALL BOTH GO TO OUR DESTINY... ENDING THE CURSE IN THE THROES OF GLORIOUS COMBAT!

THIS IS INSANE! HE'S DETERMINED TO FIGHT TO THE DEATH ...BUT I DON'T DARE LET HIM! IT MIGHT PROVE FATAL TO DRUID, WHATEVER'S HAPPENED TO HIM!

AND I DON'T DARE USE THE SWORD AGAINST HIM ... TOO MUCH RISK OF HIS BLOOD LUST TAKING OVER ME!
HEY, ERNST! WHAT DO YOU SAY WE SETTLE THIS HAND-TO-HAND?
NO!

AN UNARMED FOE IS A DEAD ONE! HOW HAVE YOU LIVED SO LONG, ANCESTOR?
I'VE BEEN LUCKY--

--TO TRAIN IN THE MARTIAL ARTS--
--WITH A FELLA NAMED CAPTAIN AMERICA!

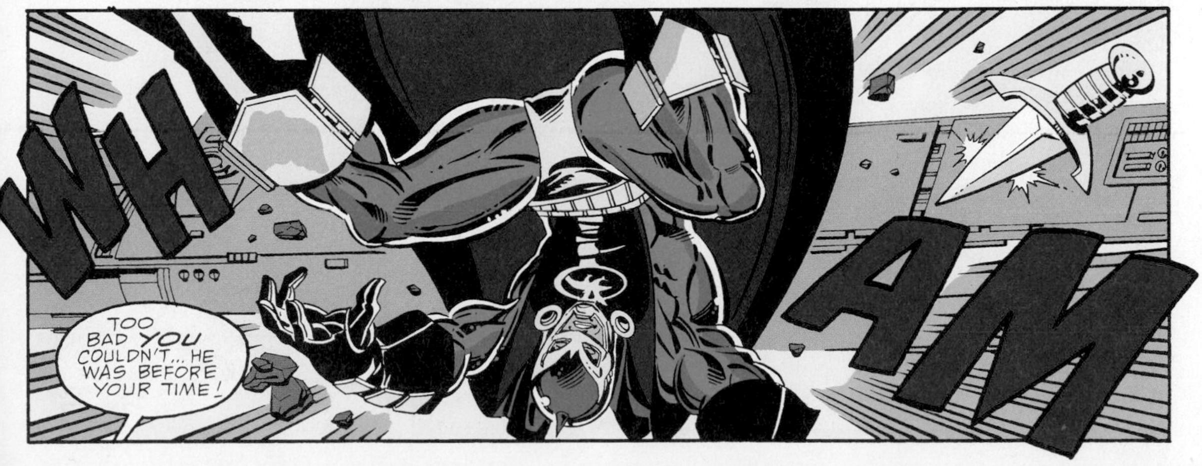
WHAM
TOO BAD YOU COULDN'T... HE WAS BEFORE YOUR TIME!

YOU CANNOT WIN... I AM BIGGER... STRONGER!

MAYBE SO...
WUDD

...BUT I'M A LOT MORE DESPERATE!
WUNK

AND I'M NOT READY TO DIE...
...NOT BY A LONG SHOT!
BTOK

I--I DID IT! I NEARLY BROKE MY FISTS ON HIS CHIN GUARD, BUT I FINALLY KNOCKED HIM OUT!
NOW WHAT DO I DO WITH HIM? BETTER YET, HOW DO I GET DOCTOR DRUID BACK?

I'LL TIE HIM UP BEFORE HE REGAINS CONSCIOUSNESS, THEN I'D BETTER CALL THE OTHER AVENGERS TO ASSEMBLE. IF WE CAN'T COME UP WITH A WAY TO FIND DRUID--

--WE'LL HAVE TO--
WAIT A SECOND--!
UHHNGH!?

DOC! ARE YOU ALL RIGHT ?!?
I THINK SO.

WHEN I KNOCKED OUT THE LAST KNIGHT IT MUST HAVE BROKEN THE SPELL THAT BROUGHT HIM HERE!
THE LAST THING I RECALL WAS PICKING UP A STRANGE VIBRATION FROM YOUR SWORD--!
DANE, WHAT THE DEVIL HAPPENED HERE?

IT'S A LONG STORY, DOC. YOU MIGHT SAY I GOT A MESSAGE FROM THE FUTURE.
I TAKE IT THE MESSAGE WASN'T GOOD NEWS!
THAT'S PUTTING IT LIGHTLY.

I HAD TO FACE MY OWN MORTALITY TODAY. I WON'T LIVE FOREVER... AND AFTER I'M GONE, SOMEONE ELSE WILL HAVE THE CURSE OF THE SWORD UNLESS--
I MUST FIND A WAY TO NEUTRALIZE THE CURSE -- OR ELSE DESTROY THE SWORD-- IN MY LIFETIME. IF I CAN'T, THOUSANDS MORE MAY BE DOOMED!
AND, UNTIL I FIND THAT CURE, I'LL HAVE TO TOTALLY REVAMP THE WAY I FIGHT. AS LONG AS THE CURSE EXISTS, THIS SWORD MUST NEVER BE DRAWN AGAINST ANOTHER LIVING FOE!
THE END?

MARVEL®

# SOLO AVENGERS™

STARRING

# HAWKEYE™

AND

# SCARLET WITCH



75¢ US
95¢ CAN
5
APR
02651



DEATH STALKS AN AVENGER!

HEADS YOU LOSE, HAWK!

THE TRIUMPH OF TRICK SHOT!™

Stan Lee presents
HAWKEYE
UNG! I'M BURNING UP! AND THE GROUND'S SO HOT! MUST HAVE DIED AND GONE TO--
NAH! MY HEAD HURTS TOO MUCH! I CAN'T BE DEAD!
HAWKEYE COSTUME, BOW, QUIVER, ...GONE!
WHERE AM I? THIS CERTAINLY ISN'T KANSAS!
LAST I REMEMBER I WAS IN PARIS...
"WHEN ARROWS FAIL!"
TOM DEFALCO STORY
MARK BRIGHT PENCILS
JOSEF RUBINSTEIN INKS
JACK MORELLI LETTERER
JANET JACKSON COLORIST
MARK GRUENWALD EDITS

YEAH, I'D GONE THERE BECAUSE OF TRICK SHOT--THE GUY WHO TAUGHT ME ARCHERY.
HE HAD CHALLENGED ME TO A DEATH MATCH!
BUT WHEN I ARRIVED, SILVER SABLE ARRESTED ME FOR HIS MURDER.

"I HAD JUST MANAGED TO ESCAPED SABLE WHEN I RAN INTO THE MAN HIMSELF--STILL ALIVE AND BREATHING!
"HE MUSTA HIT ME WITH A HYPODERMIC ARROW BECAUSE I WENT RIGHT OUT!

WHEW! I KNEW HE WAS HOLDING A GRUDGE--BUT WHY GO TO SO MUCH TROUBLE TO KIDNAP ME?
WELL, WELL, WELL! LOOK WHAT THE EASTER BUNNY LEFT ME!
KAF KAF
SOUNDS LIKE SOME-ONE'S COUGH-ING!
COUGHING?

UH-OH! SOMETHING TELLS ME THAT I'D BETTER GET MOVING!
TAP THE ARROWHEADS SO THAT THE SHAFTS LIFT INTO MY HAND!
GRAB THE BOW AND--

--MAKE IT HAPPEN!!
THIS MUST BE THE START OF TRICK SHOT'S DEATH MATCH!
TWANG
WELL, HE'S IN FOR MORE THAN HE BARGAINED FOR! A LOT MORE!

HEADS UP, TRICK! IN THE WORDS OF GOOD OL' RAMBO, "I'M COMING FOR YOU!"
GOTTA CHECK ALL THE ARROWS! THEY SEEM ALL RIGHT, BUT--

"--I CAN'T AFFORD ANY SURPRISES!"
MADAM SABLE, THE FRENCH GOVERNMENT HIRED YOU TO NEU-TRALIZE A PROFESSIONAL ASSASSIN!

YOUR PLAN TO USE THE AMERICAN ARCHER TO LEAD US TO TRICK SHOT HAS FAILED!
AND YOU'VE LOST HAWKEYE AS WELL!
QUITE TRUE, MINISTER, BUT--
MY LADY, PLEASE EXCUSE THIS INTERRUP-TION!
OUR OPERATIVES HAVE JUST LEARNED THAT A MAN FITTING TRICK SHOT'S DESCRIPTION JUST CHARTED A BOAT TO ONE OF THE UN-INHABITED GREEK ISLES!
EXCELLENT!

NOTIFY THE ASSAULT FORCE! WE LEAVE IMMEDIATELY!
THIS ISN'T GOOD! I KNOW WHAT TRICK SHOT IS CAPABLE OF DOING! IF HAWKEYE IS STILL ALIVE--

"--HE HAS THE FIGHT OF HIS LIFE ON HIS HANDS!"
COME OUT, COME OUT WHEREVER YOU ARE!

SWAK
WHAT THE--?

VERY FUNNY, TRICK! VERY...
OH, NO! NOT AGAIN!
THIP THIP THIP THIP
GEEZ! IS THIS HOW YOU TREAT ALL YOUR GUESTS?

THWAK
THWAK
THWAK
THWAK
THE VERY LEAST YOU COULD'VE DONE WAS OFFER ME A CUP OF COFFEE BEFORE YOU TRIED TO KILL ME!

NOW, I'M REAL MAD! THERE'S ABSOLUTELY NO EXCUSE FOR BAD MANNERS!
IF YOU WANT TO GET DOWN AND DIRTY--

--YOU PICKED THE RIGHT GUY!

SHUK
SHUK
YOU HEAR ME, TRICK SHOT?!

YEAH!
GUESS YOU GOT THE POINT!
SOME-THING'S REAL WRONG HERE!

TRICK IS EASILY MY EQUAL WITH A BOW! SO WHY IS HE HOLDING BACK?
UH-OH! CAN'T WORRY ABOUT THAT NOW! IT LOOKS LIKE I'VE RUN INTO A DEAD END! UNLESS THAT CAVE LEADS SOMEWHERE!
EASY DOES IT! TRICK'S GOT TO BE NEARBY!

I'M SURE HE SCOUTED THE ENTIRE ISLAND BEFORE HE BROUGHT ME HERE!
HE KNOWS THE TERRAIN AND I DON'T!
MAYBE HE WANTS ME TO ENTER THAT--

THIP THIP
WHA--?! HOW'D HE GET BEHIND ME?!
GOTTA FIND SOME COVER! FAST!

NO PLACE TO GO EXCEPT THIS CAVE!
IF I CAN GET OUT OF THE SUNLIGHT HE WON'T BE ABLE TO TARGET ME PROPERLY!

MADE IT! AND THIS BREAK IN THE WALL WILL PROTECT ME WHEN I... HEY!!

THAT'S NOT TRICK! IT'S A RIGGED UP DUMMY!
THEN THAT MEANS...

SWELL! HE USED ONE DUMMY TO TRAP AN EVEN BIGGER ONE!
BUT I'M SURE I CAN SCOOT OUT THAT OPENING BEFORE--

ER... MAYBE NOT!
SHEESH! HOW COME THOSE GUYS IN THE MOVIES ALWAYS MAKE IT OUT IN TIME?!

CLUMPF
GREAT! JUST GREAT!
NOW WHAT AM I SUPPOSED TO DO?!

HEY-- WHERE'S THAT LIGHT SUDDENLY COMING FROM?

AN EXIT!
IT'S A SAFE BET THAT TRICK'S OUT THERE JUST WAITING FOR ME!
OKAY, FELLA-- GET READY BECAUSE HERE I--

YI... YI... YIIIII!

AGGHH!

PLOOSH!

THAT DOES IT! THAT DOES IT!
I'VE HAD JUST ABOUT ENOUGH OF YOUR SCREWING AROUND!
IF IT'S A FIGHT YOU WANT-- COME OUT AND FACE ME LIKE A MAN!

NO NEED TO SHOUT, KID! I'M RIGHT HERE!
MAYBE IT'S TIME THAT WE FINALLY SETTLED THIS ONCE AND FOR ALL!
GO AHEAD, KID! MAKE YOUR MOVE!

WHAT'S THE MATTER, HOT SHOT? NEED SOME ARROWS?
THERE'S A SPARE QUIVER RIGHT IN FRONT OF YOU!

THINK YOU CAN REACH IT BEFORE I PUT THIS ARROW THROUGH YOUR HEART!?

WHAT'S WITH ALL THE TALKING?! WHY DOESN'T HE JUST TRY TO SHOOT ME AND GET THIS OVER WITH?!
HE OUGHT TO REALIZE BY NOW THAT HE CAN'T RATTLE ME!
ALL RIGHT, TRICK--

--LET'S ROCK N' ROLL!!
FWOOSH
HEY!

THAT WAS TOO EASY!
THE TRICK SHOT WHO TRAINED ME WOULDN'T HAVE ALLOWED ME TO DISTRACT HIM LIKE THAT!
PLASH
HE WOULDN'T HAVE LOST HIS BALANCE OR GIVEN ME TIME TO REACH THIS QUIVER!

WHAT THE HECK IS GOING ON?! WHY DOESN'T HE PULL OUT THE STOPS?!
C'MON, OLD MAN! THERE'S NO WAY YOU CAN ESCAPE ME NOW!
UH-OH!

NICE TRY, TRICK!
I REALLY APPRECIATE ALL THE TROUBLE YOU WENT THROUGH TO RIG THESE TRAPS FOR ME!
BUT I'VE GOT A FLASH FOR YOU, FATSO--
THIP
THIP

--YOU JUST LOST GAME, SET, AND MATCH!
I HAVE YOU NOW!!
I'M IMPRESSED KID! YOU MUST'VE FELT THAT LAST TRIP WIRE UNDER ALL THAT MUD AND SILT! YOU'RE GOOD.

ALMOST AS GOOD AS ME!
BETTER, TRICK! MUCH BETTER!

YOU SATISFIED? YOU TIRED OF PLAYING THIS STUPID GAME? IT'S OBVIOUS YOU NEVER INTEND TO GO THROUGH WITH THIS DEATH CHALLENGE!
YOU DIDN'T WANT TO KILL ME! YOU KEPT PASSING UP TOO MANY GOOD CHANCES!
DON'T BE A SAP, PUNK!

LOWERING YOUR BOW WAS A DUMB MISTAKE!
YOU'RE DEAD KID! YOU HEAR ME-- YOU'RE DEAD!!

THWIP
THWIP
THEN, SO ARE YOU!

YOU MISSED?!
THAT'S IMPOSSIBLE! YOU NEVER MISS!

YOU DID TOO, TRICK!
WHY?!
THIS AIN'T FAIR!
I SET THIS WHOLE THING UP SO YOU'D BE FORCED TO KILL ME!
YOU CAN'T FAIL ME NOW!

I WATCHED YOU! TESTED YOU!
I SENT PAID KILLERS UP AGAINST YOU-- AND YOU BEAT 'EM ALL!

YOU NEVER MISSED!
YOU WERE SUPPOSED TO KILL ME! KILL ME!

DO IT! DO IT NOW, OR I'LL BEAT YOU BLOODY!
YOU DON'T HAVE ANY CHOICE!

WHY?!
WHY?!
THOK

WHAT THE HECK IS WRONG WITH YOU?!

WHAT'S WRONG WITH ME?
I... I'M DYING!
I HAVE CANCER!

I HAVE CANCER, AND I DON'T WANT TO END MY DAYS WASTING AWAY IN SOME STINKING HOSPITAL BED OR JAIL CELL!
I'M A HITMAN, KID! I LIVED MY WHOLE LIFE BY THE WAY OF THE ARROW-- AND I WANTED TO GO OUT FIGHTING!

YOU OWE ME, KID! IT'S YOUR DUTY TO KILL ME!

YOU WERE NOTHING WHEN I FOUND YOU! NOTHING! I TRAINED YOU --GAVE YOU THE NECESSARY SKILLS TO BECOME AN AVENGER-- AND THE WORLD'S GREATEST ARCHER!
ALL YOU ARE, YOU OWE TO ME!
YOU GOTTA KILL ME!

IT'S THE PRICE I DEMAND FOR ALL I'VE GIVEN YOU!

NO WAY PAL!
SOME DEBTS JUST CAN'T BE PAID!
SNAP

YOU WERE MY LAST HOPE!
THE ONLY MAN WHO COULD'VE BEATEN ME IN A FAIR FIGHT!

WHAT AM I GONNA DO NOW?! I JUST CAN'T FACE THIS KINDA SLOW DYING!
YOU'LL FIND A WAY, TRICK! SOMEHOW, YOU'LL FIND A WAY!
I'LL DO WHATEVER I CAN TO HELP!

I OWE YOU THAT MUCH!
END.

Stan Lee presents

# SCARLET WITCH

"THE AIR IS CHILL AND DAMP.

"I AM BEING FOLLOWED.

"OF LATE, THE MAN NEVER SPEAKS, NEVER APPROACHES ME CLOSELY. BUT HE IS ALWAYS THERE, SOMETIMES OUT OF SIGHT, ALWAYS A PALPABLE PRESENCE.

"IN MY BRIEF LIFE I HAVE ESCAPED HIM **ONCE**. I FEAR THAT I WILL NOT BE ABLE TO DO SO AGAIN.

"I NEED THE HELP OF A FRIEND -- SOMEONE WHO WILL BE ABLE TO BOTH **PERCEIVE** AND TO **UNDERSTAND** MY DIFFICULTY.

"I WALK FASTER."

## "A LOVE THAT NEVER DIES"

DENNIS **MALLONEE** STORY | JOHN **RIDGWAY** ART | JACK **MORELLI** LETTERS | PAUL **BECTON** COLORS

LEONIA, NEW JERSEY.
Ahhh WANDA...
YOUR BABIES HAVE NOT LEFT YOU WITH YOUR GIRLISH FIGURE.
SHALL I GIVE UP, I WONDER, ON THE IDEA OF GETTING IT BACK?

PERHAPS IT'S A MISTAKE TO TRY TO WEAR THIS OLD GARMENT. THERE IS MUCH TO BE SAID FOR A MORE MATURE LOOK!

STILL IF MY HUSBAND PREFERS ME AS I... EH?
RAP RAP RAP RAP
WHO WOULD BE CALLING SO URGENTLY THIS LATE IN THE EVENING?

WANDA! THANK GOODNESS YOU'RE HOME! I WAS AFRAID EVEN TO STOP AND CALL!
MELINDA?! THIS IS A SURPRISE!

PLEASE! YOU HAVE TO HELP ME! YOU MAY BE THE ONLY ONE WHO CAN!
YOU'RE SHIVERING! BUT IT ISN'T THAT COLD!

CALM YOURSELF, MELINDA! WHATEVER IT IS, HYSTERIA WON'T HELP!
I KNOW...

IT MAY BE THAT NOTHING WILL HELP!
HUSH!
BUT YOU'VE BEEN KIND TO ME BEFORE, AND I NEED A KINDNESS NOW.
MY HUSBAND ISN'T HOME. A BASEBALL GAME. BUT HE'D AGREE TO LET YOU STAY FOR A TIME! FOR AS LONG AS YOU LIKE!

SIT. DRY YOUR TEARS. TELL ME ABOUT IT.
I'M NOT SURE WHERE TO...
NO! THAT'S NOT TRUE! I DO KNOW WHERE TO START. IT BEGINS WITH XANDU!

XANDU...
"I WAS DEAD, WANDA! I KNOW I WAS! BUT MY LOVER WAS A SORCERER, AND HE WOULDN'T LET MY BODY RETURN TO THE DUST!

"YOU REMEMBER. IT WAS YOUR SPIRIT XANDU STOLE TO REKINDLE THE SPARK OF LIFE WITHIN ME!*
"IF NOT FOR SPIDER-MAN'S HELP, YOU MIGHT HAVE BECOME ME. THAT WAS XANDU'S HOPE.
"BUT THAT DID NOT HAPPEN. INSTEAD, BECAUSE YOUR SPIRIT PREPARED THE WAY, I WAS ABLE TO LIVE AGAIN."
*MARVEL FANFARE #6

BUT DEATH IT SEEMS, IS RELUCTANT TO SURRENDER HIS GRIP ON THOSE WHO HAVE THOUGHT TO ESCAPE HIM!
AFTER YOU AND I PARTED COMPANY, I RETURNED TO MY HOME IN CALIFORNIA.
THERE I MET A WONDERFUL MAN NAMED JOHN KOWALSKI!
HE WAS KNOWLEDGEABLE STRAIGHTFORWARD, TOTALLY CHARMING IN HIS DIRECTNESS AND HIS SIMPLICITY.

"I COULD FEEL MYSELF FALLING IN LOVE, AND I WAS CERTAIN THAT MY AFFECTION WAS RE-TURNED.

"THEN ONE EVENING, AS WE WALKED HOME FROM A MOVIE IN WESTWOOD, THERE WAS AN ACCI-DENT!

"THERE WAS A DRUNK DRIVER AND A SIDEWALK.

"AND THE DRIVER PLOWED INTO SEVERAL PEOPLE.

"JOHN THREW ME ASIDE.
"HE WAS THE LAST TO BE HIT, HEAD-ON, WITH ENOUGH FORCE TO KILL.

"BUT JOHN KOWALSKI DIDN'T DIE...
"HE WAS ALREADY DEAD!"

"I HAD TO WATCH, IN RISING HORROR, AS JOHN KOWALSKI STIRRED HIMSELF...
"HE MOVED DOWN THE ROW OF THE INJURED AND DYING, TAKING THE LIVES OF THE DYING, ONE BY ONE, MERCILESSLY, WITH NO SYMPATHY FOR THOSE WHO WERE MERELY SUFFERING.

"DO YOU UNDERSTAND, WANDA? I HAD FALLEN IN LOVE WITH DEATH!
"JOHN KOWALSKI IS ANOTHER NAME FOR DEATH!
"I FLED FROM HIM THAT NIGHT, TERRIFIED TO THINK WHAT IT WAS HE MIGHT HAVE WANTED FROM ME!

"I PRAYED THAT I WOULD NEVER SEE HIM AGAIN."

BUT I HAVEN'T BEEN SPARED, WANDA!
I HAVE FLED FROM CITY TO CITY, AND HE HAS ALWAYS BEEN THERE, WATCHING ME. NEVER SPEAKING TO ME, NEVER MAKING ANY EFFORT TO EXPLAIN!
"I'VE BEEN HAUNTED BY DEATH THESE MANY LONG MONTHS, AND I WANT IT TO END!
"I'M ALIVE! YOU CAN SEE I'M ALIVE! WHY CAN'T HE ACCEPT THAT, AND LET ME LIVE OUT MY TIME IN PEACE?
WHY CAN'T HE... NO! HE'S HERE!
WHERE? I CAN'T SEE ANYTHI--
WAAA

WAAH WAH
THE CHILDREN!

OH, WANDA! WHAT HAVE I DONE?
WAIT HERE!
I'M SO SORRY...

KOWALSKI!
SHOW YOURSELF TO ME!

HOW DARE YOU?? MY CHILDREN! THOSE LIVES SPRING FROM ME!
DO THEY? WHAT OF IT?
POSTURE AND THREATEN IF YOU LIKE, WANDA! THERE IS NOTHING YOU CAN DO THAT WILL AFFECT ME. YOUR POWERS AFFECT PROBABILITY AND THERE IS NOTHING MORE CERTAIN FOR A HUMAN BEING THAN DEATH!

BUT I AM MORE THAN HUMAN, JOHN KOWALSKI! I AM A MUTANT WITCH! I CAN HURT YOU!
AND I WILL DO IT, UNLESS YOU PUT MY SON DOWN, NOW!
VERY WELL.

I WAS MERELY CURIOUS ABOUT THE NATURE OF CHILDREN BORN OF MAGIC.
THERE IS A VOID HERE IN THIS ONE, THAT REMINDS ME VERY MUCH OF MYSELF!

IN ANY CASE, YOUR CHILDREN WERE IN NO DANGER. THEIR TIME HAS NOT COME YET.
YOU ON THE OTHER HAND, HAVE CHEATED ME MORE THAN ONCE. A PATTERN, I OBSERVE, THAT REPEATS ITSELF AMONG YOUR FAMILY AND FRIENDS.
I'VE HAD ENOUGH OF IT!
IN THREATENING ME, YOU HAVE ISSUED ME A CHALLENGE, SCARLET WITCH!
I ACCEPT.
THE QUESTION OF WHETHER THE BEAUTIFUL MELINDA BELONGS PROPERLY TO LIFE OR DEATH CAN WAIT.
WOMAN, PREPARE YOURSELF FOR BATTLE!
"WAR THEY SAY, IS HELL!"

DEATH WEARS MANY FACES, WANDA. MINE IS ONLY ONE.
BUT EACH FACE HAS A SPECIAL DESTINY. MINE HAS BEEN TO SUFFER NEARLY FIFTY YEARS FOR MY SINS OF LIFE.
DO YOU UNDERSTAND WAR, SCARLET WITCH? DO YOU KNOW HOW MANY SOULS THERE WERE THAT DIED IN THIS WAR ALONE?

I HAVE SEEN WAR THROUGH THE EYES OF EACH OF THEM. THEIR LIVES HAVE BECOME MY OWN.

AND THROUGH THEM, I CLAIM MY DUE!
NO!

YOU PLAY WITH SHADOWS KOWALSKI! WHATEVER TRICKS YOU CONJURE, I CAN DISPEL!
PHANTOMS ARE NO THREAT! THEY'RE NOT EVEN REAL!

THEY ARE REAL TO ME.
EVERY DEATH HAS MEANING, WANDA. IF ONLY TO THE ONE WHO DIES.

"BUT PERHAPS YOU ARE RIGHT. MY WAR WAS ONE YOU NEVER LIVED. IF IT EVER BECAME REAL TO YOU, IT WAS ONLY THROUGH THE STORIES YOU HEARD AS A CHILD.
"THERE HAVE BEEN OTHERS.
WANDA...
VIETNAM!

RUN, MELINDA! THIS IS NO GAME!
I DON'T UNDERSTAND...

IS IT ENLIGHTENMENT YOU SEEK, MELINDA? I CAN OFFER THAT TO YOU AS WELL.
KOWALSKI...
YOU WILL NEVER TAKE HER!

I AM THROUGH FIGHTING SHADOWS!
NOW I AM FIGHTING YOU!
VERY GOOD!
PERHAPS YOU DO UNDERSTAND!

"THE ONLY WAY YOU CAN DEFEAT ME, WANDA, IS BY CHANGING THE RULES OF THIS CONFLICT.
"YOUR GAME, NOT MINE.
"BUT IT IS DEATH WHO RULES HERE.
"AND IF I AM TO BE BEATEN...

"THEN SOMEONE MUST TAKE MY PLACE..."
KOWALSKI...

YOUR TIME HAS ENDED. I SEE THAT NOW.
WANDA?

YOU ARE WEARY, KOWALSKI, TIRED OF THE MANTLE YOU HAVE BORNE! THERE IS NO FURTHER NEED OF YOU! I FREELY TAKE FROM YOU YOUR--
WANDA! OH, WANDA, NO!
I LOVE HIM!
WHAT?
I LOVE HIM! YOU CAN'T TAKE HIM FROM ME!
LOVE...??

YOU LOVE HIM...
YES, I LOVE HIM! DIDN'T YOU HEAR ME? I TOLD YOU THAT FROM THE START!
MELINDA...

THERE'S NOTHING TO FORGIVE.
IT'S ALL RIGHT, MY DARLING. I DO UNDERSTAND.
I WAS FRIGHTENED! I'M SO SORRY. CAN YOU FORGIVE ME?

ALL I WANTED WAS A CHANCE TO EXPERIENCE HAPPINESS. I NEVER HAD THAT IN LIFE.
YOU'VE GIVEN IT TO ME, JOHN. THAT, AND LOVE. THAT IT SHOULD COME TO ME AFTER DEATH IS A MIRACLE BEYOND MY DREAMS.

IT WAS ALL I EVER WANTED TO GIVE YOU.
I KNOW.
HOW MUCH TIME WILL WE HAVE?
I HAVE THREE YEARS TO PREPARE MY SUCCESSOR.

THREE YEARS... OR AN ETERNITY TOGETHER, MY LOVE!
WANDA!

OH, VISION! YOU STARTLED ME!
THE BALLGAME WENT INTO EXTRA-INNINGS, BUT THE METS WERE VICTORIOUS!
THE BLACK KNIGHT SENDS HIS REGARDS.

YOU SEEM DISTRACTED. IS THERE SOMETHING WRONG WITH THE CHILDREN?
NO. THE CHILDREN ARE PERFECTLY SAFE. WHATEVER HAPPENED, I WOULD HAVE SEEN TO THAT.

I LEARNED A WONDERFUL THING TONIGHT, VISION.

I LEARNED THAT EVEN IN DEATH, THERE CAN BE A LOVE THAT NEVER DIES.
FIN

MARVEL®

# SOLO AVENGERS

STARRING

# HAWKEYE™

AND THE FALCON™

75¢ US
95¢ CAN
6
MAY

APPROVED BY THE COMICS CODE AUTHORITY

02651

SANDMAN! LE PEREGRINE! HAWKEYE! FALCON! AND THE

RED SKULL II!

Stan Lee presents
ALGERIA IS FOR ARCHERS
ACHMEL! EMIL! LOOK!! IN THE ALLEY--
--AN INTRUDER!!
PUFT! PUFT!
PUFT!
YEAH, I GUESS YOU CAN CALL ME AN INTRUDER, BRIGHT EYES, BUT I'M USUALLY REFERRED TO AS AN AVENGER, AND, IN CASE YOU DON'T RECOGNIZE MY VERY DISTINCTIVE COSTUME, MY NAME IS--
STAN LEE PRESENTS WITH PRIDE!
TOM DeFALCO A WRITER QUITE DIGNIFIED!
MARK BRIGHT A PENCILER WHOSE TALENT IS BONAFIDE!
JOE RUBINSTEIN AN INKER VERY QUALIFIED!
JACK MORELLI A MASTER OF THE LETTERING GUIDE!
JANET JACKSON WHOSE COLORS WILL LEAVE YOU GOGGLE-EYED!
MARK GRUENWALD AN EDITOR QUITE SNIDE, WHO'S NEVER SATISFIED!!

HAWKEYE
THE NEWSPAPERS BACK HOME BILL ME AS THE WORLD'S GREATEST ARCHER, BUT I'M MUCH TOO MODEST TO MENTION THAT!

YOU CAN TELL THAT TO WHATEVER WESTERN GOD YOU WORSHIP, FOOL--
--BECAUSE YOU WILL SOON BE STANDING WITH HIM!

MAIS NON, GENTLEMEN!
YOU ARE QUITE MISTAKEN!

THE AMERICAN MAY BE A BIT EGOTISTICAL BUT, AS YOU CAN SEE, HE IS UNDER THE PROTECTION OF--
LE PEREGRINE, THE CHAMPION OF FRANCE!!
BUDDA BUDDA BUDDA

YOU ARE MUCH TOO NOISY, AVENGER! WE ARE BARELY FIVE MINUTES INTO THE MISSION, AND YOU HAVE ALREADY ANNOUNCED OUR PRESENCE TO THE OPPOSITION!
WHOOPS! GUESS THAT MEANS I'LL HAVE TO STAY AFTER CLASS AND REVIEW MY NOTES FOR STEALTH 101!

I AM AFRAID THAT OUR MUTUAL EMPLOYER WOULD NOT APPRECIATE YOUR ARROGANCE AND LACK OF PROFESSIONALISM!
HOWEVER, SINCE WE HAVE AL-READY LOST THE ELEMENT OF SURPRISE--

--WE MAY AS WELL DISPENSE WITH THE SUBTLETIES!
KRASH
HEY, BIRDMAN... WHY'D YOU PICK THIS PARTICULAR ROOM?

BEFORE HE DISAPPEARED, OUR MISSING AGENT MANAGED TO INFORM US THAT AN ACCESSWAY IS HIDDEN IN HERE WHICH WILL TAKE US TO OUR PRIMARY TARGET, AND...
MORE GUNMEN!
FORGET 'EM, WINGS! YOU LOOK FOR THE SECRET PASSAGE--

--WHILE I TAKE THE EASY JOB!
FWIP
FWIP
FWIP

HAWKEYE! I'VE FOUND IT!
GREAT! JUST GIVE ME A SECOND TO FINISH GAGGING THESE GUYS, AND TO LOCK THE DOOR!
I'D HATE TO BE FOLLOWED BY ANY OF THEIR FRIENDS!

HURRY! WE MUST REACH OUR TARGET BEFORE HE LEARNS THAT WE ARE HERE IN ALGERIA!
YOU KIDDING, PAL? IT'S A MIRACLE WE'VE GOTTEN THIS FAR!
THIS JOB WAS A LOST CAUSE FROM THE VERY START, AND--

"-- I STILL CAN'T BELIEVE THE WAY YOUR BOSS, SILVER SABLE, MANAGED TO CON ME INTO TAKING IT!"

NOW THAT THE FRENCH AUTHORITIES HAVE TRICK SHOT IN CUSTODY, I'D LIKE TO LEAVE PARIS AND GO HOME!
I AM AFRAID THAT THE GOVERNMENT INTENDS TO CONDUCT AN OFFICIAL INQUIRY BEFORE THAT CAN HAPPEN!
ISN'T THERE ANYTHING YOU CAN DO TO HELP ME CUT THROUGH THE BUREAUCRATIC RED TAPE?

PERHAPS, THERE IS... IF YOU WILL READ THIS DOSSIER ON THE RED SKULL.
BUT THE SKULL'S DEAD ACCORDING TO MY PAL CAPTAIN AMERICA!
DON'T YOU HAVE ANYTHING CURRENT, LIKE THIS MONTH'S ISSUE OF BULLWINKLE & ROCKY?

THIS MAN IS NOT THE ORIGINAL NAZI MENACE. HE IS AN IMPOSTOR WHO HAS BEEN OPERATING OUT OF ALGERIA SINCE THE 1950'S!
HE RECENTLY APPROPRIATED A SOPHISTICATED TIMING DEVICE WHICH IS USED TO DETONATE NUCLEAR WARHEADS!

THE MANUFACTURER HAS HIRED MY ORGANIZATION, SILVER SABLE INTERNATIONAL TO RETRIEVE IT!
ONE OF MY BEST OPERATIVES WAS ASSIGNED TO THIS CASE, BUT WE HAVE RECENTLY LOST CONTACT WITH HIM!
HE MAY BE DEAD... OR WORSE!

I INTEND TO SEND ANOTHER OPERATIVE AFTER THE DEVICE. WOULD YOU LIKE TO ACCOMPANY HIM?
AND, IF I DO..?
YOU MAY GO HOME.
YOU DRIVE A HARD BARGAIN, LADY!

A REAL HARD BARGAIN! WHEN SABLE SAID SHE WAS SENDING ANOTHER OPERATIVE, I NEVER DREAMED I'D BE PARTNERED WITH THE MOST FAMOUS CRIME-FIGHTER IN FRANCE!
I WONDER IF HER MISSING OPERATIVE IS ANOTHER COSTUMED SUPER-JOCK?
HEY, PEREGRINE, DO YOU DO ALL YOUR WORK FOR SILVER SABLE?
NON, MY FRIEND. I AM A FREELANCE OPERATIVE... LIKE YOU.
BUT I'M NOT A...
SHHHH!!

WE'RE HERE!
...A FOOL TO THINK YOU COULD STOP ME!

NOW THAT I POSSESS THE TIMER, I CAN DETONATE MY OWN NUCLEAR WARHEAD WHENEVER I CHOOSE!
THE POSSIBILITIES FOR INTERNATIONAL BLACKMAIL ARE ENDLESS!!

MASTER!! WE ARE BEING OBSERVED!!
WHAT?! KILL THEM!
KILL THE INTRUDERS!

SHEESH! LIKE I ALREADY TOLD THE GUYS OUTSIDE, WE'RE AVENGERS, PAL!
I GRANTED LE PEREGRINE AN HONORARY MEMBERSHIP FOR THE DURATION OF THIS FIGHT!
YOU ELABORATE FAR MORE THAN NECESSARY, HAWKEYE!

ONLY FISTS AND SPEED ARE NEEDED HERE... NOT WORDS!
LIGHTEN UP, FRENCHIE!

SNAPPY PATTER IS PRACTICALLY A REQUIREMENT FOR ALL US AMERICAN CRIME-FIGHTERS!

NOT ONLY DO WE OVERWHELM OUR FOES WITH OUR SKILL, DARING AND FLASHY FOOTWORK--

--WE ALSO ASSAULT THEM WITH VICIOUS VERBIAGE!
I WONDER WHO THE SKULL WAS TALKING TO WHEN WE ENTERED... AND WHAT'S WITH THIS DOME FULL OF DIRT!?

HEY! WHERE'D THE RED SKULL GO?!
I THOUGHT THAT YOU HAD ALREADY SUBDUED HIM WITH YOUR ARROWS!
NAH! I ONLY USED THEM TO ADD A LITTLE EXCITEMENT TO HIS OTHERWISE HUMDRUM EXISTENCE!
WOK
NEVER MIND! I'VE SPOTTED HIM, AND I CAN USE THIS CLOWN TO HURRY HIM OFF INTO DREAMLAND!

NO! NOT THE DOME!

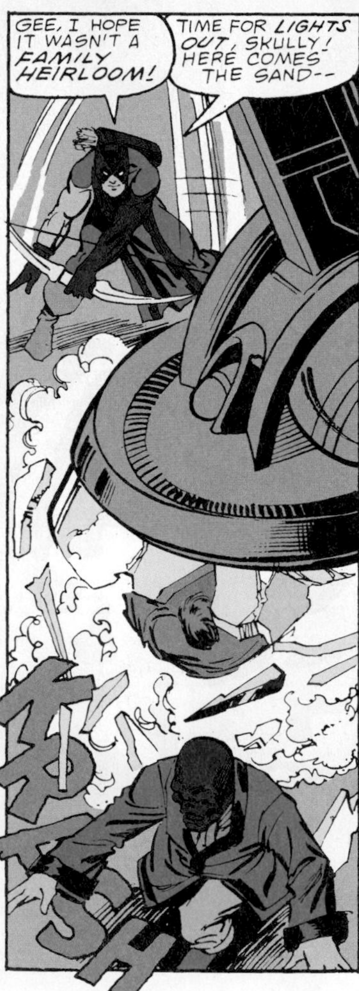
GEE, I HOPE IT WASN'T A FAMILY HEIRLOOM!
TIME FOR LIGHTS OUT, SKULLY! HERE COMES THE SAND--

--MAN!
HAWKEYE! LOOK!
I...I SEE IT... BUT I DON'T BELIEVE IT!

IT REALLY IS
--THE SAND-MAN!
YOU GOT IT, MAC!!
WHERE'S THE SKULL?
WE GOT US A SCORE TA SETTLE!

YOU WILL SETTLE NOTHING, CRETIN!!
ATTACK THEM, GUARDS... KILL THEM ALL!!

ARE YOU GUYS HERE FOR A PURPOSE--OR AM I SUPPOSED TO CARRY THE WHOLE SHOW?
DON'T GET YOUR GUMS IN AN UPROAR, SANDY! WHEN HAWKEYE'S AROUND--

--HE IS THE SHOW!!
EEEEEEEE

I TAKE IT THAT SILVER SABLE DIDN'T TELL YA THAT I WAS WORKING FOR HER!
IT MUST'VE SLIPPED HER MIND!
SHEESH! I'D HEARD THE SANDMAN HAD GIVEN UP HIS CRIMINAL WAYS--

"..BUT I NEVER EXPECTED HIM TO BE SABLE'S MISSING AGENT!"
THIS IS APPALLING! MY ELITE TROOPS ARE BEING SWEPT ASIDE AS IF THEY WERE MERE CHILDREN!

MY PLAN TO USE THIS WARHEAD FOR INTERNATIONAL BLACKMAIL HAS OBVIOUSLY FAILED! BUT I CAN STILL WIN A MODEST VICTORY--

TIK
TIK
TIK
5:42
--BY CONDEMNING THESE COSTUMED FOOLS TO DEATH!

HEY, YOU GUYS... LOOK!!
THE SKULL'S TAKIN' A POWDER!
DON'T SWEAT IT, SANDY!!
I'VE GOT A HUNCH THIS EXPLOSIVE TIPPED ARROW WILL CAUSE HIM TO CHANGE HIS TRAVEL PLANS!

EXCELLENT SHOT, HAWKEYE!
YOU CRIPPLED HIS ESCAPE CRAFT, AND I SHALL RETRIEVE HIS EJECTING SEAT!
GLOAT WHILE YOU CAN, FOOLS!
KA-BWAMM!

THE LAST LAUGH STILL BELONGS TO THE RED SKULL!
YOU HAVE FINALLY PUT AN END TO MY ILLUSTRIOUS CAREER AS AN INTERNATIONAL TERRORIST

--BUT I WILL DIE SECURE IN THE KNOWLEDGE THAT I PUT AN END TO YOU AS WELL!
Uh-Oh!
TIK TIK TIK

ER... GUYS, ANYBODY HERE WHO DIDN'T FLUNK HIGH SCHOOL SCIENCE SHOULD SPEAK UP REAL QUICK!

GET REAL, AVENGER!
I'LL JUST GUM UP THE WORKS WITH A BLAST OF SAND!

NOW, LET'S GLOM THIS BOZO'S REAL MUG!
HEY! HE'S ONLY SOME OLD GEEZER!
YOU HAVEN'T HEARD THE LAST FROM THE RED SKULL!
WHAT'RE YOU GONNA DO-- USE YER MEDICARE PAYMENTS TO BUY ANOTHER BOMB?

SOMETIME LATER...
I'M SURPRISED THE LOCAL AUTHORITIES WERE SO COOPERATIVE!
SILVER SABLE HAS A LONG REACH!
AND A MEMORY TO MATCH!

SHE SENT US TO RETRIEVE THAT TIMING DEVICE... NOT DESTROY IT!
GOSH, I HOPE SHE DON'T GET MAD... AND DOCK OUR PAY!
WHAT DO YOU MEAN OUR PAY, AMERI-CAN?!
C'MON, PEREGRINE! YA KNOW I DIDN'T HAVE NO CHOICE! WE COULD'VE ALL BEEN BLOWED UP!

PERISHING IN A NUCLEAR EXPLOSION WOULD HAVE BEEN A LOT LESS STRESSFUL THAN INFORMING SILVER SABLE THAT YOU FAILED TO COM-PLETE A MISSION!
YA REALLY THINK I MADE THE WRONG DECISION?
MAN O'MAN! I CAN'T WAIT TO DITCH THESE CLOWNS, AND HEAD HOME!
THE END... FOR NOW

DAN MISHKIN
WRITER

TOM GRINDBERG
PENCILER

JOSEF RUBINSTEIN
INKER

JACK MORELLI
LETTERS

STEVE BUCCELLATO
COLORS

OH. OKAY, NOW I GET IT.
GOOD IDEA, TOO. THE AVENGERS MOVING OUT'LL PROBABLY CUT THE CITY'S SUPER-VILLAIN ATTACK ***IN HALF!***
BUT YOU THINK THEY'D HAVE LET ME KNOW, HUH, BIRD?
FUTURE SITE OF MARIA STARK MEMORIAL ARBORETUM

YOU AIN'T IMPROVIN' OUR NEIGHBORHOOD-- YOU'RE PUSHIN' FOLKS OUT!
AN' I'M GONNA--

SIMMER DOWN, IF YOU KNOW WHAT'S GOOD FOR YOU!
I'M NO FAN OF THIS "GENTRIFICATION" EITHER, BUT BREAKING THE LAW IS NOT THE ANSWER!
EASY FOR SOME JIVE SUPER-COP TO SAY!
WRONG! I DIDN'T LEARN ABOUT THE DANGERS OF WALKING THE WILD SIDE AS THE FALCON--

--IT WAS PLAIN SAM WILSON WHO ALMOST WRECKED HIS LIFE BY CROSSING THAT LINE!
YOU THINK I WANT TO SEE THIS CHURCH TURNED TO RUBBLE?

THE CHURCH MY GRANDFATHER HELPED TO BUILD AND MY FATHER PREACHED IN?
I REMEMBER A SERMON HE ONCE TOLD--
--ABOUT HOW THE PEOPLE WITH POWER IN THIS WORLD ARE LIKE A ROCK...

...AND HOW THE REST OF US, ALL OUR VOICES AND PROTESTS, ARE NOTHING BUT RAINDROPS BEATING ON THAT BIG OLD BOULDER!
BUT GIVE US TIME, BROTHERS AND SISTERS, AND WE'LL WEAR DOWN THAT ROCK JUST AS SURE AS THE RIVER TURNS THE STONE TO SAND!
AND THAT'S OUR POWER!
RIGHT ON!
TELL IT, BROTHER!

I GUESS THAT'S ALL I'VE GOT TO SAY!
WELL, IT WAS A MOUTHFUL, SAM. AND YOUR DAD COULDN'T HAVE SAID IT BETTER.
HEY, REV'END!

THAT WAS A MIGHTY FINE SPEECH THERE, REV'END! GOOD SPEECH!
YOU DON'T HAVE TO CALL ME "REVEREND." I'M NOT--
AN' Y'KNOW, REV-- THEY SAY THAT OL' ROCK MIGHT GET SMASHED UP SOONER THAN YOU THINK!
LISSEN T'THAT SCATTERBRAIN TALK! GOTTA TELL EVERYONE 'BOUT THEM "VOICES" OF HIS.
POOR BOY'S SICK, LIONEL... HE THINKS THOSE RUSSIANS AND SPACEMEN HE'S ALWAYS ON ABOUT ARE REAL!

GOTTA GO NOW, REV! YOU NEED ME, GO TALK TO MR. MEACHUM!
ASK FOR SCATTER-BRAIN!

A VERY STRANGE YOUNG MAN... AND WHAT'S HIS CONNECTION TO A CRIME LORD LIKE VICTOR MEACHUM?
HE SURELY COULDN'T MAKE A VERY USEFUL THUG!
SO HERE'S THE THING, MISTER REAL ESTATE MAN...

...IF YA DON'T LEAVE THE NEIGHBORHOOD, SEE, I CAN'T BE RESPONSIBLE!
THEY DON'T WANT YOU HERE-- AND THEY'LL DO WHAT THEY HAVE TO TO PROTECT THEIR TURF!
NOTHIN' WE CAN DO ABOUT IT, Y'KNOW WHAT I MEAN?

THAT'S ENOUGH OF THAT, SON.
PEOPLE'S EMOTIONS ARE ALREADY RUNNING PLENTY HIGH! DON'T NEED YOUR THREATS TO STIR THINGS UP!
BUT IT AIN'T ME! IT'S THEM!

HUH?
IT'S THEM!

SORRY, MISTER, YOU'LL HAVE TO MOVE IT! TOP CLEARANCE GOVERNMENT SECURITY AREA.
BUT--
SEE THAT BARBER SHOP BEHIND ME? IT'S THE SECRET ENTRANCE TO CIA HEADQUARTERS.

YOU--YOU'RE AS CRAZY AS HE IS!
BUT I KNOW MY RIGHTS!
YOU DON'T UNDERSTAND-- IT'S OUT OF OUR CONTROL!

YOU BETTER LISTEN TO HIM, MISTER MAN!
STRANGE THINGS ARE GONNA IF YOU DON'T WATCH OUT!

WHA--? WHAT'S GOING ON??

ON YOUR WAY, LITTLE FOOL! BY THE TIME I COUNT TO THREE, OR I WILL BREAK YOUR EVERY BONE!
ONE...
B-BUT I CAN'T *LEAVE* IF YOU DON'T *LET GO!*
TWO...
SQUAWK
ATTAWAY, REDWING! DO WHAT YOU CAN TO DISTRACT HIM! BUT DON'T GET TOO CLO--

NO!
BEGONE, CREATURE, OR I SHALL FEAST ON YOUR FLESH!

DON'T MESS WITH MY *BIRD!*
CHUD
IT GETS ME *MAD!*

HEY... W-WHERE'VE WE BEEN?

AND YOU WON'T *LIKE* ME WHEN I'M MAD!
NOW JUST WHAT DO YOU THINK YOU'RE DOING?
I AIN'T DOIN' NUTHIN' REV--
IT'S THE *VOICES!*

...THEY TELL ME WHAT THEY GOTTA DO-- AND ME, I JUST LET 'EM.
AND NOW THEY'RE TELLIN' ME--
--THAT YOU GOTTA DIE!

SORRY, REV-- IT'S OUTTA MY HANDS!

HOLY--! WOULD YOU LOOK AT WHAT THAT BOY DID?
TURNED THOSE CARS INTO FLYING SAUCERS!
HOW'D HE DO THAT?

GOOD QUESTION!

HOPE I LIVE LONG ENOUGH TO FIND OUT THE ANSWER!
IT'S OBVIOUS THAT THIS "SCATTERBRAIN" IS A SCHIZOPHRENIC!
HE BELIEVES IN VOICES ONLY HE CAN HEAR--AND FEELS COMPELLED TO OBEY THEM!

AS SAM WILSON, SOCIAL WORKER, I'VE SEEN PLENTY OF PEOPLE LIKE THAT ON THE STREET!
FOLKS WHO'VE BEEN RELEASED FROM INSTITUTIONS WITHOUT ADEQUATE FOLLOW-UP -- OR WHO NEVER RECEIVED PROPER CARE AT ALL!
BUT THIS BOY CAN SOMEHOW CHANGE REALITY TO GIVE LIFE TO HIS VOICES! HE'S INCREDIBLY POWERFUL!
AND PROBABLY THE ONLY LIMIT ON THAT POWER'S THE FACT THAT HE DOESN'T REALIZE THAT HE CONTROLS IT!

RATS! I WAS HOPING I COULD LOSE THOSE SAUCERS IN A TIGHT SQUEEZE--
--BUT THEY'RE STILL RIGHT ON MY TAIL!
I'LL HAVE TO...
SKASSH

HUH?
THE "SPACESHIPS"...

"--THEY'RE REVERTING TO NORMAL!"

SCREEEEEEEEEEEEEEEEEEE
KRUNCH

GOOD THING I SAW WHAT WAS HAPPENING AND SWOOPED DOWN LOW!
WHEN THE SAUCERS BECAME CARS AGAIN, THEY DIDN'T HAVE FAR TO FALL, SO NOBODY DIED!
YET!

SCATTERBRAIN!
THAT'S WHAT THEY CALLED ME... EVER SINCE I WAS A KID!
C'MON CLOSER, REV'END! THEY ALL WANNA MEETCHA!

NO! I DIDN'T THINK THEY COULD BE SO FAST!
SON, LISTEN TO ME... I DON'T KNOW WHY YOU'RE DOING THIS, BUT--

I KEEP TELLIN' YA, REV-- I AIN'T DOIN' ANYTHING!
YOU SLOW OR SOMETHING, MAN? BACK IN SCHOOL, THEY ALWAYS SAID I WAS SLOW!

NO, I--I UNDERSTAND YOU.
AND I UNDERSTAND WHAT IT'S LIKE TO HEAR THINGS THAT NOBODY ELSE CAN!
TAKE ME, FOR IN-STANCE...

I HEAR THE VOICES OF BIRDS!
C'MON REDWING, SHOW HIM YOUR STUFF!

AND WE DON'T NEED TO LET HIM KNOW THAT OUR PSYCHIC LINK LETS YOU RESPOND TO MY THOUGHTS NOT JUST MY WORDS!
YOU KNOW THE DRILL, RIGHT, BIRD?
SHEE-OOT! LOOK AT THAT SUCKER MOVE! SAY, REV, WHAT ELSE CAN YOU MAKE HIM D--

NICE WORK, RED! SHAKE HIS CONCEN-TRATION AND HE CAN'T KEEP A MENTAL HOLD ON THESE MONSTERS!
OOFF!

AND HE WON'T BE CREATING ANY MORE OF THEM ONCE HE'S OUT COLD!
THUD

FALCON! WAIT A MOMENT, PLEASE!
I'D LIKE TO THANK YOU FOR SAVING MY LIFE--AND DEFUSING THE ENTIRE SITUATION, FOR THAT MATTER!
YOU UNDERSTAND, OF COURSE, THAT IT CAN'T EFFECT MY COMPANY'S PLANS FOR THE CHURCH PROPERTY, BUT--
BUT MAYBE IT AFFECTS MINE!
I STILL OWN THAT CHURCH--AND I JUST MIGHT BE WILLING TO FORGET THE ENTIRE TRANSACTION--
--MAYBE DEED THE PROPERTY OVER TO THE CONGREGATION INSTEAD OF SELLING THE PLACE!
YEAH? AND JUST WHY WOULD YOU WANT TO DO THAT, MR. MEACHUM?
SO PEOPLE WILL FORGET SCATTER-BRAIN WAS WORKING FOR YOU?
SO THEY WON'T GUESS YOU ENCOURAGED HIM TO USE HIS POWER, EVEN THOUGH YOU KNEW IT COULD GO WILD LIKE IT DID?
YOU GIVE THEM THE CHURCH--MY FATHER'S CHURCH--AND YOU FIGURE YOU CAN BE SOME KIND OF HERO?
NO WAY, MEACHUM! YOU CAN STEAL THEIR MONEY, BUT I'M NOT GOING TO LET YOU HAVE THEIR SOULS!
AND I'LL BUILD A NEW CHURCH BRICK BY BRICK BEFORE I'LL BE BEHOLDEN TO A SLUG LIKE YOU!
WHY YOU--! NOBODY TALKS TO VICTOR MEACUM LIKE THAT!
YOU LISTEN TO ME, FALCON! YOU'RE WALKING A VERY THIN LINE!
EVERY DAY OF MY LIFE, MAN!
END

MARVEL

© 1988 MARVEL ENT. GROUP INC.

75¢ US
95¢ CAN
7
JUN
02651

APPROVED BY THE COMICS CODE AUTHORITY

# SOLO AVENGERS

STARRING

# HAWKEYE

AND

# BLACK WIDOW

TOM DEFALCO WRITER | MARK BRIGHT PENCILS | JOSÉ MARZAN INKS | JACK MORELLI LETTERS | JANET JACKSON COLORS | MARK GRUENWALD EDITOR | LUCKY YOU READER

OH, GREAT! I FINALLY FINISH MY BUSINESS HERE SO I CAN GO HOME, AND NOW THIS!
QUIT GRIPIN', HAWKEYE. AT LEAST SILVER SABLE AND I ARE HERE TO SEE YOU OFF!
NO OFFENSE SANDMAN, BUT I'D FEEL A WHOLE LOT BETTER IF I HADN'T CHECKED THE BAG CONTAINING MY BOW AND ARROWS!

WHO ARE THESE CLOWNS, ANYWAY?
JUST A BUNCH A' CHEAP THUGS WHO STARTED MAKIN' HEADLINES A FEW WEEKS AGO.
WHAT SHOULD WE DO ABOUT THEM, BOSS LADY?
NOTHING!

AS AN AVENGER, HAWKEYE MAY FEEL COMPELLED TO GET INVOLVED IN THIS MATTER...
...BUT WE ARE PROFESSIONAL MERCENARIES, AND ONLY RISK OUR NECKS WHEN WE HAVE A PAYING CLIENT!
HEADS UP! TH' PUNKS ARE MAKIN' A MOVE!

YOU!! COME HERE!
THE REST OF YOU-- LISTEN UP!

THIS GIRL WILL BE THE FIRST TO DIE IF THERE IS ANY RESISTANCE!!
ERIC!! HERE COMES AIRPORT SECURITY!

DROP YOUR GUNS! SURRENDER! OR MY MEN WILL BEGIN FIRING INTO THE CROWD!
THE PENALTY FOR HIJACKING IS DEATH! SO WE HAVE NOTHING TO LOSE!

I'M WARNING YOU--! THIS IS NO BLUFF!
ALL RIGHT! ALL RIGHT! WE... SURRENDER!
EVERY-ONE! GET ON YOUR STOMACHS! LAY DOWN!! NOW!!

DO NOTHING TO BRING YOURSELF TO OUR ATTENTION!
WE INTEND TO KILL A HOSTAGE EVERY HALF HOUR UNTIL THE FRENCH GOVERNMENT MEETS OUR DEMANDS--AND FREES THE HEROIC BARTO-VIAN PATRIOTS WHO WERE ARRESTED LAST WEEK!

SOME PATRIOTS! THEY GOT NAILED TRYIN' TO PLANT A BOMB ON A BUS FULL'A SCHOOL KIDS!
HEY, SILVER, I USUALLY KEEP A SPARE DOLLAR FOR EMERGENCIES! YOU INTERESTED?

ARE WE TALKING CASH?

YOU MEN KNOW WHAT TO DO... PICK AN APPROPRIATE VICTIM... SOMEONE WHO WILL LOOK GOOD FOR THE TELEVISION CAMERAS!
THE REST OF YOU COME WITH ME... WE MUST MAKE CERTAIN THE ENTIRE TERMINAL IS SECURE!

NOW--!
KEEP YOUR HEAD DOWN, FOOL, UNLESS YOU WANT THE ENTIRE WORLD TO WATCH AS WE EXECUTE YOU IN THE GLORIOUS NAME OF--
OLYMPIAN

AW, SHUT UP! IT'S REAL EASY TA FLAP YER JAWS WHILE YOU'RE HOLDIN' ALL THE WEAPONS, BUT LET'S SEE HOW TOUGH YA ARE NOW!

LOOK! WE'RE BEING ATTACKED!
YOU TWO DEAL WITH THE SANDY CREATURE... WHILE I ATTEND TO THIS STUPID AMERICAN!
HE SHALL BE THE FIRST HOS-TAGE TO DIE!
I DOUBT IT, PAL!

EVEN WITHOUT MY BOW AND ARROWS, I'M MORE THAN A MATCH FOR ANY TEN OF YOU!
FWAP
NO ONE IS DYING TODAY! NOT AS LONG AS MY FRIENDS AND I HAVE ANYTHING TO SAY ABOUT IT!

WAY TO GO, SILVER! I DIDN'T REALIZE YOU COULD USE THOSE HALF MOON GIZMOS ON YOUR BELT AS WEAPONS!
THEY ARE CALLED CHAIS, HAWKEYE!
YEOW!
THWAK
YOU WILL FIND THEM LISTED UNDER "EXPENSES" ON THE ITEMIZED BILL I INTEND TO GIVE YOU!

MAGNIFICENT! IT BARELY TOOK YOU A FULL MINUTE TO SUBDUE ALL THOSE TERRORISTS!
IS THERE ANYTHING WE CAN DO TO HELP?
WHY DON'T YOU AND YOUR BUDDIES GO AND FIND SOME MORE GUNS TO SURRENDER TO THE BAD GUYS!?
BE NICE, SANDMAN!
WE MAY HAVE TO WORK FOR THESE PEOPLE SOMEDAY!

WHERE ARE YOU GOING, HAWKEYE?
TO FIND MY GEAR!
YOU HELP THE SECURITY GUARDS GET THE CIVILIANS TO SAFETY!
THEN, WE'LL TAKE CARE OF ERIC AND THE REST OF HIS BARTOVIAN BLOW-HARDS!

WHY DON'T WE JUST LET THE LOCAL AUTHORITIES HANDLE IT FROM HERE?
BECAUSE THAT'S NOT MY STYLE, LADY!
I JUST CAN'T SIT ON THE SIDELINES WHILE LIVES ARE IN DANGER!

HEY, FELLAS! WHERE CAN I FIND THE LUGGAGE BOUND FOR FLIGHT 207 TO LOS ANGELES?
YIIII!!
I GUESS THEY HEARD ALL THE COMMOTION UPSTAIRS AND DON'T WANT TO GET INVOLVED!

OH, WELL. LOOKS LIKE I'M GOING TO HAVE TO DO THIS THE HARD WAY!

A FEW FRANTIC MINUTES LATER...
YAHOO! THERE'S MY BAG!
I'D RECOGNIZE IT ANYWHERE THANKS TO THAT GOOFY RIBBON MY WIFE TRAINED ME TO TIE TO MY LUGGAGE!

GOOD OL' ARROW KIT!
CONSIDERING THE WAY THIS TRIP'S BEEN GOING, I'M LUCKY THE AIRLINE DIDN'T ACCIDENTALLY SHIP IT TO GUAM!

NO TIME TO PUT ON MY ENTIRE COSTUME!
I'LL JUST SETTLE FOR MY MASK AND TUNIC!
GOTTA HURRY--!

"SILVER SABLE AND SANDMAN MAY BE IN OVER THEIR HEADS AND DESPERATE FOR MY HELP!"

I MAY NOT BE PARANOID ABOUT KEEPING MY CIVILIAN IDENTITY A SECRET, BUT I'M GLAD I ALWAYS TRAVEL UNDER A FAKE NAME!
OTHERWISE MY REAL ONE WOULD BE PUBLIC KNOWLEDGE AFTER TODAY!

"WHAT'S GOING ON UP THERE? I DON'T HEAR ANY GUNFIRE. HOPE EVERYTHING'S STILL UNDER CONTROL!"

AT LAST! MY BOW'S AT THE PROPER TENSION, I HAVE PLENTY OF ARROWS--
GUESS IT'S FINALLY TIME TO--

"--ROCK 'N' ROLL!"

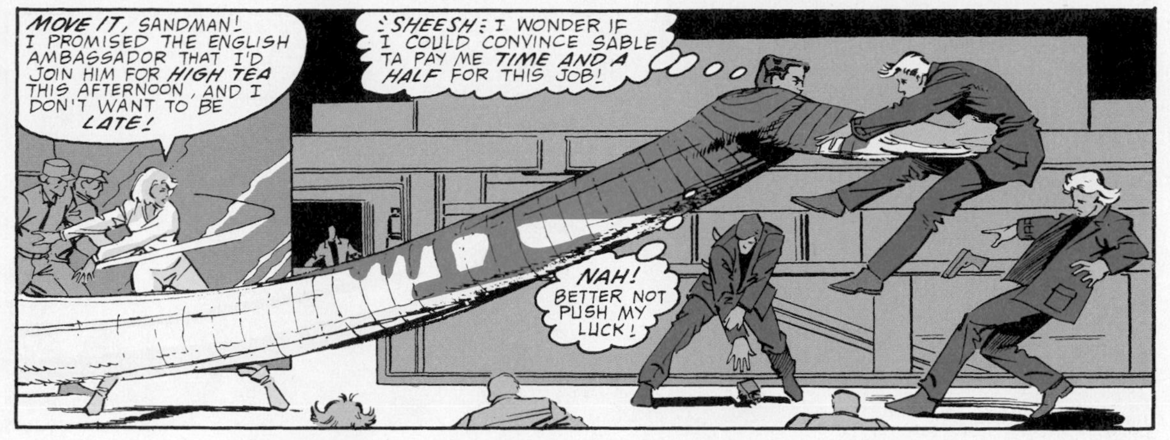
MOVE IT, SANDMAN! I PROMISED THE ENGLISH AMBASSADOR THAT I'D JOIN HIM FOR HIGH TEA THIS AFTERNOON, AND I DON'T WANT TO BE LATE!
SHEESH! I WONDER IF I COULD CONVINCE SABLE TA PAY ME TIME AND A HALF FOR THIS JOB!
NAH! BETTER NOT PUSH MY LUCK!

THAT'S THE LAST OF THEM BUMS IN THIS AREA!
HEY! WHERE'S MISTER MOUTH!? WHAT HAPPENED TA HAWKEYE? HE'S THE ONE WHO GOT US INTO THIS FIGHT IN THE FIRST PLACE!
HE WENT DOWN TO THE LOWER LEVEL... WHERE THEY KEEP THE BAGGAGE!

"MAYBE HE'S STILL THERE!"
KEEP DOWN!
PLEASE DON'T FORCE US TO KILL ANYONE UNTIL AFTER THE NEWSMEN HAVE ARRIVED!

KA-THUNK
KA-THUNK
WHAT THE--?

HI THERE! I'M HAWKEYE!
FLY ME TO OBLIVION!
DON'T LOOK SO SURPRISED AT MY ACCOMMODATIONS, OSWALD! ONLY THE FANTASTIC FOUR TRAVEL FIRST CLASS ALL THE TIME!
WE AVENGERS ARE DOING OUR BIT TO DECREASE SPENDING, AND EASE THE WIDENING TRADE DEFICIT!

SOMETHING'S WRONG!
I CAN'T SEEM TO REACH ANY OF THE OTHER TEAMS!
GEORGE! CLAUDE! ISAAC! SCOUT THE AREA AND MAKE SURE THAT IT IS STILL SECURE!
WE WILL DO AS YOU COMMAND, ERIC... FOR THE GREATER GOOD OF OUR NOBLE CAUSE!

SHUT UP! AND GET MOVING!
RIGHT NOW, I'M MORE CONCERNED WITH THE GREATER GOOD OF OUR LIVES!
YES, SIR!
HEY! WHAT'S THIS STUFF ON THE --

--FLOOR!?

PWOOM

A
WHAT WAS THAT?
I DON'T THINK WE WANT TO KNOW!
EVERYONE OUTSIDE! NOW!
IT'S TIME WE REGROUPED, AND REASSESSED OUR SITUATION!

ERMIN
GEE, THAT'S AN EASY ONE... IT STINKS!

SORRY, GENTLEMEN, BUT YOUR ESCAPE FLIGHT HAS BEEN CANCELED!
THE AIRLINE REGRETS ANY INCONVENIENCE THIS MAY CAUSE, AND IS ALREADY ARRANGING ACCOMMODATIONS FOR YOU AND YOUR FRIENDS--
--FOR THE NEXT TWENTY OR THIRTY YEARS!
HE'S ONLY ONE MAN! WASTE HIM!
DP

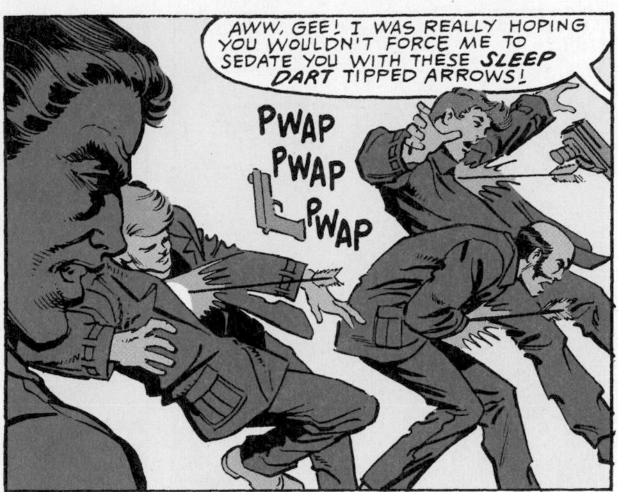
AWW, GEE! I WAS REALLY HOPING YOU WOULDN'T FORCE ME TO SEDATE YOU WITH THESE SLEEP DART TIPPED ARROWS!
PWAP
PWAP
PWAP

KEEP OUT! DON'T PUSH ME, HERO!
I SWEAR I'LL SHOOT!!

GO RIGHT AHEAD!
THE GIRL'S LIFE MEANS NOTHING TO ME!
WHO ARE YOU?
I'M SILVER SABLE, A PROFESSIONAL BOUNTY HUNTER--

--AND I'M ONLY CONCERNED WITH COLLECTING THE REWARD THE FRENCH GOVERNMENT PAYS FOR CAPTURED TERRORISTS LIKE YOU!
YOU CAN'T BE SERIOUS!

CAN'T I?
YOU KILL HER, I KILL YOU! IT'S YOUR CHOICE!
EITHER WAY, I COLLECT MY FEE!

NO! I CAN'T BELIEVE YOU'RE-- ARRGH!
TAKE YOUR SLIMY HANDS OFF ME, CREEP!
WAY TO GO, GIRLIE!
STOMP

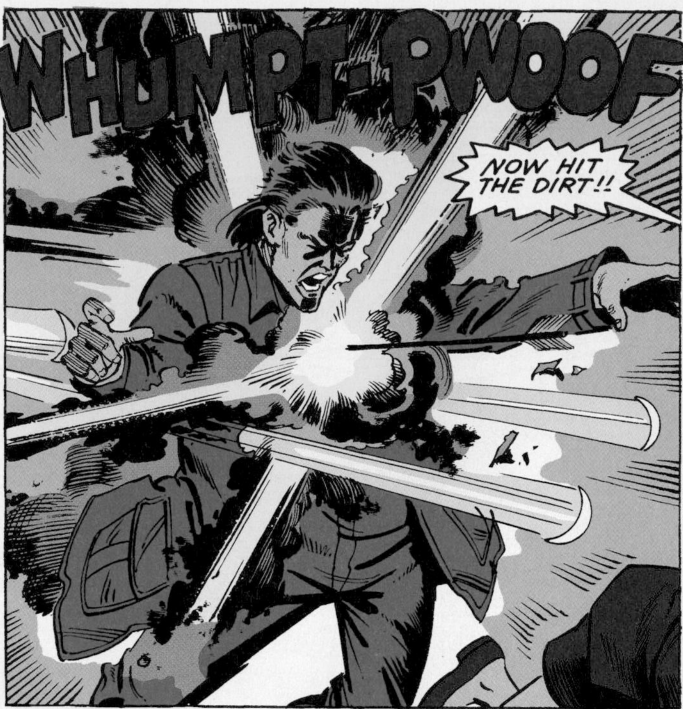
WHUMPT-PWOOF
NOW HIT THE DIRT!!

LATER...
Uh-Oh! HERE COME THE COPS!
ADIOS, HAWKEYE! I MAY OCCASIONALLY WORK FOR SABLE, BUT SOME GUYS STILL CONSIDER ME A CRIMINAL!
LATER, SANDY! IT'S BEEN A GAS WORKING WITH YOU!
THE AUTHORITIES WILL TAKE CARE OF YOU NOW, MISS.

ER, SILVER, WHAT YOU SAID ABOUT THE GIRL... YOU WERE KIDDING, RIGHT?
I MEAN, YOU COULDN'T POSSIBLY HAVE BEEN SERIOUS!

SABLE--?
SABLE--?

SOMETIME LATER...
WHAT A DAY!
IT TOOK AWHILE, BUT I FINALLY MANAGED TO DUCK THE AUTHORITIES, AND QUIETLY SLIP ABOARD THIS PLANE!

AT LONG LAST! I'M ON MY WAY HOME!
MAN, I CAN'T WAIT TO SEE MOCKINGBIRD AGAIN!
I HATE BEING SEPARATED FROM HER!

HEY! WHAT'S THIS?
SOMEONE MUST'VE SLIPPED THIS INTO MY POCKET WHEN I WASN'T PAYING ATTENTION!

IT'S FROM SILVER SABLE!
NO! SHE WOULDN'T! SHE COULDN'T!

SHE DID!
INTERNATIONAL
INVOICE
BILLED TO THE AVENGER KNOWN AS HAWKEYE:
ONE DOLLAR (AMERICAN) FOR SERVICES RENDERED

HA HA HA HA
THE END. FOR NOW!

Stan Lee presents
BLACK WIDOW
IT IS A RAINY TUESDAY EVENING ON MANHATTAN'S UPPER WEST SIDE. FOR NATASHA ROMANOFF -- DANCER, SPY ADVENTURER AND RESERVE AVENGER, IT IS AN EXCELLENT OPPORTUNITY TO RELAX IN A MANNER MOST WOULD FIND CONTRADICTORY!
--AND IN THE LOCAL NEWS, THE KREMLIN HAS GRANTED PERMISSION FOR ONE OF RUSSIA'S MOST FAMED CITIZENS TO SEEK ADVANCED OPTICAL SURGERY IN THE UNITED STATES! TASS NEWS AGENCY HAS RELEASED THAT--
THE TOKEN
BOB LAYTON PLOT/SCRIPT/INKS JACKSON GUICE PLOT/PENCILS JACK MORELLI LETTERS PAUL BECTON COLORS

--FAMED BOLSHOI BALLET INSTRUCTOR OKSANA BOLISHINKO HAS COME TO NEW YORK TO UNDERGO SPECIALIZED EYE SURGERY AT MT. SINAI HOSPITAL!

THE SIXTY-TWO YEAR OLD MS. BOLISHINKO WILL BE HELD IN "PROTECTIVE CUSTODY" AT THE SOVIET EMBASSY TO AVOID THE AMERICAN PRESS CORPS AND THE DROVES OF HER ADMIRERS!

OKSANA!

I--I DON'T BELIEVE IT! SHE'S HERE--IN THE STATES!!

MY BALLET MASTER!!

HOW LONG HAS IT BEEN? ELEVEN YEARS? HOW MUCH SIMPLER LIFE WAS THEN! MY WHOLE LIFE REVOLVED AROUND PLEASING MY INSTRUCTOR!

I WAS TO BE PRIMA BALLERINA OF THE BOLSHOI! I STILL WEAR THE MEDALLION SHE GAVE ONLY TO HER PREMIERE STUDENTS!

I REMEMBER THE DAY--AS IF IT WERE YESTERDAY!

<I WANT YOU TO HAVE THIS SMALL TOKEN, NATASHA! YOU HAVE MADE AN OLD, BROKEN-DOWN DANCER VERY HAPPY!>

<THANK YOU, MASTER! I'LL TRY TO MAKE YOU SO PROUD OF ME!>

THREE YEARS LATER, I WAS RECRUITED BY THE K.G.B. AND TRAINED TO BE AN UNDER-COVER OPERATIVE! ALL THOSE YEARS SHE GAVE ME, AND I BETRAYED HER--FORSAKING MY ARTISTIC DISCIPLINES!
THE IRONY OF IT IS THAT A FEW YEARS AFTER BECOMING THE BLACK WIDOW--I DEFECTED TO THE UNITED STATES!
PERHAPS BETRAYAL IS IN MY NATURE--LIKE MY NAMESAKE!

BUT NOW, I MIGHT HAVE AN OPPORTUNITY TO MAKE AMENDS!
Eh? SOMEONE'S IN THE APARTMENT AND--I THINK I KNOW WHO IT IS!

<DRESSED FOR AN EVENING ON THE TOWN, EH, CZARINA?>
THIS IS AMERICA, IVAN. IN ENGLISH PLEASE!
DON'T DO IT, NATASHA.
I WAS DOWN AT NICOLA'S HAVIN' A COLD ONE WHEN I SAW THE NEWS REPORT!

THE K.G.B. HAS A STANDING DEATH SENTENCE ON YOUR HEAD! IF YOU SET FOOT ON SOVIET SOIL--YOU'RE AS GOOD AS DEAD!
I KNOW YOU LOVE ME, IVAN--BUT YOU'VE GOT IT ALL WRONG!
'TASHA--I'VE LOOKED AFTER YOU SINCE YOU WERE AN ORPHANED CHILD--I KNOW YOU!

WHEN YOU WERE A SPY, YOUR ONE WEAKNESS WAS YOUR CONSCIENCE! DON'T LET YOUR GUILT MAKE YOU DO SOMETHING STUPID!
DON'T BE SILLY, OLD FRIEND. I MERELY RAN OUT OF CAVIAR AND WAS ON MY WAY OUT TO THE 7-11 FOR MORE!

TA-TA, DARLING!

THE DOWNPOUR CONTINUES, AS THE HOURS PASS...
PATIENTLY, SHE WAITS FOR THE OPPORTUNITY SHE NEEDS--TRYING DESPERATELY TO IGNORE THE ELEMENTS ASSAULTING HER...

UNTIL...
FINALLY! I THOUGHT THAT NO ONE WOULD EVER LEAVE THE COMPOUND!

WELL, I'D BETTER MAKE UP MY MIND! ONCE I GO IN THERE--
--THERE'S NO TURNING BACK!

AFTER A DEEP BREATH OF RESOLVE SHE USES THE TINY SUCTION DEVICES IN HER BOOTS AND GLOVES TO CLING TO THE INSIDE OF THE RAPIDLY CLOSING GARAGE DOOR!
PIERCING BLUE EYES SCAN THE SURROUNDINGS--SEARCHING FOR WHAT HER ESPIONAGE-TRAINED MIND KNOWS SHE WILL INEVITABLY FIND...
THERE IT IS--

--IT'S THE EVER-PRESENT SURVEILLANCE CAMERA!

WHIRRR
NO TIME TO DISCONNECT IT... I'LL BE SPOTTED IN A FEW MORE SECONDS!

I MUST USE MY WIDOW'S BITE!
KA-CHAM
SHA-RAK

<YURI--WE'VE GOT A MALFUNCTION ON THE GARAGE LEVEL!>

<HAH! THEY'RE AMERICAN MADE! THEY MALFUNCTION CONSTANTLY, COMRADE!>
<B-BUT I THOUGHT I SAW A G-GIRL ON THE SCREEN JUST BEFORE IT WENT BLANK!>
<THOUGHT? BAH! I'LL GRAB BORIS AND HAVE A LOOK DOWN THERE! NOTIFY THE COLONEL THAT WE'RE CHECKING OUT A GLITCH!>

MOMENTS LATER, ON THE PARKING LEVEL...
<MUST'VE HAD A CIRCUIT BURN OUT-- SMOKE IS EVERYWHERE!>
<NEXT TIME WE BRING OUR OWN EQUIPMENT FROM LENINGRAD!>

<LOOK AT THIS, BORIS!
<CURIOUS-- IT LOOKS LIKE IT'S BEEN-->

--SHOT!!
SHA-RAK

<LENIN'S GHOST!! IT'S THE ACCURSED BLACK WIDOW! YOU MUST BE INSANE TO COME HERE!
<PERHAPS YOU'RE RIGHT, COMRADE! BUT NOT HALF AS CRAZY AS-->
BLAM
BLAM
BLAM

<--YOU TO THINK YOU CAN STOP ME!>
KER-WONK

IF THEY FOLLOW PROCEDURE-- CONTROL WILL SEND SOMEONE TO SEARCH FOR THE MISSING GUARDS SOON!
I MUST ACT SWIFTLY! NO MORE MISTAKES!

EVERY MOMENT I WASTE WILL INCREASE MY CHANCES OF BEING--

--CAUGHT!!

FREEZE! BAT AN EYELASH AND I WILL KILL YOU!

YOU WILL RETURN TO THE U.S.S.R., WIDOW, TO BE TRIED AND EXECUTED AS THE TRAITOR YOU ARE! YOU HAVE BETRAYED US ALL!!

WRONG CHOICE OF WORDS--

KER-CHOK

LIAR!!

IT ANGERED ME TO BE CALLED A BETRAYER! GUESS IT FEELS -- TOO CLOSE TO THE TRUTH?

I DARE NOT LET MY EMOTIONS CLOUD MY REASONING AGAIN!
NOW TO FIND OKSANA ON THE MONITOR SYSTEM!

AFTER A FEW ANXIOUS MOMENTS...
THE DANCE STUDIO! OF COURSE!
LEVEL 3 -- ROOM 16

JUST TO INSURE WE'LL BE SAFE FROM PRYING EYES--
SHA-RAK

QUICKLY, SHE STEALTHILY MAKES HER WAY THROUGH THE SOVIET EMBASSY, TAKING A ROUTE FEW COULD FOLLOW... THEN...
ALL THAT STANDS BETWEEN ME AND MY GOAL IS THE LONE MAINTAINANCE MAN!
I ALMOST FEEL SORRY FOR HIM!

SECONDS LATER...
< WHA... THE WIDOW! >
< FORGIVE ME, COMRADE, FOR WHAT I MUST NOW DO! >

KER-CHOK
⟨YOU THINK ME BUT A HELPLESS VICTIM, EH, SPY?!⟩
⟨I AM IGOR KULGARIAN--EASTERN BLOCK MARTIAL ARTS CHAMPION FOR SEVEN YEARS AND I'M--

--NO EASY PREY!!⟩
WHAM
KER

⟨YOU ON THE OTHER HAND, WILL BE CHILD'S PLAY TO DISPATCH!⟩
KER-WHAP

⟨I HAPPEN TO KNOW A FEW MOVES MYSELF, COMRADE KULGARIAN!⟩
⟨UNFORTUNATELY, I DON'T HAVE THE TIME TO WASTE SPARRING WITH YOU, SO--

⟨--SLEEP WELL!!⟩
SHA-RAK
ARGHH!!

⟨LUCKILY FOR YOU... MY BITE WAS SET ONLY ON STUN, "COMRADE"!⟩

WITH HER HEART POUNDING IN HER THROAT, THE BLACK WIDOW APPROACHES HER FORMER MENTOR...
SHE-SHE'S BLIND!
<TEACHER--I HAVE COME TO BEG F-FORGIVE-NESS!>
<H-HELLO...? WHO IS THERE? I--I CAN HEAR SOMEONE!>
<CZARINA! IT WARMS MY HEART TO HEAR YOUR VOICE AFTER ALL THESE YEARS!>
<COME CLOSER, CHILD.>

THERE IS A MOMENTARY SILENCE AS NATASHA KNEELS BEFORE THE BLIND INSTRUCTOR. THEN--
<YOU SHOULD NOT HAVE COME, NATASHA! YOU ARE IN THE GRAVEST DANGER!!>
<I DON'T CARE ABOUT THAT, MADAME BOLISHINKO...>

<I-I'VE COME TO... R-RETURN THIS MEDALLION TO YOU!>
<I-I HAVE BE-TRAYED YOUR T-TRUST IN ME! AND YOUR DEDICATION IN MY ARTISTIC PROWESS!>
<THIS BELONGS TO A T-TRUE DANCER--NOT SOMEONE LIKE M-ME!>
THE BLIND WOMAN SMILES THINLY, THEN--

<POOR CHILD... YOU'VE MISUNDERSTOOD MY INTENTIONS, HAVEN'T YOU?>
<LISTEN TO ME--IN RUSSIA, YOU BECOME WHAT THE PARTY DECIDES YOU WILL BE! YOU WEREN'T THE FIRST STUDENT I'VE LOST TO THE K.G.B. RECRUITING PROGRAM, AND I FEAR, NOT THE LAST!>

<GRANTED, YOU WERE A GREAT DANCER, BUT-- THE BLACK WIDOW IS RESPECTED AND FEARED BY THE KREMLIN! IT IS YOUR TRUE CALLING!>
<I MERELY GAVE YOU THE TOKEN BECAUSE-->
<--I LOVED YOU, MY DEAR!>

<NOW--NO MORE SELF-INCRIMINATIONS! GO--AND BE AS PROUD OF YOURSELF AS I AM!>
<HOLD IT, ROMANOVA!>

⟨NONE OF YOUR TRICKS! ONE MOVE AND YOU'RE BOTH DEAD!⟩

⟨YOU'RE BLUFFING.⟩

⟨TRY ME.⟩

⟨NOW THAT I HAVE YOUR ATTENTION--⟩
⟨--I THINK THAT IT IS TIME FOR YOU TO LEAVE, WIDOW. GO AND DO NOT RETURN!⟩

⟨Y-YOU'RE LETTING ME GO?⟩
DO AS HE DEMANDS NATASHA! ALL MY LOVE GOES WITH YOU, MY CHILD!
AND, AS THE BLACK WIDOW DEPARTS--

⟨THE BUREAU WILL HAVE YOUR HEAD FOR THIS, COLONEL.⟩
⟨I KNOW, MADAME.⟩
⟨YOU'RE A GOOD BOY, SASHA. YOU MAKE AN OLD WOMAN PROUD.⟩

⟨IT WAS THE LEAST I COULD DO, MADAME... AFTER ALL...⟩
⟨I KNOW EXACTLY HOW SHE FEELS.⟩
END

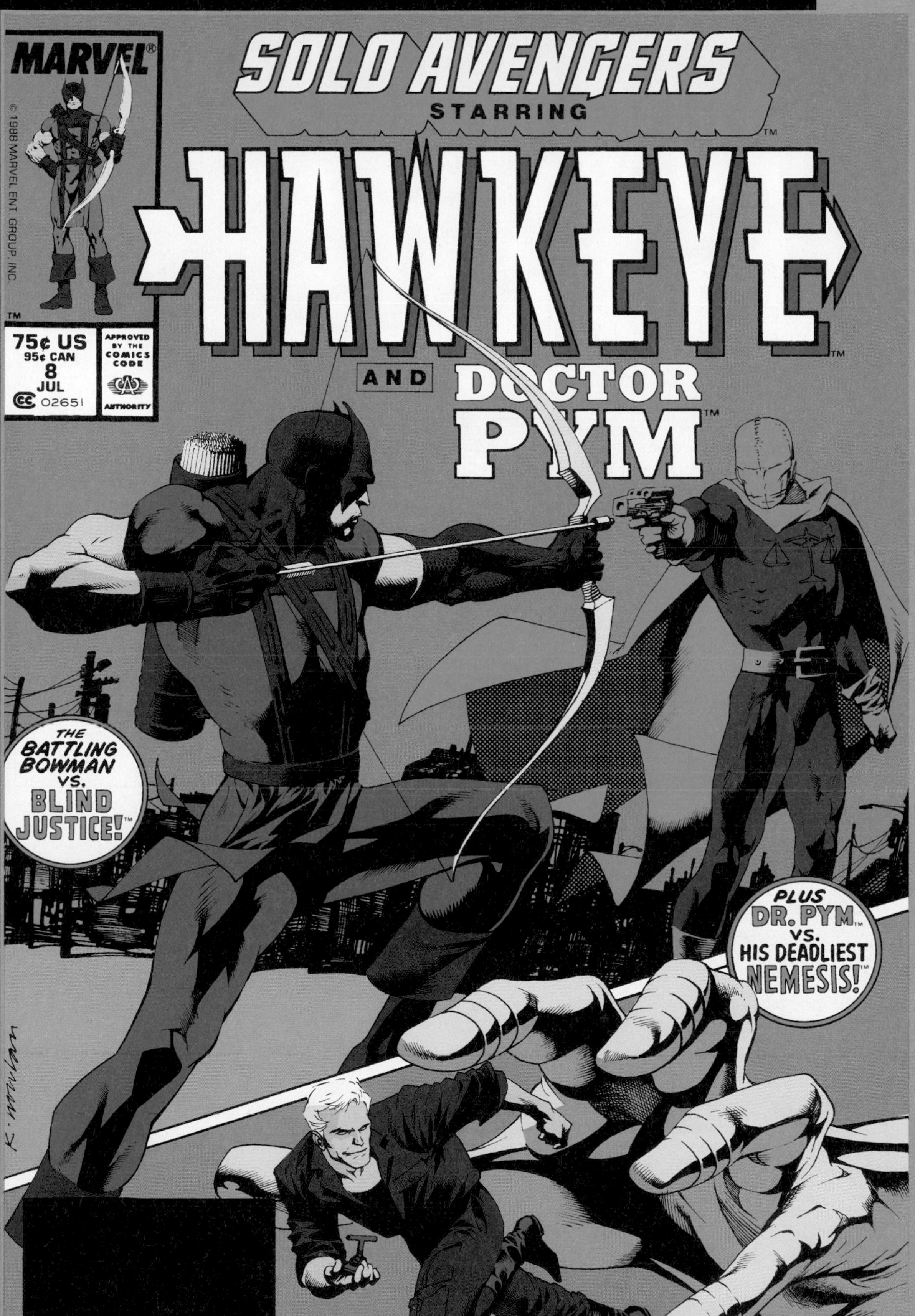
MARVEL
SOLO AVENGERS
STARRING
HAWKEYE
AND DOCTOR PYM
© 1988 MARVEL ENT. GROUP, INC.
75¢ US
95¢ CAN
8
JUL
02651
APPROVED BY THE COMICS CODE AUTHORITY
THE BATTLING BOWMAN VS. BLIND JUSTICE!
PLUS DR. PYM VS. HIS DEADLIEST NEMESIS!
K. MORGAN

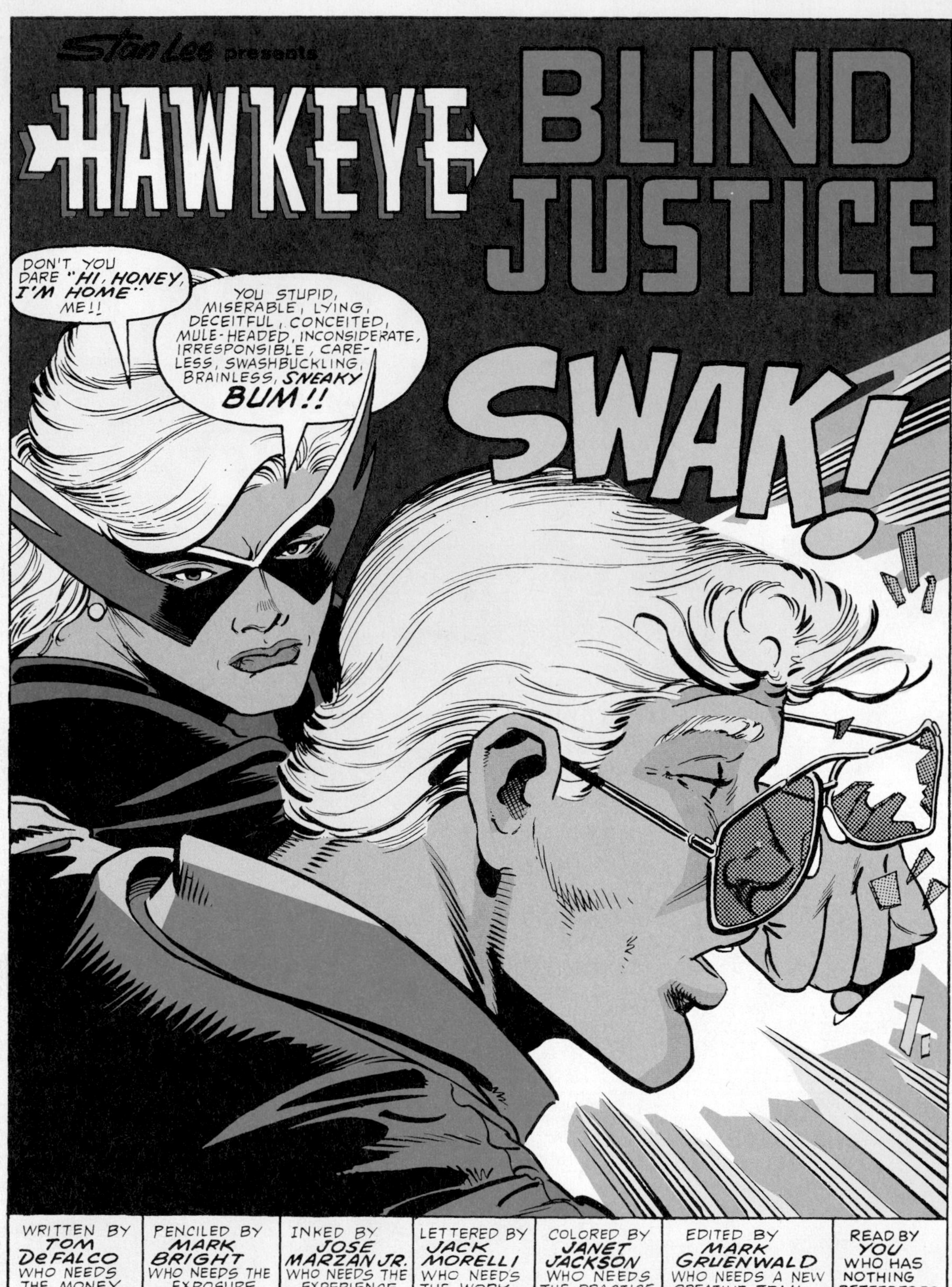


| WRITTEN BY TOM DeFALCO WHO NEEDS THE MONEY | PENCILED BY MARK BRIGHT WHO NEEDS THE EXPOSURE | INKED BY JOSE MARZAN JR. WHO NEEDS THE EXPERIENCE | LETTERED BY JACK MORELLI WHO NEEDS THE WORK | COLORED BY JANET JACKSON WHO NEEDS THE PRACTICE | EDITED BY MARK GRUENWALD WHO NEEDS A NEW CREATIVE TEAM | READ BY YOU WHO HAS NOTHING BETTER TO DO |
|---|---|---|---|---|---|---|

IN CASE YOU'VE FORGOTTEN, YOU KNOCKED ME OUT WITH A GAS ARROW LAST WEEK SO THAT YOU COULD GO TO PARIS--
--AND RISK YOUR WORTHLESS LIFE IN SOME IDIOTIC, MACHO GOON BATTLE TO THE DEATH WITH YOUR FORMER MENTOR, TRICK SHOT!
AND, NOW, YOU HAVE THE COLOSSAL NERVE TO COME WALTZING BACK HERE WITH A BIG SMILE ON YOUR UGLY FACE!
WOULD YOU HAVE FELT BETTER IF I HAD MOON-WALKED IN WITH A FROWN?

ARRGGHH!!

SLAM!
WELCOME BACK, HAWKEYE! THE OL' WEST COAST AVENGERS' COMPOUND HAS BEEN A LITTLE TOO QUIET AND BORING SINCE YOU'VE BEEN GONE!
THANKS A LOT, WONDER MAN!

THAT MOON-WALK LINE WAS A CLASSIC!
YOUR WIFE WAS PRETTY STEAMED! THINK SHE'LL EVER FORGIVE YOU?
OF COURSE SHE WILL! MOCKINGBIRD IS CRAZY ABOUT ME!

BESIDES, I KNOW HOW TO HANDLE WOMEN!
AND THEY CALL DAREDEVIL THE MAN WITHOUT FEAR!
SURE, BUT NO ONE KNOWS IF HE'S MARRIED!

AND SO, SOMETIME LATER...
HEY, PAL! ANYTHING BIGGER WILL COST YOU A FORTUNE!
HEY, PAL, ANYTHING SMALLER WILL COST ME MY LIFE!
Flowers by FRANCESI

AND MAKE THE CARD OUT TO "MY VERY LOVING AND BEAUTIFUL WIFE!"
THINK WE SHOULD ALSO ADD "FORGIVING" AND "UNDERSTANDING" TO THAT?
MISTER, FROM THE DESPERATE WAY YOU SOUND, YOU COULD ADD DIAMOND EARRINGS AND A MINK COAT-- AND STILL BE IN TROUBLE!
WELL, I WAS PLANNING ON INCLUDING A BOX OF BUTTERCRUNCH!

HEY, FRANCESI!!
WHAT THE HECK ARE YOU STILL DOING HERE!

WE WARNED YOU TO CLOSE SHOP!
WE TOLD YOU WE DON'T WANT YOUR KIND IN OUR NEIGHBORHOOD!

YEAH! EITHER YOU GET OUT-- OR WE GET NASTY! UNDERSTAND?!
PUT HIM DOWN!
STAY OUT OF THIS, MISTER!

YOU PUNKS HAVE BEEN WATCHING TOO MUCH MIAMI VICE!
YOUR TOUGH GUY ROUTINE IMPRESSES NOBODY!
KEEP BACK, OLD MAN!
I'M WARNING YOU!

OLD MAN?
OLD MAN??
:SHEESH: YOU REALLY KNOW HOW TO HURT A GUY!
BUT, THEN, SO DO I!!

GRAB HIM!
HE CAN'T STOP US ALL!
I'LL SCRAMBLE HIS BRAINS!
MAYBE I'M NOT MISTER OBJECTIVE, BUT THE ODDS SEEM A BIT LOPSIDED TO ME!

WHAT SAY WE EVEN THEM UP A BIT?

OF COURSE, I SUPPOSE I'D HAVE TO TIE BOTH HANDS BEHIND MY BACK--AND WEAR A BLINDFOLD--IN ORDER TO GIVE YOU GUYS A FIGHTING CHANCE!

YOU SEEM TO BE THE LEADER OF THIS PACK!
HEY! YOU'RE ONLY A TEEN-AGER!
THE PUENTES KID!

MAYBE WE ARE TEENAGERS, BUT WE CAN STILL TAKE OUT A LOSER LIKE YOU!
WHERE'S YOUR SMART MOUTH NOW, MACHO MAN?

YOU OKAY, MISTER?
YEAH, THEY ONLY HURT MY PRIDE!
TALK ABOUT CARELESS! MAY-BE I AM GETTING OLD!

THEY GOT AWAY, BUT WE CAN STILL DESCRIBE THAT ONE PUNK TO THE POLICE!
NO! NO COPS! I DON'T WANT ANY TROUBLE! I JUST WANT TO RUN MY SHOP IN PEACE!

SOMETIME LATER...
OW! THAT STINGS!!

DON'T BE SUCH A BIG BABY! IT'S ONLY YOUR HEAD-- AND NOT ANYTHING YOU USE MUCH!
YOU CAN'T EVEN BUY FLOWERS WITHOUT GETTING INTO TROUBLE!
LISTEN, HONEY, I'M REAL WORRIED ABOUT FRANCESI!

HE SAW THAT KID'S FACE, AND I THINK HE RECOGNIZED HIM!
THERE HAVE BEEN A FEW REPORTS OF AN EXTORTION RING IN THE NEIGHBORHOOD!
IF IT'LL MAKE YOU FEEL ANY BETTER, WE CAN LOOK INTO THEM--

"--AND KEEP AN EYE ON FRANCESI IN THE PROCESS!"
WELL, THIS IS REAL EXCITING--
--BUT NOT THE WAY I PLANNED ON! SPENDING OUR FIRST NIGHT BACK TOGETHER!

I'M SORRY ABOUT THAT, HONEY!
JUST TELL ME ONE THING, HAWK-- ARE YOU MORE WORRIED ABOUT FRANCESI--OR THAT "OLD MAN" CRACK THAT KID MADE?
THAT'S COLD, MOCK, REAL COLD.
HEY, LOOK WHAT'S PULLIN' INTO FRANCESI'S BACK ENTRANCE!

LIMOUSINES?!

UH-OH! THAT ONE WITH THE GAG IS THE KID WHO THREATENED FRANCESI-- BUT WHO ARE THOSE TWO GOONS?

SOMETHING'S REAL WRONG WITH THIS PICTURE!
LET'S MOVE CLOSER, AND FIND OUT WHAT'S GOING ON!

GOOD EVENING, MY YOUNG FRIEND. YOUR NAME IS PUENTES, IS IT NOT?
AS I UNDERSTAND IT, YOU AND A FEW OF YOUR ASSOCIATES WISH TO DICTATE TO ME HOW THIS NEIGHBORHOOD IS RUN!

YOU WANT MY PEOPLE TO STOP THREATENING THE LOCAL STORE OWNERS, DON'T YOU?
YOU BELIEVE YOURSELF TO BE A MAN OF INFLUENCE! A TOUGH GUY!

YOU'RE A PUNK!
SWAPP
IF THAT BUSYBODY CUSTOMER HADN'T INTERFERED THIS AFTERNOON, I WOULD HAVE SIGNALED MY BOYS TO WASTE YOU!

I DON'T BELIEVE IT! FRANCESI'S THE BAD GUY!
WELL, AT LEAST YOU GOT THE PART ABOUT AN EXTORTION RACKET RIGHT!

I WANT THE NAMES OF ALL YOUR FRIENDS! NOW!

KEE-RASH!
WHAT THE?!
WHO'S THAT?!

PWOOM PWOOM
I AM THE TRUE SERVANT OF JUSTICE...
BLIND JUSTICE!!
RALPHIE!? YOU KILLED RALPHIE!
NO, MERELY JOLTED HIM INTO UNCONSCIOUSNESS!

JUSTICE IS NOT SERVED BY PUNISHING THE SERVANT FOR THE CRIMES OF THE KING!
YEAH, WELL, YOU'RE DEAD, MISTER!
LET'S GO, MOCK!

BUDDA BUDDA
FALL DOWN! BLAST YOU-- FALL DOWN!
YOU ARE WASTING AMMUNITION, MY FRIEND--

--MERE BULLETS CANNOT STOP THE CAUSE OF JUSTICE!
HMM... IT APPEARS THAT I'M NOT THE ONLY ONE THAT USES ELECTRO-SHOCKS TO STUN HIS ENEMIES!

THANK YOU FOR YOUR TIMELY ASSISTANCE, AVENGER!
PLEASE ALLOW ME TO RETURN THE FAVOR!
PWOOM PWOOM

WHERE IS FRANCESI?
JUSTICE DEMANDS THAT HE DIE FOR HIS CRIMES!
WHAT?! YOU CAN'T BE SERIOUS, PAL!

HAWKEYE, YOU-- AND OTHERS LIKE YOU--CHAMPION THE PRINCIPLES OF LAW AND ORDER, BUT I-- AND I ALONE-- SERVE THE CAUSE OF TRUE JUSTICE!

FORGET IT, BUSTER! THERE'S NO WAY I'M GONNA LET YOU KILL ANYONE... NOT EVEN A CREEP LIKE FRANCESI!
OOO
BLAST! HE MANAGED TO DODGE BENEATH MY ADHESIVE-TIPPED ARROW!

YOU ARE WELL-INTENTIONED, AVENGER, BUT MISGUIDED!

THE SCALES OF JUSTICE DEMAND TO BE BALANCED!

MOCKING-BIRD??
WHAT ARE YOU WAITING FOR, HANDSOME??
GO GET THAT LOONY!

I CAN EASILY HANDLE THINGS HERE!
RIGHT!

THAT'S FAR ENOUGH, FRANCESI!
TAKE IT EASY, MISTER! DON'T DO ANYTHING RASH!
MAYBE WE CAN MAKE A DEAL.

I'VE HEARD ALL ABOUT YOU! YOU'RE A MURDERER! A MAD DOG!
PLEASE DON'T KILL ME! I'M BEGGING YOU! I'LL PAY YOU ANYTHING! ANYTHING!
YOU OFFER ME MERE WEALTH!?

I DESIRE NOTHING SAVE JUSTICE!
NO! NO!! I DON'T DESERVE TO DIE!!

PUT IT DOWN, MR. MASK!
NO, HAWKEYE, I CANNOT ALLOW THIS CRIMINAL TO ESCAPE HIS JUST PUNISHMENT!
AND I CAN'T ALLOW YOU TO KILL HIM!
THEN KILL ME!

STOP IT! STOP IT!! THIS ISN'T FAIR! I DESERVE A FAIR TRIAL! A CHANCE TO DEFEND MY--
ARGH!

OH MY GOSH! THE STRAIN WAS TOO MUCH FOR HIM!
HE'S HAVING A HEART ATTACK!!

WHERE ARE YOU GOING?
WE'VE GOT TO GET HIM TO A HOSPITAL!
WHY? JUSTICE DEMANDS THAT HE DIE!
LET HIM!

NO! YOU CAN'T JUST TOSS AWAY A HUMAN LIFE LIKE IT WAS A SOILED TISSUE!
I COULD STOP YOU, JUSTICE-- OR WHATEVER YOU CALL YOURSELF-- WITH JUST ONE QUICK ARROW IN THE BACK!

BUT I HAVE MORE IMPORTANT THINGS TO DO!
UNNGH...
TAKE IT EASY, OLD MAN! I'LL GET YOU TO A HOSPITAL--

"--I SWEAR I WILL!"
THESE CHARGES, WHICH BLIND JUSTICE USED, ARE PRETTY AMAZING!
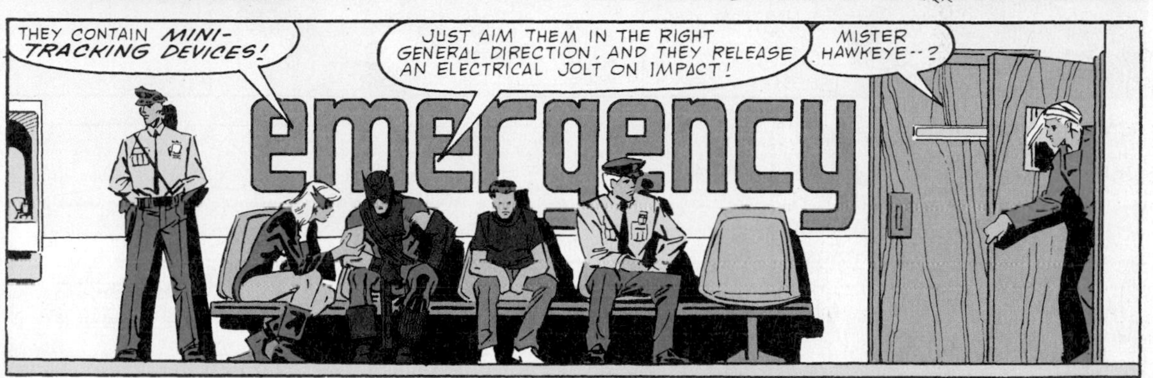
THEY CONTAIN MINI-TRACKING DEVICES!
JUST AIM THEM IN THE RIGHT GENERAL DIRECTION, AND THEY RELEASE AN ELECTRICAL JOLT ON IMPACT!
MISTER HAWKEYE--?
emergency

MR. FRANCESI HAS PASSED ON. I'M SORRY.
ALL RIGHT! ALL RIGHT!

THAT JUSTICE DUDE HAS THE RIGHT IDEA! WASTE THE BADDIES!
PUT A LID ON IT, PUENTES!
HEY, HAWK...

NEXT ISSUE

MORE ON THE MYSTERIOUS BLIND JUSTICE! PLUS A SPECIAL APPEARANCE BY A CERTAIN CREATURE OF THE NIGHT!!

JUSTICE KILLS

Stan Lee presents

# DOCTOR PYM

MIKE W. BARR
WRITER

LARRY ALEXANDER
PENCILS

JOSÉ MARZAN
INKS

JACK MORELLI
LETTERS

PAUL BECTON
COLORS

I WANT TO PARK UP *HERE!* ANY PROBLEM?

Uh, N-NOT A *ONE* PAL!

# ANOTHER WORD FOR *REVENGE*

THANKS, I APPRECIATE IT.
YOU HOVER RIGHT THERE, ROVER, UNDERSTAND?
GOTCHA, DR. PYM!
HEY, AIN'T THAT THE ANT-MAN GUY?
NEVER MIND THAT! HOW DO WE GET THE DEPARTMENT TO SPRING FOR CARS LIKE THIS FOR US?

I HEARD THAT OFFICER'S QUESTION ABOUT MY NAME, BUT I COULDN'T TAKE TIME TO SET HIM STRAIGHT NOW--I HAD BUSINESS TO ATTEND TO...
LT. ISHMAEL'S OFFICE, PLEASE?
DOWN THAT HALL, FIRST DOOR ON YOUR LEFT!
L.A.P.D

WREET
HOLD IT RIGHT THERE, MISTER! METAL DETECTOR SAYS YOU'RE CARRYING AN ARSENAL! THOUGH I CAN'T FIGURE WHERE!
AN ARSENAL? I DON'T--

OH, OF COURSE! HERE, OFFICER!
YOU KIDDIN'? THOSE TOYS?

THEY LOOK LIKE TOYS, BUT THEY DO A LITTLE GROWING UP!
WHOA!

THEN, AT MY MENTAL COMMAND, THEY SHRINK BACK DOWN AGAIN--OUT OF SIGHT, IF NOT OUT OF MIND.

HOPE THEY DON'T TAKE UP TOO MUCH SPACE OFFICER!
I THINK I CAN SQUEEZE 'EM IN SOME-WHERE...

LT. ISHMAEL
ROBBERY
HELLO, LIEUTENANT. I SUPPOSE YOU'RE PRETTY TIRED OF THE "CALL ME ISHMAEL" JOKE, Eh?
YES... ESPECIALLY SINCE I'VE NEVER BEEN ABLE TO MAKE IT MORE THAN HALFWAY THROUGH MOBY DICK. SIT DOWN, MR... ER... IS IT GIANT-MAN OR--?
JUST "DR. PYM" WILL BE FINE. THANKS.
...AND I'LL STAND, IF YOU DON'T MIND. WHY DID YOU WANT TO SEE ME, LIEUTENANT?
SOME PRETTY STRANGE GOINGS-ON, LATELY, GIANT-- DR. PYM.
THREE ROBBERIES COMMITTED OVER THE PAST WEEK THAT DON'T FIT ANY MODUS OPERANDI WE'VE EVER HEARD OF...
...LAST NIGHT, HUNDREDS OF THOUSANDS OF DOLLARS OF STATE OF THE ART EQUIPMENT WAS STOLEN FROM MORGAN-STERN ELECTRONICS...
...TWO NIGHTS AGO, WHAT LOOKS LIKE THE SAME THIEF CLEANED OUT THE JEWELRY OF THE ENTWILER FAMILY...
...AND FOUR NIGHTS AGO, EXPERIMENTAL MEDICAL VACCINES GOT HEISTED FROM THE NEW CENTURIES LABS!
SOUNDS LIKE YOU'VE GOT YOUR HANDS FULL ALL RIGHT, LIEUTENANT... BUT WHAT AM I DOING HERE? IF YOU WANT THE AVENGERS' HELP...
IT'S A LITTLE MORE SERIOUS THAN THAT, DR. PYM. YOU SEE, IN ALL THREE ROBBERIES, THE SECURITY SYSTEMS WERE EITHER EVADED OR DEACTIVATED...
...ALMOST AS IF THE THIEF WAS THE SIZE OF AN ANT...
...AND THE VAULT DOOR WAS TORN OFF AT THE NEW CENTURY LABS AS THOUGH THE THIEF HAD THE STRENGTH OF A GIANT!
WHAT?! ARE YOU ACCUSING ME OF--
MY FIRST RESPONSE WAS A SURGE OF RIGHTEOUS INDIGNATION...

...BUT HE WAS ONLY DOING HIS JOB... AND LOOKING AT IT FROM HIS POINT OF VIEW, I COULDN'T BLAME HIM.
SORRY, LIEUTENANT...
LT. ISHMAEL
ROBBERY

...WITH MY HISTORY OF MENTAL INSTABILITY, I CAN'T BLAME YOU FOR THINKING OF ME... BUT I'M INNOCENT.

I'D APPRECIATE IT IF YOU COULD BACK THAT UP WITH AN ALIBI DR. PYM.
LOOK, I'M NOT THE ONLY GUY AROUND WHO CAN CHANGE SIZE, YOU KNOW...

THERE'S A NEW ANT-MAN...
...THERE'S A NEW, EVIL YELLOWJACKET-- YOU'D HAVE TO CHECK THE EAST COAST AVENGERS ABOUT THEIR WHEREABOUTS.
ALL THAT'S TRUE, DR. PYM...

...BUT YOU WERE THE FIRST TO SHRINK, AND YOU'RE HERE IN TOWN...
TWO OBVIOUS CLUES THAT ANYONE WHO WANTED TO FRAME WOULD KNOW!

I THOUGHT OF THAT... MUST BURN YOUR FANNY THAT SOMEONE HATES YOU THAT MUCH, HUH? WOULD MAKE ME WANT TO GO OUT AND--
SAVE THE PSYCHOLOGY 101, LIEUTENANT --I'VE ALREADY DECIDED TO HELP YOU FIND WHO-EVER IS BEHIND THIS.
HUH?! YOU THINK THAT'S WHAT I WANTED ALL ALONG!?

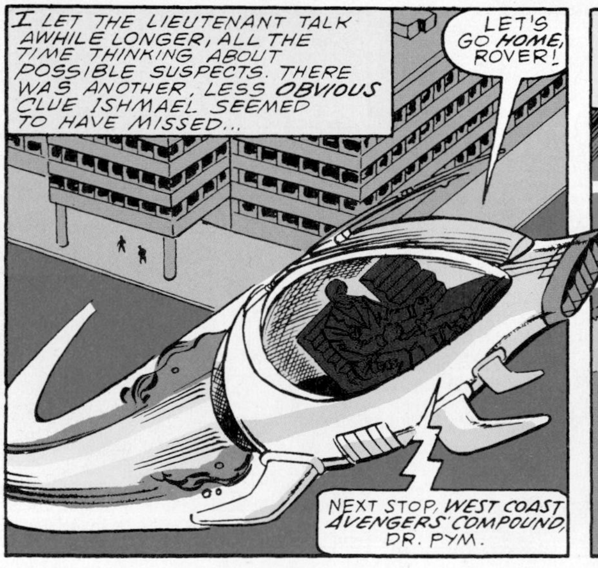
I LET THE LIEUTENANT TALK AWHILE LONGER, ALL THE TIME THINKING ABOUT POSSIBLE SUSPECTS. THERE WAS ANOTHER, LESS OBVIOUS CLUE ISHMAEL SEEMED TO HAVE MISSED...
LET'S GO HOME, ROVER!
NEXT STOP, WEST COAST AVENGERS' COMPOUND, DR. PYM.

AND IT WAS ALL I NEEDED TO GO TO WORK. ACCORDING TO THE THIEF'S ESTABLISHED PATTERN, HIS NEXT SCORE WOULD BE TOMORROW NIGHT.

WHICH GAVE ME MORE THAN ENOUGH TIME TO DO A LITTLE PLANNING OF MY OWN. IT FELT GOOD TO WORK ON WIRES AND CIRCUITRY AGAIN...
...NOT THAT MY MECHANICAL PARTNER NECESSARILY SHARED MY ENTHUSIASM.

WE'VE BEEN SITTING AROUND ALL DAY, DR. PYM! I'M GETTING RUSTY! AND ALL YOU'RE DOING IS WORKING ON THOSE DUMB GADGETS!
IF I'M CORRECT, THESE "GADGETS" WILL PROVE VALUABLE TONIGHT, ROVER!

BUT UNTIL I NEED THEM, LET'S JUST PUT THEM OUT OF HARM'S WAY.

AND NOW WE'RE READY TO GO! SATISFIED, ROVER?
YOU BET, BUT--WHAT ABOUT THE OTHER AVENGERS? AREN'T YOU GONNA TELL THEM?

NO ROVER. THE THIEF BEHIND THIS HAS MADE IT PERSONAL!
AND I'M MORE THAN HAPPY TO ACCOMMODATE HIM!
THAT SOUNDS LIKE I SPRANG INTO ACTION RIGHT AWAY...

...BUT AFTER RUNNING A FEW ERRANDS, NIGHTFALL FOUND US HOVERING ABOVE LOS ANGELES, AND ROVER AS PATIENT AS EVER.
THIS IS BORING, DR. PYM. WHEN IS SOMETHING GONNA HAPPEN?
TONIGHT, I HOPE, ROVER. BUT IF NOT, WE'LL JUST WAIT UNTIL--

THAT'S WHAT WE'VE BEEN WAITING FOR, ROVER! WHICH BUG IS IT!?
I'M GETTING A FIX ON IT NOW, DR. PYM ...LET'S SEE...
BEEP EEP BEEP

...IT'S THE BUG YOU PLANTED IN ECKMAN'S ELECTRONICS DR. PYM. IT'S PICKED UP CYBERNETIC IMPULSES INSIDE THEIR PLANT!
GOOD! I KNEW HE'D STICK TO HIS PATTERN!
I DON'T GET IT, DR. PYM! HOW'D YOU KNOW?
AND WHY'D WE ONLY PLANT THOSE CYBERNETIC SENSORS IN PLACES BEGINNING WITH "E"?

ACTIVATE ACID SPRAY, ROVER!
OKAY... BUT WON'T THAT SET OFF THE BURGLAR ALARM?
SSST
I HOPE SO! I'M COUNTING ON IT TO BRING THE POLICE SO THEY CAN SEE ME BAG THIS GUY!

YOU'RE TALKING LIKE YOU KNOW WHO'S BEHIND THIS, DR. PYM!
JUST LIKE I KNEW TO PLANT THE SENSORS IN PLACES BEGINNING WITH "E" ROVER! THE MAN FRAMING ME WAS SIGNING HIS NAME TO THE ROBBERIES...

"HE ROBBED NEW CENTURY LABS, ENTWILER JEWELERS MORGANSTERN ELECTRONICS"...

ECKMAN'S ELECTRONICS BEGINS WITH "E"--AND THAT'S THE NEXT LETTER IN THE NAME OF--
SPOTLIGHT ON ROVER!
RIGHT, DR. PYM!

DR. NEMESIS!!
LOOKS LIKE A SLIGHT CHANGE OF PLAN IS IN ORDER, DR. PYM! INSTEAD OF FRAMING YOU, I'LL HAVE TO HUMILIATE YOU!

THAT'S RIGHT, NEMESIS, TRY TO CONVINCE YOURSELF THAT YOU STILL HAVE A PLAN -- THAT IT HASN'T GONE UP IN FLAMES!
SUCH HOSTILITY, PYM! AREN'T YOU EVEN CURIOUS AS TO WHERE I'VE BEEN ALL THESE YEARS?!

THAT'S NO MYSTERY, NEMESIS!
OH NO?

"NO. I KNEW YOU WERE CAUGHT IN MY EXPERIMENTAL SHRINKING BEAMS WHEN YOU TRIED TO ROB MY HOUSE..."
*MICRONAUTS #40-41.

AND I ALSO KNEW IT WOULD WEAR OFF -- LIKE IT DID -- AND RETURN YOU TO YOUR NORMAL SIZE.
RIGHT AS USUAL, PYM! I DECIDED TO TAKE MY REVENGE BY FRAMING YOU FOR MY ROBBERIES -- AFTER ALL, "NEMESIS" IS ANOTHER WORD FOR REVENGE!

BUT I MUST SAY I PREFER TAKING OUT MY REVENGE ON YOU PERSONALLY! IT'S UNSCIENTIFIC, I SUPPOSE, BUT CERTAINLY SATISFYING!
I WAS JUST THINKING THE SAME THING, NEMESIS!

BUT I INTEND TO BE THE ONE WHO WALKS AWAY!
ROVER! TAKE HIM!!
AGGHHH!
FOOSHT

GONE! ROVER! DID YOU SEE WHERE THEY WENT?
NO, DR. PYM. I THINK HE SHRUNK!
"I'D FIGURED AS MUCH!"

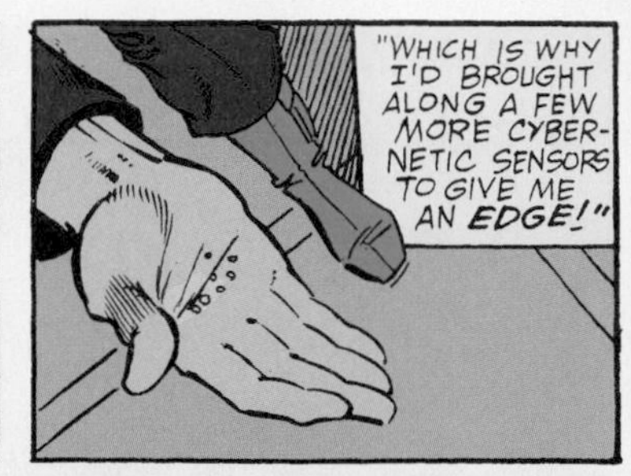
"WHICH IS WHY I'D BROUGHT ALONG A FEW MORE CYBER-NETIC SENSORS TO GIVE ME AN EDGE!"

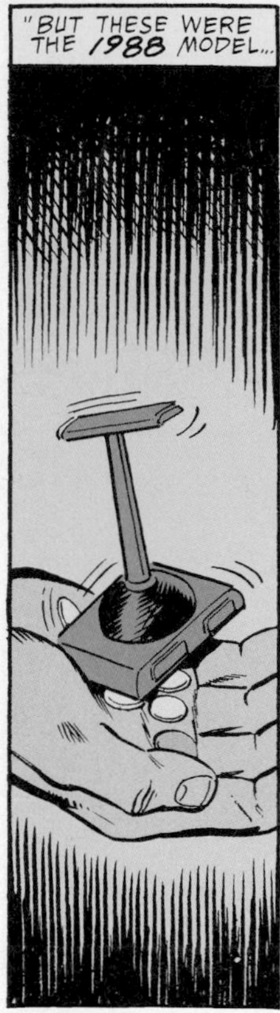
"BUT THESE WERE THE 1988 MODEL...

"...AND THEY DIDN'T HAVE TO WAIT FOR NEMESIS TO COME TO THEM!"
GO GET HIM, GUYS!

FOUND HIM ALREADY? GOOD WORK BOYS!

WHY NOT SURPRISE ME, NEMESIS? SURRENDER, AND SAVE US ALL SOME--
"I'D FORGOTTEN THAT EVEN REDUCED, HE STILL HAD THE PROPORTIONATE STRENGTH OF A FULL-SIZED MAN...

"IT'S NOT MUCH WHEN YOU'RE GOING UP AGAINST THE HULK...
BROKK!

"BUT AGAINST THE AVERAGE JOE, IT'S QUITE AN ADVANTAGE, AS NEMESIS KNEW!
MY ANKLE!! MUST'VE PICKED UP AN UNWELCOME HITCHHIKER!

BUT I'VE GOT SOMETHING FOR THAT THAT'S BETTER THAN FLEA POWDER!
KLIK

ARGH!
"AS I'D HOPED, A SECOND OR TWO OF CYBERNETIC FEEDBACK, CHANNELLED THROUGH THE SIZE-CHANGING CIRCUITRY IN HIS HELMET...
"...AND HE'D CHOOSE THE BETTER PART OF VALOR, QUICKLY...
DON'T GO AWAY MAD, NEMESIS...!
I'M NOT GOING AWAY AT ALL, PYM--!
MY LORD!
I JUST WANTED TO GIVE YOU A LOOK AT THE LAST THING YOU'LL EVER SEE!!
"TALK ABOUT TURNING THE TABLES! OVER THE YEARS, SOME CYNICS ASKED ME HOW JUST 'BEING BIG' PUT ME IN THE LEAGUE OF THUNDER GODS AND SUPER-SOLDIERS!
"IF THEY COULD SEE NEMESIS NOW, THEY WOULD REALIZE, AS I DID FOR THE FIRST TIME, WHAT IT IS LIKE TO FACE AN OPPONENT TALLER THAN A DINOSAUR!

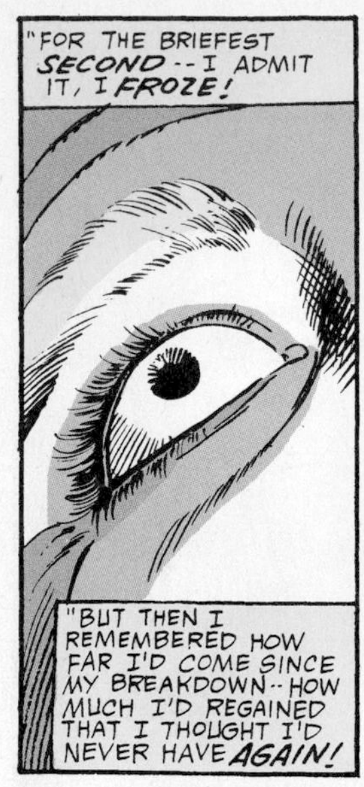
"FOR THE BRIEFEST SECOND -- I ADMIT IT, I FROZE!
"BUT THEN I REMEMBERED HOW FAR I'D COME SINCE MY BREAKDOWN -- HOW MUCH I'D REGAINED THAT I THOUGHT I'D NEVER HAVE AGAIN!

"AND I FOUND THE STRENGTH TO MOVE!
BOK
ROVER!!

RIGHT HERE, DR. PYM! BOY, THAT WAS CLOSE, HUH?
IT WON'T HAPPEN AGAIN! GO INTO EVASIVE MANEUVERS NOW...

...AND LET HIM CLUTCH AT STRAWS AWHILE!

GO, ROVER! KEEP HIM SO BUSY, HE DOESN'T NOTICE ME BACK HERE!
OKAY, DR. PYM!
"I COULD HAVE GIVEN NEMESIS ANOTHER SHOT OF FEEDBACK...

"BUT THAT WOULD ONLY HAVE ANGERED HIM, AND I WANTED TO END THIS, AND END IT QUICKLY. I ALREADY HAD AN IDEA AS TO HOW TO DO IT...

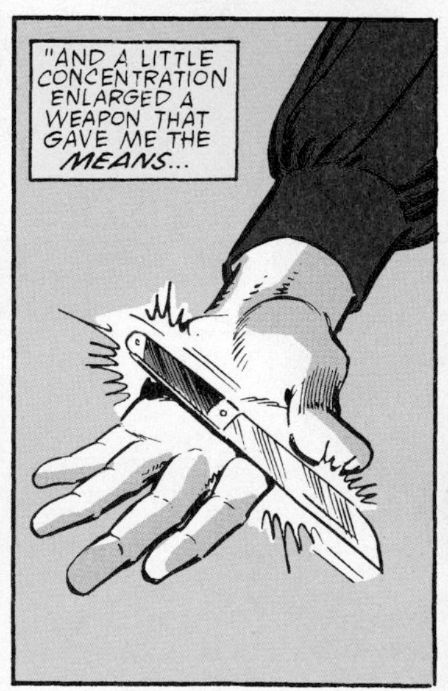
"AND A LITTLE CONCENTRATION ENLARGED A WEAPON THAT GAVE ME THE MEANS...

BLAST IT, PYM, ALL YOU'RE DOING IS DELAYING IT!
"NEMESIS HAD NEVER SPOKEN A TRUER WORD...

"THOUGH NOT QUITE IN THE WAY HE THOUGHT.
RIIPP

PYM? WHAT ARE YOU DOING BACK THERE?
"WHAT I WAS DOING WAS PREPARING A LITTLE LAYING ON OF HANDS.

"SPECIFICALLY MY HANDS. YEARS OF SHRINKING AND ENLARGING MYSELF HAD GIVEN ME THE POWER TO REDUCE OR INCREASE THE SIZE OF ANYTHING...
...INCLUDING HUMANS!
STOP IT! STOP IT! OR I'LL--

"NEMESIS'S POWER WAS IN HIS HELMET CIRCUITRY... ONCE HE WAS OUT OF CONTACT WITH THAT...
UNGHH!
"IT WAS OVER.

"A SINGLE THREAD ENLARGED FROM HIS COSTUME GAVE ME THE MEANS TO KEEP NEMESIS OUT OF TROUBLE!
PYM? DR. PYM?

"THEN THE CAVALRY ARRIVED!
OH, HERE YOU ARE! WHO'S THIS!?
HE CALLS HIMSELF DR. NEMESIS. BUT I'M SURE HE'LL BE GLAD TO TELL YOU MORE!

GOOD WORK, DR. PYM... SORRY FOR THE HARD FEELINGS!
HEY, AREN'T YOU THAT GOLIATH GUY?
I WAS. A LONG TIME AGO.

BUT NOW I ANSWER TO THE NAME OF PYM.
"DR. PYM."
END

MARVEL®

# SOLO AVENGERS

STARRING

# HAWKEYE™

AND

# HELLCAT!™

75¢ US
95¢ CAN
9
AUG
02651

APPROVED BY THE COMICS CODE AUTHORITY



TM

MAD DOGS AND
MYSTERY MEN!

Stan Lee presents
HAWKEYE
IN THE SERVICE OF
JUSTICE
I'M REAL PLEASED THAT YOU COULD FIT ME INTO YOUR BUSY SCHEDULE, SPEEDO EVEN THOUGH I DID SHOW UP WITHOUT AN APPOINTMENT!
NOW, ABOUT THAT INFORMATION I REQUESTED..?!
GAKK Y-YOU'RE CRAZY, HAWK-EYE! I CAN'T HELP YOU!
I KNOW ZERO-- ABSOLUTELY NOTHING ABOUT THAT CREEP, BLIND JUSTICE!

TOM DEFALCO THE SULTAN OF SCRIPTING · MARK BRIGHT THE PRINCE OF PENCILS · JOSE MARZAN JR. THE EMPEROR OF EMBELLISHING · MORELLI THE LORD OF LETTERS · JACKSON THE COUNTESS OF COLORS · MARK GRUENWALD THE BABYSITTER OF BOZOS

I DON'T HAVE TIME FOR ANY MORE FUN' N'GAMES, SPEEDO!
TELL ME HOW TO FIND JUSTICE-- AND DO IT QUICKLY-- BECAUSE I'M ABOUT TO GET REAL ANNOYED WITH YOU-- AND YOU DON'T WANT THAT TO HAPPEN!
STAY COOL, PAL! I'D GIVE HIM TO YOU ON A SILVER PLATTER IF I COULD -- HONEST!
PLEASE BELIEVE ME!!

WHY SHOULD I??
BECAUSE THAT BLASTED VIGILANTE LIVES TO STICK IT TO WISE GUYS LIKE ME!
HE'S BAD FOR MY BUSINESS!
EVERYBODY ON THE STREET WANTS A PIECE OF HIM-- ME INCLUDED!

ALL RIGHT SPEEDO, I'LL BUY YOUR ACT... THIS TIME!
BUT YOU'RE STILL AN A-ONE WEASEL --AND I'M GONNA KEEP MY EYE ON YOU!

YOU JUST BETTER WATCH YOURSELF, HERO! I INTEND TO BURN YOU!
BURN YOU BAD!

AND SO, SOMETIME LATER...
CALM DOWN, SPEEDO!
I CAN'T CALM DOWN, BOSS!

THAT CRAZY AVENGER--HAWKEYE--JUST TRASHED MY ENTIRE GANG!
WE'VE GOTTA DO SOMETHING ABOUT HIM--AND I MEAN NOW!
I UNDER-STAND, SPEEDO--AND I AM FULLY PREPARED TO SANCTION THE APPROPRIATE ACTION!

HOWEVER, ONE MUST REALIZE THAT KILLING AN AVENGER IS NOT A LOW-RISK PROPOSITION!
WE MUST BE PREPARED TO ACCEPT THE CON-SEQUENCES FOR THIS ACTION--

--UNLESS WE CAN ARRANGE FOR ANOTHER PARTY TO APPEAR GUILTY!
I LIKE THE WAY YOU THINK, BOSS! WHO YOU GOT IN MIND?

UNDER THE CIRCUMSTANCES, I BELIEVE THE COSTUMED ADVENTURER KNOWN AS BLIND JUSTICE IS THE MOST APPROPRIATE CANDIDATE!

LATER, ACROSS TOWN, IN THE COMPOUND HEADQUARTERS OF THE WEST COAST AVENGERS...
YOUR QUICK QUIPS AREN'T GOING TO SAVE YOU THIS TIME, ARCHER!
NO PROBLEM! IF YOU WANT TO PLAY HARD BALL--

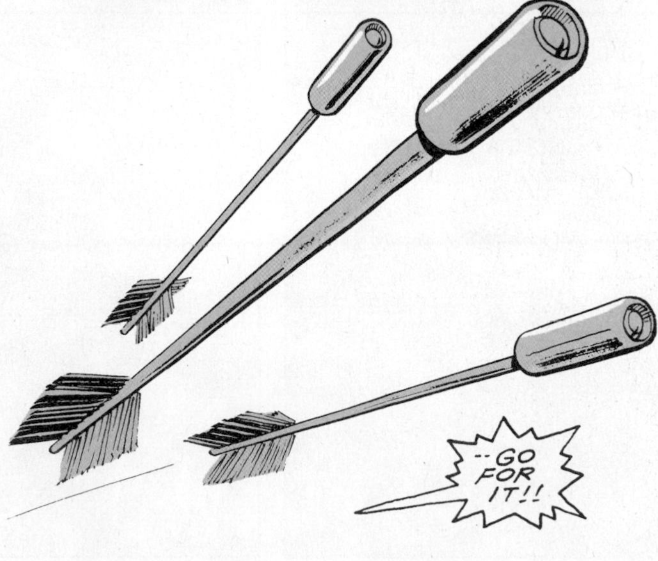
--GO FOR IT!!

I DON'T CARE WHAT YOU ASK--AS LONG AS YOU STAY OUT OF MY WAY--AND ALLOW ME TO FINISH MY DAILY WORKOUT!
RUMOR HAS IT THAT YOU ARE CURRENTLY INTERESTED IN A MYSTERIOUS GENTLEMAN WHO CALLS HIMSELF BLIND JUSTICE!

MAYBE--MAYBE NOT! WHAT'S IT TO YOU, MISS ROGERS?
I'M A REPORTER--AND THE PUBLIC HAS A RIGHT TO KNOW IF THIS CHARACTER IS A HYPER-ACTIVE VIGILANTE--

"--OR A COMMON STREET CRIMINAL WHO'S BENT ON WIPING OUT HIS COMPETITION?"
WHAT'S THE DEAL, ZIPPER?

LET'S JUST SAY THAT MY BOSS, SPEEDO, IS PLANNING ON HOSTING A PARTY TONIGHT!

A SURPRISE PARTY FOR HAWKEYE AND BLIND JUSTICE!
COUNT US IN!!
INTERESTING!

I DON'T CARE WHAT MOTIVATES JUSTICE!
I JUST KNOW HE ALWAYS LEAVES A TRAIL OF BODIES BEHIND HIM--
--AND HE MUST BE STOPPED!

TELEPHONE, HAWK!
SOUNDS LIKE YOUR FRIEND SPEEDO, TRYING TO DIS-GUISE HIS VOICE!
THANKS, MOCK-INGBIRD!

LISTEN UP, HOT SHOT! SOMETHING BIG IS GOING DOWN ON THE DOCKS TONIGHT!
MAYBE YOUR BOY WILL BE THERE!
THANKS FOR THE TIP!

HE BOUGHT IT, ZIPPER!
GREAT, BOSS! IF JUSTICE DOES SHOW UP, WE CAN BAG 'EM BOTH!

HOURS LATER, NIGHT ENGULFS THE CITY...
IT IS MID-NIGHT, THE WITCHING HOUR...

BUT, IT IS NOT A WITCH THAT HAUNTS THE CITY THIS NIGHT...
I'M RUNNING LATE!
BUT I HAD TO MAKE SURE NONE OF THE OTHER AVENGERS FOLLOWED ME!
THIS HAS GOT TO BE A SOLO SHOW!

CAN'T AFFORD ANY MISTAKES!

BLASTED PIGEONS!
I DIDN'T SEE THEM IN THE DARK!

TALK ABOUT EMBARRASS-ING!
I'M REAL GLAD NO ONE CAN SEE ME NOW!

BETTER CHECK OUT THE AREA!
SPEEDO DIDN'T INVITE ME HERE AS A GESTURE OF GOOD WILL!
URGKK!

THAT'S ODD--!
NOTHING'S STIRRING!

I WAS SO SURE THERE'D BE A RECEPTION COMMITTEE!

UGNN!
UFF!
GOSH! I HOPE THIS IS THE RIGHT DOCKS!
I MIGHT NOT GET INVITED TO ANOTHER AMBUSH IF I SCREWED UP THIS ONE!

I WISH SOMETHING WOULD HAPPEN!
I'M STARTING TO FEEL LIKE A REAL JERK WITH ALL THIS SKULKING AROUND!
MAYBE I'D BETTER TURN UP MY OL' HEARING AID-- IN CASE I'M MISSING SOMETHING!
KLIK
Uh-oh! DID I JUST HEAR A GUN GO :CLICK:?

BLAST HIM!!
BLOW HIM AWAY!!
BUT BLIND JUSTICE AIN'T HERE YET!
FORGET 'IM-- AND ICE THE ARCHER!

GOOD OL' SPEEDO! I SHOULD'VE HAD MORE FAITH IN HIM!
THAT SLIME-BUCKET NEVER COULD RESIST AN OPPORTUNITY TO SET ME UP!
HOPE HE DIDN'T PAY THESE BOZOS IN ADVANCE! THEY SHOOT SO BADLY, THAT MY ONLY PROBLEM IS--

--WHO TO TAKE OUT FIRST!

MAYBE I SHOULD TEST SOME OF MY NEW TRICK ARROWS AGAINST THIS BUNCH!
NAH! THEY'RE NOT WORTH THE EFFORT!
'SCUSE ME, PAL!

--BUT I NEED SOME QUICK COVER!
WISH I HAD PACKED MY BOXING GLOVE ARROW! THIS IS THE KIND OF FIGHT THAT PRACTICALLY DEMANDS IT!

IF IT IS COVER YOU SEEK, HAWKEYE--
--I SHALL BE HONORED TO PROVIDE IT!
THE SHROUD?!

HEY, WHAT'S GOING ON??
WHERE'D THAT BLACK MIST COME FROM ??
WHO CARES!? SCATTER!!

NICE GOING, SHROUD! WHAT AM I SUPPOSED TO DO NOW?
I CAN'T FIGHT IF I CAN'T SEE!
DO NOT FEAR AVENGER!

I AM THE HAND OF DARKNESS!

THE MASTER OF THE NIGHT SHIFT!

I SHALL BE YOUR FISTS! YOUR FURY!

I WILL STRIKE IN YOUR STEAD!
THIS IS RIDICULOUS!

TOTALLY RIDICULOUS!

WHAT'S WRONG, BOSS?
I'M FURIOUS, ZIPPER! FURIOUS! I PAID GOOD MONEY TO SEE THAT BIG-MOUTHED, BOW-SLINGING STOOGE GET STOMPED--

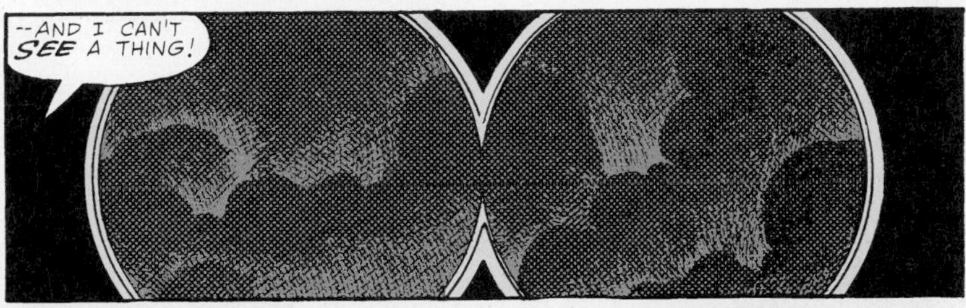
--AND I CAN'T SEE A THING!

NOT ONE BLASTED THING! I COULD TAKE POT SHOTS AT EVERY SOUND MY HYPED-UP HEARING PINPOINTS....
BUT I MIGHT HIT THE DARK-NIGHT DINGBAT!
WAIT'LL I GET MY HANDS ON THAT GLORY-GRABBING GOON!

IT IS OVER, HAWKEYE! THE BATTLE IS ENDED!
NO FOOLIN'!

HEY, PAL, IF I HAD WANTED TO SIT ON THE SIDELINES, I WOULD'VE BOUGHT TICKETS TO WRESTLEMANIA!

I WAS TRYING TO PROLONG THIS STUPID FIGHT UNTIL BLIND JUSTICE SHOWED UP.. AND YOU BLEW IT!!
CALM YOURSELF, AVENGER...

--THE MAIN CULPRITS HAVE YET TO BE APPREHENDED!
Uh-Oh! I THINK WE'VE BEEN SPOT-TED, ZIPPER!

WE'D BETTER MAKE TRACKS BEFORE... Uh, ZIPPER?
ZIPPER?

HE HAS ALREADY DESERTED YOU, SPEEDO!
YOU!
DO NOT REACH FOR YOUR GUN, SPEEDO!

YOU ARE NEITHER FAST NOR LUCKY ENOUGH TO ESCAPE YOUR JUST PUNISHMENT!

YOU TRIED TO KILL AN AVENGER, TONIGHT!
JUSTICE DEMANDS THAT YOU ARE THE ONE THAT DIES!
AW, C'MON... CAN'T YOU TAKE A JOKE?
I WAS JUST HAVING A LITTLE FUN WITH HAWKEYE!

OH, NO! THAT JOKER WHO JUST STEPPED INTO VIEW-- IT'S BLIND JUSTICE!
I'VE GOT TO DISTRACT HIM BEFORE HE CAN BLAST SPEEDO!

WHAT THE--?!
LOOKS LIKE HAWK DID ME A GOOD TURN! IT'S A REAL SHAME HE DOESN'T SHOOT TO KILL!
BLAM
BLAM

PWOOM
BUT I DO, SPEEDO!
ARRGH!!

JUSTICE!!
NO! NO! THIS ISN'T THE WAY I WANTED IT TO END!

I DIDN'T REALIZE SPEEDO WAS PACKING!
HIS TYPE USUALLY LEAVES THE ROUGH STUFF TO HIS HIRED HELP!
YOU CAN'T BLAME YOURSELF, HAWKEYE!

PERHAPS IT IS BETTER THIS WAY! JUSTICE WOULD HAVE NEVER SURVIVED A PRISON TERM!

A LAST! HE KNOWS TRUE PEACE... TRUE JUSTICE!
DOES HE? I WONDER.
THE END
FOR NOW!

"YOU'RE ABOUT TO MEET A WOMAN WHOSE MOTHER IMMORTALIZED HER IN A SERIES OF POPULAR COMIC BOOKS...

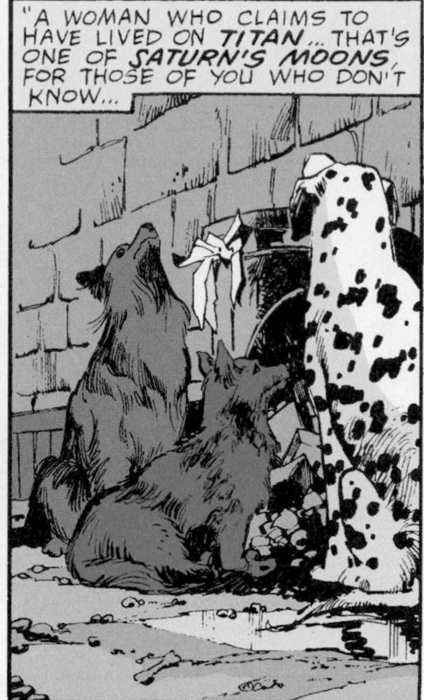
"A WOMAN WHO CLAIMS TO HAVE LIVED ON TITAN... THAT'S ONE OF SATURN'S MOONS, FOR THOSE OF YOU WHO DON'T KNOW...

"A WOMAN WHO SWEARS SHE'S MARRIED TO THE SON OF THE DEVIL...

"UNUSUAL? WELL KEEP IN MIND THAT SHE'S BEEN AN INTEGRAL PART OF BOTH THE AVENGERS AND DEFENDERS--

"-- AND SHE'S CURRENTLY HALF OWNER OF THE SAN FRANSISCO-BASED "HELLSTROM INVESTIGATIONS, INC." -- A SELF-PROCLAIMED GHOSTBUSTING TEAM, AND NO, HER PARTNER ISN'T BILL MURRAY."

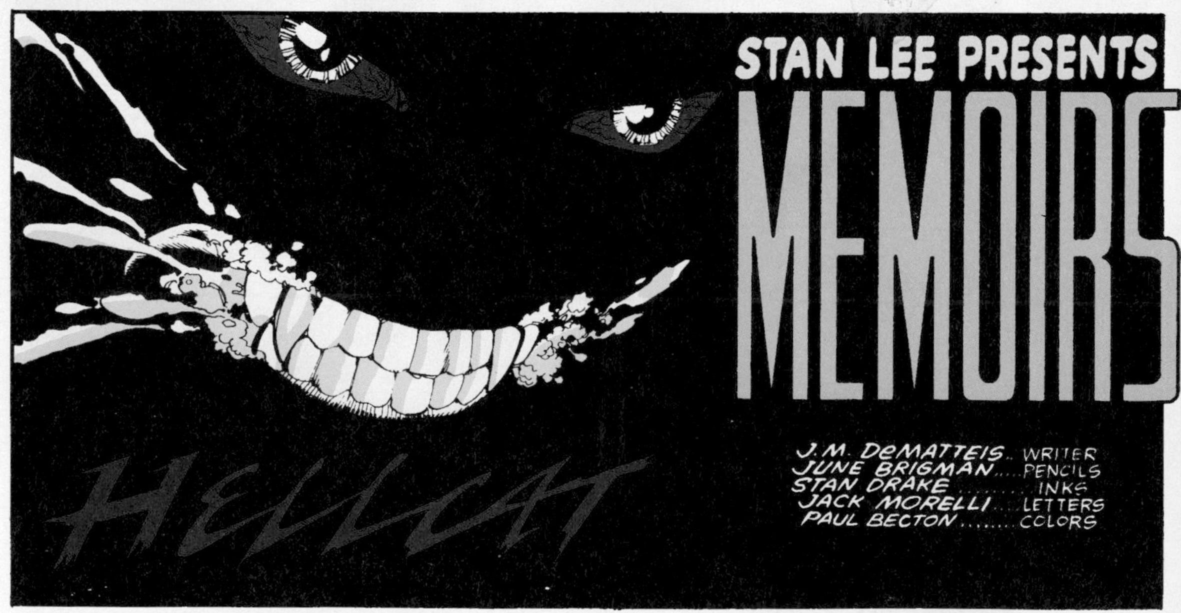
STAN LEE PRESENTS
MEMOIRS
HELLCAT
J.M. DeMATTEIS.. WRITER
JUNE BRIGMAN.... PENCILS
STAN DRAKE....... INKS
JACK MORELLI.... LETTERS
PAUL BECTON........ COLORS

"SHE'S HERE TODAY TO TELL US ABOUT HER JUST-PUBLISHED BOOK--

"--A LOOK BACK AT HER EXTRAORDINARY LIFE AND CAREER.
ab

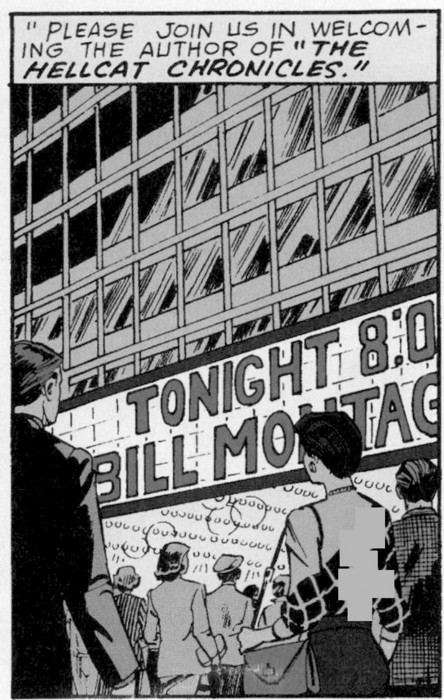
"PLEASE JOIN US IN WELCOMING THE AUTHOR OF "THE HELLCAT CHRONICLES."
TONIGHT 8:0
BILL MONTAG

MS. PATSY WALKER HELLSTROM!
THANK YOU, BILL.
I THINK I'M GONNA THROW UP!

WELCOME, PATSY!
A PLEASURE TO BE HERE, BILL!
LIAR!
THIS BOOK OF YOURS, WHICH CLAIMS TO BE A FACT-BASED MEMOIR--

IT'S NOT A CLAIM, BILL. IT'S THE TRUTH!
WELL, SOME PEOPLE HAVE SUGGESTED THAT THERE'S MORE IMAGINATION AT WORK HERE THAN--
SOME PEOPLE ARE WRONG, BILL!
WHY AM I DOING THIS??

"DO I DETECT SOME NERVOUSNESS ON YOUR PART, PATSY?"
"WELL, MAYBE A LITTLE!"
"WHY?"
"WELL, YOU DO HAVE A REPUTATION AS A RATHER... AGGRESSIVE INTERVIEWER."
"DO I?"

"WELL, YOU OF ALL PEOPLE SHOULD KNOW THE DIFFERENCE BETWEEN REPUTA-TION AND REALITY..."
"HMMM."
"YOUR HUSBAND, DAIMON HELLSTROM, IS A GOOD CASE IN POINT. THIS ABSURD CLAIM THAT HIS FATHER IS THE DEVIL..."

THINK I'LL RIP HER EYES OUT.

FIRST OF ALL, HIS FATHER'S NOT THE DEVIL... HE'S A DEVIL... ONE OF THE...
YOU DO SAY IN YOUR BOOK THAT MR. HELLSTROM IS THE SON OF SATAN, DON'T YOU?
MY... UH... FATHER-IN-LAW TOOK THE NAME OF THE BIBLICAL SATAN, BUT HE WASN'T...
FATHER-IN-LAW?

IT'S... UM... ALL EXPLAINED VERY CLEARLY IN CHAPTER FIFTEEN!
FRANKLY, IT CONFUSED THE HECK OUTTA ME!
WELL -- THEN MAYBE WE SHOULD TALK ABOUT SOMETHING YOU'LL HAVE A LITTLE LESS TROUBLE UNDERSTANDING!

"FINE. YOU SPENT A NUMBER OF YEARS WITH A GROUP OF SO-CALLED SUPER-HEROES?"
"WHICH GROUP?"
"THE DEFENDERS."
"Uh-Huh."

"AND, CORRECT ME IF I'M WRONG... THREE MEMBERS OF THAT GROUP WERE MUTANTS?"
ON THE AIR
STUDIO A

"ACTUALLY, WHEN I WAS WITH THE DEFENDERS, THE ONLY MUTANT IN THE GROUP WAS THE BEAST. ICEMAN AND ANGEL JOINED LATER."

THEN YOU LEFT BECAUSE OF THE INFLUX OF MUTANTS?
WHAT? NO, OF COURSE NOT!
THEN YOU SUPPORT THE MUTANT CAUSE?
EXACTLY WHAT IS THE MUTANT CAUSE, BILL?--
--YOU BIG JERK!!

WELL, SOME PEOPLE WOULD HAVE US BELIEVE THAT MUTANTS WANT TO OVERTHROW NORMAL HUMAN SOCIETY AND SET THEMSELVES UP AS A --

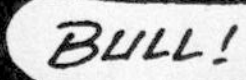

BULL!

MUTAPHOBIC BULL!
FIRST I'LL MURDER MY AGENT. THEN MY PUBLISHER. THEN...

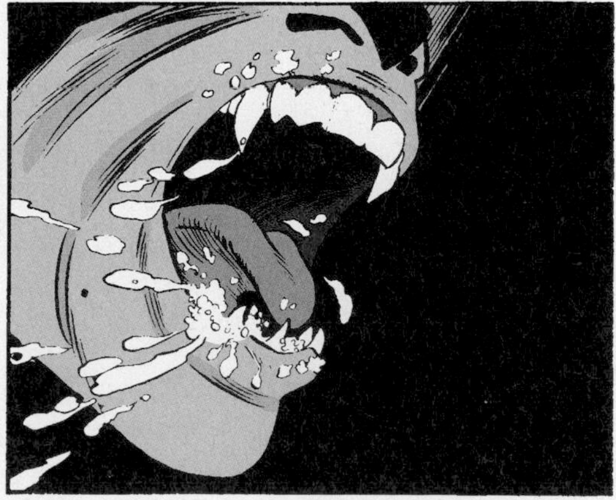

LOOK, I'M NOT HERE TO DEBATE HOT POLITICAL ISSUES. MY BOOK IS ABOUT ONE LIFE... A WOMAN STRUGGLING TO FIND HER IDENTITY IN THE 1980'S!
I DIDN'T REALLY SAY THAT!

FINE. LET'S PUT A MORE PERSONAL FOCUS ON THIS.
YOU DEVOTE CONSIDERABLE SPACE TO YOUR FIRST MARRIAGE TO ROBERT BAXTER, A MILITARY HERO--

--WHO'S CURRENTLY SPENDING TIME IN A FEDERAL PRISON FOR HELPING THE SECRET EMPIRE IN THEIR ATTEMPTS TO START WORLD WAR III!!

MY MARRIAGE TO BUZZ WAS A MISTAKE! I DIDN'T LOVE HIM! I WAS REBELLING AGAINST MY MOTHER... LOOKING FOR A WAY OUT OF --
I'VE GOT--
A QUESTION.
Uh... WE'RE NOT TAKING AUDIENCE QUESTIONS JUST Y--
--A QUESTION!!

BUZZ?! Ohh!!
BLINDED BY THE STUDIO LIGHTS! DIDN'T SEE HIM UNTIL--
UHH! MY THROAT--! IF I MOVE, HE'LL RIP IT OPEN--!

WHY DO YOU TELL SO MANY LIES ABOUT ME??
SOME KIND OF POISON IN HIS FAKE FANGS-- I'M-- I'M--

HELLO--

--DARLING.

OOOO... MY HEAD FEELS LIKE...
BUZZ BAXTER!! YOU SON OF A--

TUT-TUT, DARLING, SWEARING WAS NEVER YOUR STYLE. HAVE YOU REALLY CHANGED THAT MUCH?
AND PLEASE, DON'T CALL ME BUZZ. CALL ME MAD-DOG. IT'S SO MUCH MORE DRAMATIC.
WHERE ARE WE? WHAT AM I DOING IN THIS--

WE'RE IN A WAREHOUSE, IF YOU MUST KNOW. LOWER MANHATTAN.
AND I SLIPPED YOU INTO YOUR HELL-CAT COSTUME. THOUGHT IT WOULD BE A NICE TOUCH.
YOU PUT THIS ON ME? YOU TOOK OFF MY--?!
I ENJOYED IT. IT'S NICE TO KNOW YOU HAVEN'T CHANGED COMPLETELY.

YOU'RE SUPPOSED TO BE IN PRISON!
I WAS. BUT I STILL HAVE FRIENDS IN HIGH PLACES. I GOT OUT.
OBVIOUSLY.
SO WHAT'S IT GONNA BE, BUZZ? AM I GONNA HAVE TO KICK THE ALPO OUT OF YOU LIKE LAST TIME --WHEN YOU TRIED TO STOP MY MARRIAGE TO DAIMON?*
*NEW DEFENDERS #125!
YOU DON'T UNDERSTAND, DO YOU? YOU NEVER DID!

OH, I UNDERSTAND, ALL RIGHT!
DON'T BE A FOOL, PATSY! YOU'RE STILL DISORIENTED FROM MY BITE!
REMEMBER ??
HE'S RIGHT, I FEEL DROWSY--WOOZY--EVERY MOTION MAKES ME DIZZY!

MY ARM!

TEETH'RE HOLLOW, LIKE A SNAKE'S. FILLED WITH NASTY CHEMICALS. I COULD'VE KILLED YOU IF I'D WANTED TO!
MY ARM...

BUT I DON'T WANT TO KILL YOU!
LISTEN TO ME. I WANT TO MAKE YOU UNDERSTAND.
YOU'RE SICK,

I LOVE YOU, PATSY! WE...WE WERE ONCE SO IMPORTANT TO EACH OTHER! WE SHARED SO MUCH! WE--
WE SHARED NOTHING! I NEVER LOVED Y--
WHY DO YOU KEEP LYING?!

YOU KNOW WHAT IT'S LIKE TO WATCH SOME-ONE YOU LOVE CHANGE... TURN AWAY FROM YOU?

YOU... YOU WERE SUCH A SWEET, INNOCENT GIRL. SOMEONE TO BE HELD AND CHERISHED AND PROTECTED.

BUT THEN-- THEN YOU STARTED GETTING IDEAS ABOUT BEING INDEPENDENT... GETTING A JOB... FINDING YOUR-SELF!
WHAT WAS THERE TO FIND, PATSY?!?

I COULD'VE GIVEN YOU EVERYTHING! WHY WOULDN'T YOU LET ME??

THE ONLY THING YOU EVER GAVE ME WAS PAIN!
SHUT UP AND LET ME TALK!!

WHY DO YOU THINK I ASKED THE BRAND CORPORATION TO TURN ME INTO MAD-DOG?
I DID IT-- FOR YOU!

YOU'D BECOME AN AVENGER ... A COSTUMED HERO. I WANTED TO PROVE THAT I COULD DO IT TOO! THAT I COULD--
NO! I WAS A PATRIOT! BRAND AND THE SECRET EMPIRE WERE TRYING TO SAVE THIS COUNTRY!!
YOU SAID IT YOURSELF BUZZ. I BECAME A HERO. YOU BECAME A CRIMINAL!
KEEP RANTING, BUZZ! MAYBE YOU WON'T NOTICE ME GETTING READY TO POUNCE!

OH, WHY DO WE HAVE TO ARGUE ABOUT THE PAST? I'VE MADE MISTAKES! I'M SORRY! LET ME MAKE IT UP TO YOU!

COME AWAY WITH ME. WE... WE CAN BE A TEAM! MAD-DOG AND HELLCAT! JUST LIKE HAWKEYE AND MOCKINGBIRD! THE VISION AND--
YOU'RE OUT OF YOUR MIND!

YOU'VE REWRITTEN THE PAST... AND NOW YOU'RE TRYING TO CREATE SOME FAIRY TALE FUTURE!

I LOVE YOU, PATSY, AND YOU LOVED ME. ONCE. BUT I SEE NOW-- THAT YOU BELIEVE ALL THOSE LIES YOU WROTE IN YOU BOOK!

I SEE NOW--
--THAT I HAVE TO KILL YOU.

AROOO

I WROTE THE TRUTH!

I NEVER LOVED YOU!

NEVER!!

KRAK

YES, YOU DID.

YES...
...YOU...

I DID.

ALL THESE YEARS... I'VE BEEN TRYING SO HARD TO PULL AWAY FROM THE PERSON I USED TO BE... FROM THE **MONSTER** YOU'D BECOME--

--THAT I FORGOT.

**NO**... I DIDN'T FORGET.

I JUST REFUSED TO LET MYSELF **REMEMBER**.
POLICE
POLICE
THE END.

MARVEL

# SOLO AVENGERS

STARRING

# HAWKEYE

AND

# DOCTOR DRUID

75¢ US
95¢ CAN
10
SEPT
02651





HAWK ROCKS L.A.--

--AS THE OCCULT AVENGER BATTLES THE MAGIC BENEATH MANHATTAN!

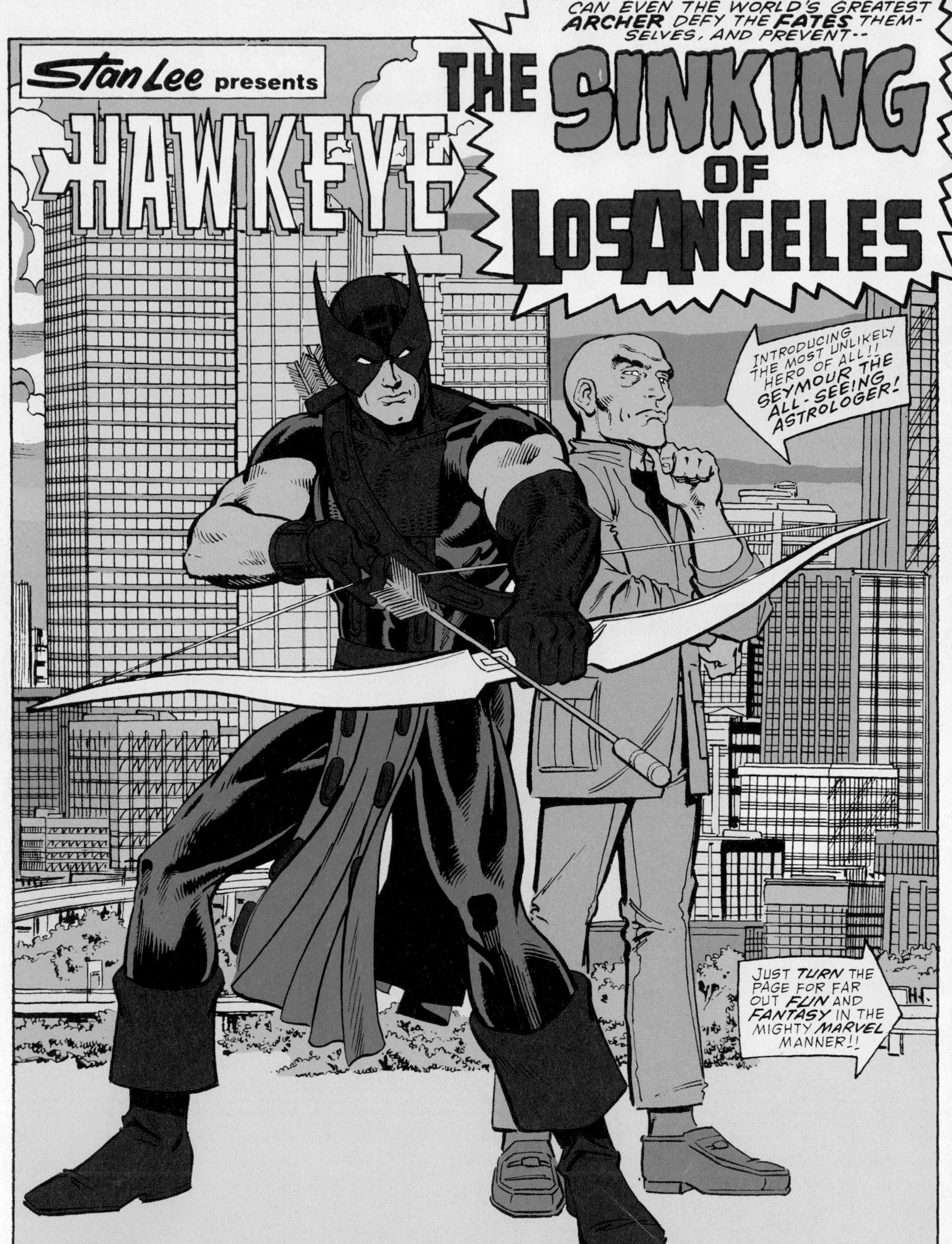


TOM DeFALCO A WRITER WITHOUT PEER! MARK BRIGHT THE PENCILER OF THE YEAR! JOSÉ MARZAN AN INKER YOU SHOULD CHEER! MORELLI LETTERS CLEAR! JACKSON COLORS WITHOUT FEAR! MARK GRUENWALD AN EDITOR WHO WANTS A NEW CAREER! LUCKY YOU GET TO SIT AND JEER!

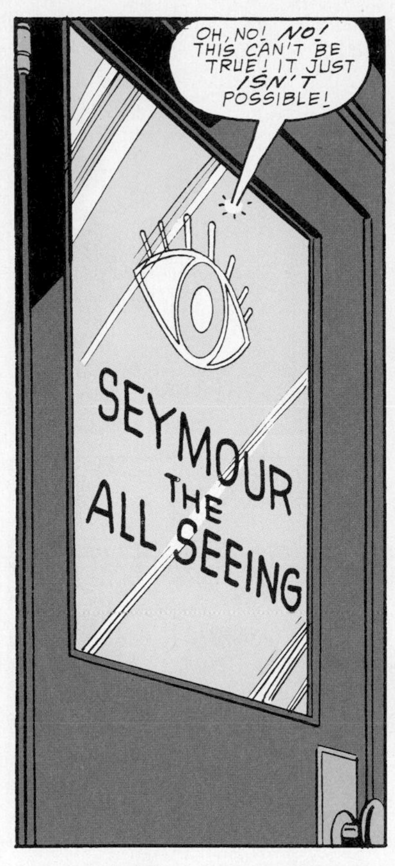
OH, NO! NO! THIS CAN'T BE TRUE! IT JUST ISN'T POSSIBLE!
SEYMOUR THE ALL SEEING

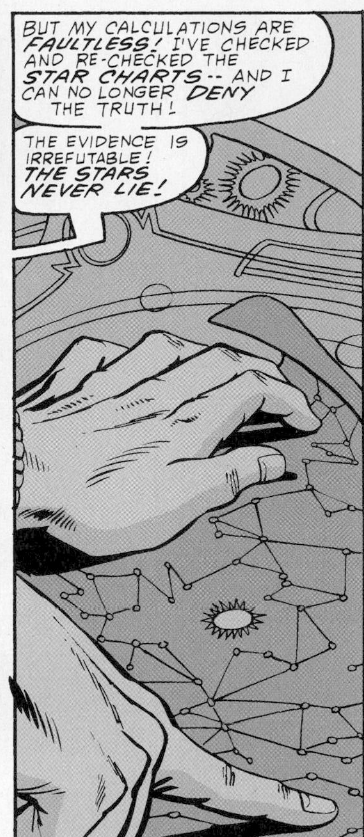
BUT MY CALCULATIONS ARE FAULTLESS! I'VE CHECKED AND RE-CHECKED THE STAR CHARTS-- AND I CAN NO LONGER DENY THE TRUTH!
THE EVIDENCE IS IRREFUTABLE! THE STARS NEVER LIE!

I ONLY HOPE I HAVE DISCOVERED THIS IN TIME!!
82147.43
DBABILITY
094.00106

GOOD AFTERNOON. YOU HAVE REACHED THE EDITORIAL OFFICES OF THE LOS ANGELES JOURNAL. HOW MAY WE HELP YOU?
LISTEN CLOSELY, YOUNG LADY! THIS IS SEYMOUR, THE ALL-SEEING ASTROLOGER, AND I HAVE SOME ASTOUNDING NEWS!

ACCORDING TO MY CALCULATIONS, THE CITY OF LOS ANGELES WILL SINK INTO THE SEA AT PRECISELY TWELVE NOON TODAY!

YOU MUST WARN THE PEOPLE, AND EVACUATE THE CITY BEFORE-- HELLO? HELLO?!
KLIK

HELLO, LADIES AND GENTLEMEN! WELCOME TO THE
1988 LOS ANGELES MANUFACTURERS EXPOSITION!
THIS IS A REAL PLEASURE, HAWKEYE!
I AM SO THRILLED THAT THE CHAIRMAN OF THE WEST COAST AVENGERS COULD BE HERE ON OUR OPENING DAY.

--ESPECIALLY SINCE THE MAYOR ARRANGED FOR US TO DISPLAY THE PRICELESS STAR OF ANGELS ATOP OUR SCALE MODEL OF THE CITY!

OF COURSE, I'M SURE YOUR PRESENCE HERE WILL GUARANTEE A FEW THOUSAND EXTRA PATRONS FOR THE EXPO!
YOU DON'T HAVE TO PUMP UP MY EGO, MR. JOHNSTON!
I KNOW THAT THE STAR IS THE REAL STAR TODAY!

THIS EXPO IS VERY IMPORTANT TO ME CAREER-WISE!
THE MAYOR HIMSELF ASKED ME TO CHAIR IT!
AND IF IT'S A SUCCESS, MY POLITICAL FUTURE IS GUARANTEED!

UH, SURE, JOHNSTON... GLAD TO HEAR IT!
ALL RIGHT, KID, QUIT CLOWNING AROUND AND TELL ME HOW TO SPELL "THADEUS"!

AT THAT EXACT MOMENT, OUTSIDE THE EXPOSITION CENTER...
WE'VE GOT TROUBLE, CHIEF! THEY'VE HIRED HAWKEYE TO BABYSIT THE DIAMOND!
NO PROBLEM! HE'S THE WEAKEST AVENGER OF ALL!
HE NEEDS A REAL GOOD DAY TO MEASURE UP TO THE WASP!

NEUTRALIZE HIS ARROWS AND HE'S NOWHERE!
OUR SUPERIOR WEAPONRY WILL CRUSH HIM AS EASILY AS THIS CONCRETE COLUMN!

MEANWHILE, AT A LOCAL TELEVISION STATION...
KLAF
YOU SHOULD HAVE SAID NO TO DRUGS, MAN!
B-BUT YOU MUST BELIEVE ME--!

"--THE CITY IS IN GREAT DANGER!"
NOT A BAD SHOW! NICE EXHIBITS AND REALLY WELL ORGANIZED! JOHNSTON DOES GOOD WORK!

EVEN THE TOURISTS ARE ACTING WELL-MANNERED AND CIVILIZED!
THIS HAS ALL THE MAKINGS OF A REAL FUN DAY!
JUST LOOK AT THAT JERK! HE'S STRUTTING AROUND AS IF HE DOESN'T HAVE A CARE IN THE WORLD!
WE'LL FIX THAT! TAKE HIM OUT-- NOW!

NO CAN DO, PAL! I'D JUST GET BORED AND FALL ASLEEP!

BESIDES, THIS EXPLOSIVE-TIPPED ARROWHEAD OUGHT TO KEEP YOU OCCUPIED JUST LONG ENOUGH--

BWOOM

--FOR ME TO REGAIN MY FOOTING AND SEE HOW BADLY YOU DAMAGED MY STASH!

HEY!! HE'S GETTING AWAY!

FROM THE WAY THE SHAFTS ARE RATTLING AROUND IN THE QUIVER, I WONDER IF ANY OF MY ARROWS SURVIVED INTACT ?!
Ah, HERE'S ONE!

I CAN CERTAINLY PUT IT TO GOOD USE -- BUT WHAT DO I DO FOR AN ENCORE?

I MIGHT HAVE TO DO SOMETHING DRASTIC -- LIKE USE MY BRAINS FOR A CHANGE!
NAH! NO SENSE GOING OVERBOARD!
LOOK! HE'S RACING INTO THAT GIANT STEREO SPEAKER!

YOU'RE TRAPPED, ARCHER! THERE'S NO WAY YOU CAN ESCAPE US NOW!
GIVE UP! WE'LL HEAR YOU IF YOU MAKE A MOVE!

THAT WON'T BE ALL YOU'LL HEAR, BUSTER-- THANKS TO MY HANDY-DANDY SONIC ARROWHEAD!

ELSEWHERE, AT THAT VERY SECOND...
WHAT AM I GOING TO DO? I'VE TRIED THE NEWSPAPERS, THE RADIO AND TELEVISION STATIONS--AND NO ONE BELIEVES ME!
OH, NO! LOOK AT THE TIME! THERE'S LESS THAN NINE FULL MINUTES TO GO!

THE EXPOSITION CENTER--!! IT'S CROWDED WITH UNSUSPECTING TOURISTS!
I'VE GOT TO WARN THEM BEFORE IT'S TOO LATE!

THEY HAVE A RIGHT TO KNOW ABOUT THE DANGER!

MEANWHILE, INSIDE...
SQUEEK
SKWAAK

KEE-RASH
I NEVER THOUGHT THAT BEING 80% DEAF IN BOTH EARS WOULD BE SUCH AN ADVANTAGE AT TIMES!

OF COURSE, I'LL HAVE TO REMEMBER TO REACTIVATE MY MINIATURE HEARING AIDS IN TIME TO HEAR THE APPLAUSE OF MY ADORING PUBLIC!
THIS CLOWN IS OUT FOR THE COUNT--AND I FINALLY FOUND MY STURDY TEAR-GAS ARROW, WHICH I CAN USE ON HIS FRIENDS!

SNAP
WHOOPS! I GUESS IT WASN'T AS FIRM AS I THOUGHT!

BLAST HIM! DON'T GIVE HIM TIME TO NOCK ANOTHER ARROW!

GET SERIOUS, MAN!
THE WAY MY LUCK'S BEEN RUNNING, I COULD NOCK A DOZEN ARROWS AND STILL BE IN HOT SOUP!

I COULDN'T HAVE PLANNED THIS ANY BETTER!
THOSE IDIOTS WILL KEEP HAWKEYE BUSY, WHILE I MAKE OFF WITH THE STAR OF ANGELS!
WATCH THE RAILING, BOYS!

MISTER, WE'VE GOT TO GET THESE PEOPLE OUT OF HERE-- AND EVACUATE THE CITY!
HUH? WHO ARE YOU??

I AM SEYMOUR THE ALL-SEEING --AND THE STARS HAVE INFORMED ME THAT THE CITY OF LOS ANGELES WILL SINK INTO THE SEA AT PRECISELY TWELVE NOON!
GET AWAY FROM ME, YOU NUT!

I HAVE ENOUGH PROBLEMS WITHOUT LISTENING TO A LUNATIC!
MY EXPOSITION IS IN RUINS--AND SO IS MY POLITICAL FUTURE!
B-BUT THE CITY IS ON THE VERGE OF DESTRUCTION! THE STARS NEVER LIE!

KFLOOOSH
WHAT THE??
YIII!!
SMILE, FELLAS! I WANT TO IMMORTALIZE THIS SPECIAL OCCASION --AND DON'T FORGET I ALREADY WARNED YOU ABOUT THE RAILING!

T-THAT SUDDEN FLASH... BLINDED ME... EVEN WITH MY SUNGLASSES!
GOSH, YOU GUYS LOOK A LITTLE DIZZY! YOU'D BETTER LIE DOWN-- FOR ABOUT AN HOUR OR SO!

YOU MUST BE FEELING VERY PROUD OF YOURSELF, HAWKEYE!
WELL, I'LL CHANGE THAT! THIS GLOVE IS LINED WITH LEAD PELLETS!
UNGH!

THE LIVING SEA
F-FINALLY FOUND THE STAR... BUT I STILL NEED A FEW MORE SECONDS...

"...FOR MY EYES TO CLEAR!"
OKAY, PAL! YOU'VE HAD YOUR TURN! NOW LET'S SEE IF YOU CAN TAKE PUNISHMENT AS WELL AS YOU DISH IT OUT!
WOK

GUESS NOT.

HEADS UP, ARCHER! THE GAME JUST WENT INTO EXTRA INNINGS!

LIVING SEA
I'M CERTAIN I CAN BLOW YOU APART LONG BEFORE YOU'LL EVER FIND AN ARROW THAT STILL WORKS!
GOT TO DO THIS STRICTLY BY FEEL -- AND I WON'T GET A SECOND CHANCE!

MAKE YOUR MOVE WHEN YOU FEEL LUCKEEEEE!!
LUCK IS FOR LOSERS! WINNERS RELY ON SKILL!

OH, NO! WHEN HE SLAMMED INTO THE TABLE HE CAUSED THE SCALE MODEL OF THE CITY TO... TO ... I DON'T BELIEVE IT! THAT LITTLE GUY WAS RIGHT!

OF COURSE! THE CITY OF LOS ANGELES SANK AT THE STROKE OF NOON, JUST AS I PREDICTED!
THE STARS NEVER LIE!

A FEW HOURS LATER...
HOW DID YOU KNOW WHAT WAS GOING TO HAPPEN AT THE EXPOSITION TODAY?
DOES THE SINKING OF THE SCALE MODEL BODE ILL FOR THE REAL CITY?
ANY OTHER PREDICTIONS, SEYMOUR!?
WILL MADONNA AND SEAN STAY TOGETHER?
WHAT ABOUT DAVID AND MADDIE?
WILL REED AND SUE REJOIN THE FANTASTIC FOUR?

PLEASE! PLEASE! YOU'RE EMBARRASSING ME! I'M A SCIENTIST-- MY PREDICTIONS REQUIRE HOURS OF STUDY, CONCENTRATION, AND CALCULATIONS!
I WILL NOT PERFORM FOR YOU LIKE A TRAINED SEAL--AND WASTE MY SPECIAL SKILLS ON MORE CELEBRITY NONSENSE!

I HAVE DECIDED TO FOCUS ALL MY ATTENTIONS ON POLITICS--ON THE FUTURE OF THIS GREAT NATION--AND THE MAN WHO IS DESTINED TO BE OUR PRESIDENT IN THE YEARS AHEAD!
I'M TALKING ABOUT RICHARD OBADIAH JOHNSTON!

WELL, WELL, SEEMS LIKE YOU'RE PICKED TO BE # 1 WITH A BULLET!
PLEASE, HAWKEYE, DON'T MENTION BULLETS WHEN YOU TALK ABOUT THE PRESIDENT!
YOU SURPRISE ME, JOHNSTON! I DIDN'T FIGURE YOU FOR THE TYPE TO BELIEVE IN ASTROLOGY!

I'M NOT... BUT I DO BELIEVE IN BACKING A WINNER. MAYBE THE LITTLE GUY CAN SCORE AGAIN!
AT THE VERY LEAST, I MAY END UP THE PRESIDENT OF A SMALL CORPORATION!
I WISH YOU THE BEST OF LUCK, PAL!
YOU'RE GONNA NEED IT!!
END.

MANHATTAN...
WE 'POLGIZE FOR DA DELAY ON DA NUMBER SIX UPTOWN LOCAL...
YOU GOTTA REALIZE HOW IMPORTANT THIS IS, ANTHONY...
DOCTOR DRUID
SOME NEW YORKERS CONSIDER RIDING THE SUBWAYS A DAILY HORROR.

CUDDETTER REPORTS A SICK PASSENGER ON BOARD...
THE LETTERMAN SHOW CAN BE A BIG PUSH FOR YOUR NEW BOOK!
THE GRAFITTI, THE FILTH.

WE SHALL BE RESUMIN' NORMAL SERVICE MOMEN-TARILY...
DELAYS, PETTY THIEVES, DERELICTS OF HUMANITY.
I MEAN OCCULT BOOKS JUST DON'T MOVE LIKE THEY USETA...

WATCH DA CLOSIN' DOORS...
NEW YORKERS SHOULD THANK THEIR GOD EVERY DAY THAT THEY ARE SPARED THE TRUE HORRORS THAT EXIST.
ONE WAY
NOT WITH SHIRLEY MACLAINE DOING HER--
--ANTHONY?
TOKEN SACRIFICE

ANCIENT CELTIC RUNES COVERING A NEW YORK CITY SUBWAY TRAIN? IT'S EARTH MAGIC... TAPPING INTO THE POWER OF THE PLANET SIMILAR TO MY OWN ABILITIES...

BUT WHERE MY POWERS ARE USED IN QUEST OF ANSWERS TO THE UNKNOWN, THESE RUNES SPELL OUT A RITUAL...

...OF HUMAN SACRIFICE!

PLEASE...
YOU'VE GOT TO HELP!
THE OLD MAN IS FIVE STEPS AWAY... FIVE STEPS... TO PERHAPS UNRAVELLING THE MYSTERY...

FIVE STEPS TOO FAR.
KEERAKLE
NO!

THE OLD ONE-- BELONG TO ME-- AND DISCIPLES--
--SO WE COME AGAIN.
REMEMBER.
I FEEL-- YOU ARE MAN-- OF POWER!
I TELL YOU--
WAY HE

DO NOT ATTEMPT--
--YOUR POWER--
--AGAINST MINE!

THE WORDS CHILL THE AIR IN THE WAKE OF HER DEPARTURE ...
ALL RIGHT, FOLKS, AIN'T NOTHIN' TA SEE,,,
WHO'D BELIEVE IT, HUH?! GOOD THING THERE'RE PEOPLE HERE WHO CAN HANDLE IT!
INDEED.
...BUT NOTHING CAN QUELL THE FIRE BURNING INSIDE ME: MY NEED TO KNOW MORE.

YOU'LL NO DOUBT ADVISE AGAINST THIS, CHARLES,,,

BUT I MUST ASK YOU TO CONVEY MY APOLOGIES TO MR. LETTERMAN.
WHAT ARE YOU TALKING--?!
WHERE DO YOU--?! THAT SHOW'S A NATIONAL PUSH FOR YOUR BOOK SALES! THIS IS YOUR LIFE!

IT'S NOTHING WHEN COMPARED TO MASTERING THE UNKNOWN! THAT IS MY LIFE!
THE TUNNELS STRETCH INTO THE UNDERGROUND, A NETWORK OF MAZES...

A WARREN OF DARKNESS. JUST AS SHE WAS ABLE TO SENSE MY POWER, I, TOO, CAN SENSE HER MYSTIC ENERGIES.
BUT, WHERE MY ABILITIES ARE REFINED--REQUIRING CAREFUL INCANTATIONS --HERS ARE CRUDE-- ABLE TO STRIKE AT ANY MOMENT...
A DANGER I NEED TO BE EVER MINDFUL OF AS THE IRON IN THESE WALLS PLAYS HAVOC WITH THE RELIABILITY OF MY OWN POWERS.

BUT I CAN STILL PROVIDE SOME CONVENIENCES.
ROUGH-HEWN WALLS CHISELED BY CRUDE TOOLS ...

...OR CLAWED BY MONSTROUS TALONS!
KILL--
AUUMPH!
WHERE FIRST THERE IS BUT ONE...

...THERE ARE SOON MANY!
NO--KILL MAN--
KILL FOR HER--PRIESTESS--
TOO MANY TO FIGHT.
KILL FOR STONE-CUTTER!
NO TIME TO DRAW THE RUNES.. TO PREPARE THE CHANTS I WOULD NEED TO REPEL THEM.
KILL HORRIBLE LIGHT--

ONLY CHANCE--

--TO USE THE ONE THING THAT'S ALWAYS DRIVEN BACK CREATURES OF THE NIGHT.

SHRSIIZZLE
AAAIIIEEEE!

STONECUTTER.
NOW SHE HAS A NAME.

AND A PURPOSE: A CELTIC MAZE OF POWER!
A PASSING TRAIN TRIGGERS THE SPELL...
TRANSPORTING A SUBWAY FULL OF INNOCENTS TO...?
THERE IS A WAY TO FIND OUT.

AND AS MY LIGHT GROWS DIMMER...
AND AS I CAN HEAR STONE-CUTTER'S CREATURES BEGINNING THEIR APPROACH...

I KNOW THAT IT IS EITHER LET THEM TAKE ME ON THEIR TERMS...

...OR CONFRONT THEM ON MINE!

THERE IS A RUMBLE OF MOTION.
A VIOLENT LURCHING FROM SIDE TO SIDE.
A FETID GUST OF WIND THAT TEARS ME APART AS THE DARKNESS CLOSES AROUND ME...

SOME NEW YORKERS BELIEVE THAT TRAVELING THE SUBWAYS IS PURE TORTURE. BUT AS HELLISH AS THE SUBWAYS HAVE BECOME...

...EVEN THE TRANSIT AUTHORITY NEVER INTENDED FOR ONE OF THEIR TRAIN YARDS TO BE USED QUITE THIS WAY...
I PROMISED-- YOU FOLLOWED I--WE--WAITED LONG! SOON FREE!
THIS LAST ONE-- OTHER HUMAN FALL--
--UNDER KNIFE!

POWER STRONG-- HUMAN NO ESCAPE--
WE CUT CHAIN TO-- LOWER WORLD!

LAST KILL--

WE ROAM-- FOREVER RULE-- UPPER WORLD!

IT IS OBVIOUS WHAT WILL HAPPEN IF THEY SUCCEED IN THEIR RITUAL...
BUT I CANNOT HELP BUT WONDER WHAT WILL HAPPEN IF THEY FAIL...
IF ALL THE MYSTIC ENERGIES HELD IN CHECK BY THIS CIRCLE OF POWER WERE SUDDENLY FREED.

WHAT WOULD HAPPEN, I WONDER, IF SOMETHING WERE TO OCCUR THAT WOULD...

...DISRUPT THE FESTIVITIES?
RRRUMMBLE

HUMAN OF POWER I GAVE-- WARNING!

NOW I TAKE--
LIFE!

THE IRON IN THE TRAINYARD DISRUPTED MY POWER--
--CHANGING AN EARTHQUAKE INTO AN EARTH TREMOR!
LEAVING THEIR CIRCLE OF POWER STANDING!
AND STONE-CUTTER'S CREATURES OUT FOR MY BLOOD.

SOME MINDS ARE WEAK...
EASILY BROUGHT AROUND TO MY WAY OF THINKING.
ULF!
AGK

OTHERS ARE NOT SO EASILY DISPATCHED...

...FORCING ME TO RISE ABOVE THE SITUATION.
URF!

LAST CHANCE--WE FREE! I LOVED BY-- MY PEOPLE!
NO... PLEASE... HELP...
THERE IS STILL A CHANCE SHE COULD SUCCEED.

STILL A CHANCE I CAN FIND THE ANSWERS TO HER QUESTIONS...
THANK GOD...
NO!
NO...

NOT OLD ONE-- THEN--

BUT YOU!
THERE ARE SEVERAL WAYS TO STOP HER...

INSTEAD, THE EARTHQUAKE DOES IT FOR ME...
IRON ONLY DISRUPTED THE SPELL FOR A MOMENT.
RRMBLE
NOW IT CUTS BACK IN--

--FULL STRENGTH!
KRASH
THE DELICATELY BALANCED CIRCLE IS BROKEN!

FOR SOME, THE END IS QUICK AND PAINFUL!

FOR OTHERS THERE IS ONLY PAIN.
FAILED! NO--
LOVE FOR ME-- SO MUCH--
WORK! STILL--
--IN--
--CHAINS!

SHE IS FIVE STEPS AWAY... FIVE STEPS TO PERHAPS A FEW MORE ANSWERS...
THEN THE REST OF THE SUBWAY CARS BEGIN TO TOPPLE...
TO THE GROUND...
...TOWARD THE OLD MAN.
AND PURSUIT--

--MUST BECOME PRESERVATION!

WOW
THWAKUM
IN THE TRAINYARD ALL THAT REMAINS...

...DUST, SHATTERED SUBWAY CARS.
AND A BRUISED AND BATTERED OLD MAN.
YOU'VE SUSTAINED SOME INJURIES, A BROKEN LEG, SOME SPRAINED MUSCLES...
YOU...YOU LET HER GET AWAY!
THIS SHOULD ALLEVIATE SOME OF THE DISCOMFORT.
YES.
BUT, W-WHY? I'M JUST AN OLD MAN.
BEFORE I WAS AN AVENGER BEFORE I KNEW ANYTHING OF THE OCCULT, I WAS A DOCTOR...

WHILE MY FASCINATION WITH THE UNKNOWN CAN NEVER BE SATED, I CANNOT PERMIT A FELLOW TRAVELER TO FACE LIFE'S ULTIMATE UNKNOWN BEFORE ITS NATURAL HOUR.
D.G. CHICHESTER & MARGARET CLARK WRITERS
LEE WEEKS ARTIST
JACK MORELLI LETTERS
PAUL BECTON COLORS

# SINGLE FILE

c/o MARVEL COMICS GROUP
387 Park Avenue South
New York, New York 10016

Attention correspondents: if you don't want your full address printed, please be sure to tell us so!

## MARK'S REMARK'S

I've always liked "split books." When TALES TO ASTONISH, TALES OF SUSPENSE, and STRANGE TALES broke up and begat INCREDIBLE HULK, SUB-MARINER, CAPTAIN AMERICA, IRON MAN, DR. STRANGE, and SHIELD, in 1968, as far as I was concerned the first era of the Marvel Age was over. Sure, Marvel attempted split books again two years later with ASTONISHING TALES (featuring Ka-Zar and Doctor Doom) and AMAZING ADVENTURES (featuring the Inhumans and the Black Widow), but neither book lasted more than twelve issues before full-issue stories took over and the second feature was eliminated. For me, some of the best Hulk, Subby, Cap, Iron Man, Doc, and Fury stories were told in 10-page segments and the heroes' adventures lost that certain something when they expanded.

Ever since I started working at Marvel in 1978, I harbored a secret plan to create or revive at least one split book. Now, a hair shy of ten years later, I've gotten my wish with the premiere of SOLO AVENGERS! (Yeah, I know "Solo Avengers" is an oxymoron — contradiction of terms — since "solo" means *one* and "Avengers" is *plural*, but if you think of it as "SOLO adventures of the AVENGERS" it won't bother you as much, will it?) It's true that Bob (Special Projects) Budiansky almost got a split book off the ground (featuring Sandman in one feature and Vision and the Scarlet Witch in the other) a few years ago, and Carl (Punisher) Potts succeeded in reviving STRANGE TALES (featuring Cloak & Dagger and Dr. Strange) currently on its ninth issue, but all that means is certain other oldtimers share my fondness for the format.

Okay, so I like the format already. As an editor, it offers me something other books don't — *variety*. As much as I like working with my regular teams on their regular assignments, I crave variety once in awhile, the opportunity to work with other talented writers and artists without adding regular ongoing books to my already-burgeoning editorial stable. Not only that, but there are also certain creative types who are not willing or able to commit to a regular monthly book or regular creators on other books who have a hankering to do something different once in awhile. Books like this are a haven for these folks, and I get to work with them all!

So enough talk about generalities. Let's get down to specifics. The purpose of SOLO AVENGERS (besides giving your editor his jollies — ahem!) is to give the various Avengers some more space to strut their stuff. What with two teams of Avengers, each of which has at least seven active members, and over a dozen currently inactive Avengers who are undoubtedly having adventures we don't get to hear about, there are plenty of candidates for solo stories. In the group books we never have the chance to see 11 pages of solo action for a given member so we really get an in-depth look at the character. Here in SOLO, we'll be able to do just that. This is the place where exciting new character developments can and will occur which will affect the solo Avengers' lives and become part of their status quo in the pages of their team book. This is the place where personal foes will premiere, giving those heroes who never had their own series before the makings of a rogue's gallery. This is the place where you will see the solo Avengers challenged to their utmost, without another Avenger around to back them up. My hope is that each 11-page feature will serve as a "pilot film" or tryout feature to test the waters to see if any of our solo Avengers is deserving of his or her own feature. It's up to you to write and let us know.

Originally, I wanted to make both features in SOLO rotating, so that every month you'd be surprised by which two Avengers got their shot at the spotlight. But I soon realized that that would be placing this book in double jeopardy. Not only was I uncertain if Marveldom at Large shared my passion for split books, I was also taking a big gamble by not giving readers some idea of what to expect every month — in other words, a regular feature. So, in order to insure the longevity of this book, I decided to take the character who seems to be the most popular Avenger who doesn't have his own solo book — *Hawkeye* — and make him a continuing feature. That way, every month, you readers will know at least half of what you'll get for your hard-earned quarters — a frenetic Hawkeye adventure. And, with any luck, you'll like the agonizing archer's *co-star* to boot! (And if Hawkeye proves to be the superstar we think he is, why, we'll just have to give him his own book and promote some other Avenger to our lead slot!)

After eliminating the four Avengers (present and past) who currently have their own solo books (namely, Captain America, Iron Man, Thor, and the Hulk), who does that leave eligible for our co-feature slots? Well, on the East Coast, we have Captain Marvel, the Black Knight, She-Hulk, the Sub-Mariner, and Doctor Druid. On the West Coast, there's Mockingbird, Wonder Man, Tigra, Moon Knight, and the dynamic Doctor Pym. As for the ranks of the inactives and reserves, there's the Wasp, Hercules, the Black Widow, the Black Panther, the Falcon, Moondragon, Binary (the original Ms. Marvel), Quicksilver, the Scarlet Witch, the Vision, Hellcat, Starfox, the Beast (now with X-Factor), and Mantis. If I really wanted to stretch it (with reader approval, of course!), we could also feature the Thing and Espirita (who were offered membership but declined), honorary members Stingray and Rick Jones, and friends of Avengers, Ant-Man and Paladin. Let me know if you only want official members past and present to appear, or if we can play fast and loose now and then.

The HAWKEYE feature will be brought to you each issue by Tom DeFalco (THOR scribe and spanking new editor in chief), Mark Bright (IRON MAN penciler) and Josef Rubinstein (MARVEL UNIVERSE inker). with top pros like these, you know what good stuff to expect. The co-feature this issue — Mockingbird — also written by Tom, features the artistry of Jim Lee (whose credits include ALPHA FLIGHT) and Al Williamson (who's currently embellishing DAREDEVIL). Next issue our co-feature will star none other than the current head of the East Coast Avengers, Captain Marvel, in a story produced by AVENGERS writer Roger Stern, CAPTAIN AMERICA penciler Kieron Dwyer, and NEW MUTANTS co-creator Bob McLeod. And the month after that . . . ? Well, let's not get too ahead of ourselves, okay?

Address your comments, quips, and (ulp) criticisms about SOLO AVENGERS to *Single File* at the address above. And please put your address on your *letter* not on the envelope which is thrown away when the mail's opened! Till next time, Go Solo!

—Mark Gruenwald

## MARK'S REMARKS

Seeing as how I won't have any mail on our premiere issue of SOLO AVENGERS for another month or two (and I'd feel guilty running a blank page here), I thought I'd respond to some of the mail that my *Mark's Remarks* column running in my other books (AVENGERS, WEST COAST AVENGERS, and IRON MAN) has been getting in recent months. The most controversial column I've done since my "Death of the No-Prize" essay in my very first M's Rems has certainly been "How *Not* To Break Into the Comics Industry" which ran in WEST COAST AVENGERS #22. It seems that a number of you took my listing of seven things you can do that will hurt your chances of landing an assignment in professional comics the *wrong way*. In the words of one correspondent, "I'm amazed that you could publish these commandments without realizing that you sound a bit arrogant yourself, or at best, supremely disdainful." It was not my intent, in writing that particular column, of course, to be arrogant or disdainful. If I were truly arrogant and disdainful I wouldn't have even addressed the subject at all, preferring to keep the process of "going pro" as mysterious and foreboding as possible.

But before I delve into a point by point analysis of what I said, why I said it, and what I meant by it, let's review those seven points so we all know what I'm talking about. In brief, they were: 1) Have a whole bunch of different career goals, not just comics. 2) Don't get good at any one thing first . . . be a little good at a lot of things. 3) Don't be willing to sacrifice or put yourself out in any way. 4) Submit a million things at the same time. 5) Submit material that isn't quite comics to be evaluated. 6) When an editor criticizes some aspect of your work, argue with him or her. And 7) Develop arrogance, smugness, and obnoxiousness in your dealings with the person you want to get work from. Now then, one correspondent (you'll note that I'm not identifying my critics by name — it's not my intent to pick on anybody's opinions in a forum where I get the last word) wonders why I took the *negative* approach to the essay. Why didn't I write "*How To* Break Into the Comics Industry" instead of "How *Not* To"? The reason for that is that there's *not* just one way to break into comics, and I felt it would be misleading to list what might be construed as the recipe for going pro.

All right then, on to the specific points. First, the career goals issue. When I first began investigating how to make comics my career, I was asked by a renowned comics artist who I showed my art samples to, "If you couldn't do comics for a living, what would you do?" I said, "I don't know . . . go into advertising, teach art, something like that." He said, "To make it into professional comics, you must have no viable career alternative to fall back on. If you do, you won't be hungry, desperate, or motivated enough to do whatever it takes to become a professional." Now this seemed like pretty extreme advice to take at the time. On the other hand, I followed it, and look where I am today, passing along the same advice. I truly believe that it takes drive and determination to make it in this business, and there's no greater drive than survival. I wanted to get into comics and I was willing to do whatever it took. (This invokes my third tip: be willing to make sacrifices.) I left my comfortable home in the midwest to move to New York (where the main publishers are headquartered), having no job (not even a job offer), few acquaintances, and but $600 in savings to live on. I struggled for six months, depleting my savings, living in a one room garret, and trying to get a job with one of the comics companies, before I finally had to take a file clerk job with a major bank to put food on the table. Did I compromise my career goals by taking that clerk job? Was I ruining my motivation to get in the comics industry? No, "file clerk" was never a career, it was just a job to tide me over till I could get into my career. One correspondent writes, "Only a fool pulls up roots and faces an uncertain financial picture without a firm job offer in hand." He's right. And I was a fool to take the chance on my talent as I did, but it was a gamble I was willing to take, and one that I was determined to make work. The same correspondent goes on to say that an editor should "give someone an offer in writing before you expect them to go to the expense of relocation." I agree, that sure would be nice, but that's not the way the business works. Nobody wanted me to be in the comics industry except *me*. No one would have missed me had I not gotten in. It was up to *me* to prove myself to the people I wanted to hire me. Moving to where the jobs are was necessary, I felt, to put myself in a position to so prove myself. *The comics industry owes no one a living.*

In my second point, I cautioned against not specializing in any one of the various disciplines in comics. Again, I pulled this *caveat* straight from my own experience. My own early submissions portfolios showed I could do *all* of the various disciplines in comics — writing, penciling, inking, lettering, coloring, editing — *halfway decent*. But the industry does not want people *halfway* good at something, it wants someone who is *all the way* good at something. You don't get an assignment until you have mastered the minimal professional standards of the particular discipline (and even that is no guarantee). All my half-skills did not add up to one full skill at anything I could be expected to be hired for. Virtually no one breaks in by being hired to do more than one discipline at a time. For example, John Byrne and Frank Miller were hired by Marvel as pencilers. Only after demonstrating their mastery of the one discipline did they branch out into others (inking and writing). But if a person is halfway good at something, is it too much to expect that a company will hire you and work with you to bring your half-skills up to full-skills? Yes, that *is* too much to expect. Unlike certain other professions where there is on the job training, the *comics industry owes no one an education*.

My third point, about the willingness to make sacrifices, was pretty well covered in my discussion of the first point, so I'll move on.

My fourth point was about the counter-productiveness of bombarding an editor with so many samples at once that it would take a great deal of patience and perseverence to wade through them all. This is no idle gripe. An editor has only so much time to devote to screening samples, and if one person tries to make too big a presumption on an editor's time, that person has a strike against him or her before the editor even looks at the work. One should submit only a representative sample of his or her work, not the collected body of it. The object is to get the editor to *want* to look at your work, not scare him or her off. Sending samples through the mail is a very impersonal way of breaking in the business, but most editors I know don't want to give anyone a personal interview unless he or she's previewed the person's work in advance. It is important to remember that editors don't want to have to edit your samples to get to the good stuff buried in there. *Editors owe no one a disproportionate amount of their time.*

My fifth point was about only submitting material appropriate to the various comics disciplines in your samples. While I exaggerated the type of inappropriate material to submit (poems and record reviews for writing samples, still life watercolors and charcoal portraits for art samples), I continue to be amazed at the not-quite-comics material I am shown. Prose short stories do not demonstrate to me that a person can write a comic book synopsis. Full page pin-ups do not demonstrate to me that a person can tell a story through a sequence of panels. (Marvel's need for prose short stories and single page pin-ups is very minimal.) I am also shown comic book plots that don't have Marvel characters in it, and sample comic pages that don't have Marvel characters on them. How am I supposed to know if a person understands the Marvel characters enough to write about them or can draw Marvel characters to look like they're supposed to from samples like that? An aspiring professional has to demonstrate his or her ability to handle the characters the company published in the format the company publishes them. *Editors can only judge your ability and suitability by what you give them.*

My sixth point concerned justifying, apologizing for, or arguing on behalf of your submissions. None of that will get you anywhere. You must assume that the editor is always right in knowing just what it is he or she is looking for. Explaining why a certain piece of work is not your best ("My hand hurt the day I drew it.") won't make it any better or make the editor want to buy it any more. *Your work should speak for itself.* If it doesn't, you're in trouble.

My seventh point is closely related to the sixth, and concerns attitude. It always amazes me when people who want me to hire them demonstrate discourteousness or obnoxiousness ("cop an attitude"). Do these aspiring professionals really expect me to hire someone who gets on my nerves? I try to treat people as fairly as I can, but I'm human, and I can be as aggravating as the next man. On the other hand, I'm not the one looking for the job. Anyone who maligns one of the people I'm currently using makes no points with me. In essence, that person is criticizing my judgment for hiring who I did. If anyone questions my qualifications to judge his or her work, I feel no need to list them. If someone doesn't know my qualifications or doesn't recognize the authority of my position, then why in the world is he submitting his work to *me*? They'd do better to submit to a person whose qualifications they know, whose authority they recognize.

The correspondent who gave my previous column the most trouncing asks me in light of the "grouchiness" of "How Not to Break Into the Comics Industry" if I truly *am* looking for new writers and artists. The truth of the matter is *no*, I am *not* personally on a great quest to find new talent for the comics industry. After all I've got top professionals doing all the books I edit at present. Certain other editors devote more of their time to hunting and cultivating tomorrow's talent than I do, while certain other editors devote even less. On the other hand, Marvel, as a company, is committed to finding and hiring all the top talents there are. That's why we have a Submissions Editor whose full-time job it is to review the work of would-bes. But me personally? No, my great quest is to put out great books. If new talent can do what my old talent can't, *then* I'm interested. My personal goal is the *product* of top talent, not the *process* of finding them. I'm willing to bet that most people who are in the position to hire people would admit the same if pressed for an answer. You see, while I'm not looking for new talent, I'm confident that new talent is looking for *me* (or someone like me). And if my tips on how not to break in were helpful (either in my original short-winded exaggerated version or this long-winded soft-sell version), I feel like I've done something to put all you aspiring top talents a little more "in the know."

More of Mark's Remarks to Reader Mail on *Mark's Remarks* next month!

—Mark Gruenwald

## MARK'S REMARKS

Occasionally, I get requests from aspiring writers who want to know exactly what format we like to see plots in. While there's no strict universally-accepted format (as there is for movie and TV scripts), the basic rule of thumb is this: to double space, put your name/title/book and issue number/page at the top of each page, and to break down the plot page by page. Still confused? All right, here's an example . . . the actual plot of the first two pages of this issue's lead story, which our artist drew the story from!

*Tom DeFalco*
*SOLO AVENGERS #4*
Hawkeye
"The Great Escape"
Plot for 11 pages
*Submitted: June 15, 1987*

*1: Splash panel/credits/title copy/indicia: We open this chapter in the continuing saga of the life of the world's greatest archer just as our hero is being tossed in the clink. We are deep within a very ornate castle which is located somewhere in France. The "clink" is not quite a dungeon room, but it does have bars on its windows . . . and the only piece of furniture is a bed. A heavy wooden door will bar the place.*

*In the opening scene, Hawkeye is being shoved into the room by a few members of Silver Sable's WILD PACK. (These agents all wear a distinctive costume.) Silver Sable coldly watches the action. Behind Silver is a well-dressed member of the French government. Hawkeye is wearing his mask and his pants. (His boots, gloves, tunic, shirt and weapons have all been confiscated.) In this first panel, Silver will be apologizing for the accomodations, but she hopes that Hawkeye will understand . . . after all, he has been arrested for murder. (The murder of Trick Shot.)*

*2. Hawk claims he's innocent and demands a lawyer.*

*Silver responds that they are keeping him here . . . until the French government can sort out all of the messy legal issues . . . what with Hawk being an Avenger and all. She hopes he'll enjoy his stay, and the door is slammed on him. No sooner does the door slam, than Hawk looks around the room, and at the bed. It should be real obvious to our readers that he's already planning his escape. We will follow Silver and her people to a large gym (Please show an outside view of castle before we begin the workout.) where she begins one of her classic work outs. Perhaps we should have her fighting five guys with swords . . . or, if you prefer, staffs . . . in any event, Silver will be involved in a practice session . . . one filled with a lot of dangerous action. Check her previous appearances for reference. And, while she is so occupied, we'll get in some exposition, and bring our readers up-to-date on what's happening . . . because she'll be having a conversation throughout the entire scene. She will be conversing with the representative of the French government. It seems the French have hired Silver to get Trick Shot . . .*

And that's how it's done. Thanks, Tom — this is the easiest M's Rems I've yet to write!

—Mark Gruenwald

## MARK'S REMARKS

One of the things I told writers submitting stories to SOLO AVENGERS is that I wanted to see new villains. After all, most of the individual Avengers who have never carried their own feature don't have a lot of foes they can call their own and here would be a good place to give them some. Now I know that creating new super-villains is no mean feat (this from the man who gave the Marvel Universe Armadillo and the Slug), and one of the hardest parts is coming up with a good name. That's what I want to talk about this outing.

During my recent move to another office, I unearthed a document written circa 1978 by Marvel writer *Peter Gillis* and his brother *Robert*. What it is is a handy-dandy guide to creating thousands of valid villain (and hero) names by combining two simple words to make a compound word. Herewith, for your edification, and by kind permission of the Brothers Gillis is . . .

**THE PATENTED GILLIS SUPERDUDE NAME MAKER**

(Pick one from Column A and one from Column B — and presto! you have a character name.)

| COLUMN A | COLUMN B |
|---|---|
| Dark | Lord |
| Fire | Master |
| Shadow | Sword |
| Black | Dragon |
| Moon | Rider |
| Spider | Slayer |
| Iron | Witch |
| Night | Hawk |
| Star | Stealer |
| Ring | Destroyer |
| Power | Thief |
| Ruby | Force |
| Scarlet | Flame |
| Silver | Wizard |
| Mind | Light |
| Sun | Warrior |
| Hell | Arrow |
| Sea | Shark |
| Air | Demon |
| Doom | Queen |
| Green | King |
| Red | Wing |
| Sky | Storm |
| Time | Dancer |
| Earth | Mask |
| Grey | Knight |
| Wing | Guardian |
| Phantom | Axe |
| Blood | Stalker |
| Hawk | Eagle |
| Crimson | Mane |
| Winter | Star |
| Plague | Fire |
| Wind | Serpent |
| Dragon | Flower |
| White | Shadow |
| Death | Phantom |
| Dream | Skull |
| Thunder | Wolf |
| Dawn | Tiger |
| Wind | Singer |
| Were | Spear |
| Mad | Eye |
| | Bird |
| | Fox |

See how simple it is? Hey, readers, how many names of established characters can you find by putting together a word from Column A and Column B?

—Mark Gruenwald

## MARK'S REMARKS

Why am I doing this? Why do I write three or four of these columns a month? Do I write these columns out of some over inflated sense of ego — as if what I have to say is so darn important that it's worth eating up a third of my letters page space? Well, I do have things to say — that should be obvious — and obviously I think they're worth obliterating 1/3 of this page for. But, is it purely *ego*? I don't know. I can think of a number of egotistical things to do that wouldn't involve as much thought or work as writing this column.

I guess I write M's Rems because I'm a frustrated educator (my dad was a teacher and it must have rubbed off on me a bit). I get a certain pleasure out of explaining things, imparting information, and sharing ideas about subjects I know and like. And yes, letting my opinions be known, as well. I'm hardly an objective writer — I admit it. This column probably has two opinions for every fact presented. Of course, I'm as entitled to my opinions as anyone else is to his. The difference is that my opinions get to go in magazines with circulations of several hundred thousand.

Sometimes a few of those several hundred thousand potential readers (I can't be sure that just because they bought the book, they're reading my column) write in to respond to my Remarks. Some say they liked what I wrote, others say they didn't. I would not be truthful if I didn't say that it disturbs me to read negative reactions to my writing; while I know that everyone is different and can't love and approve of everything I write, I can never deny that everyone is entitled to his own reaction.

The major thrust of criticism I get is that I come off like a smug, arrogant, know-it-all. I don't think I am one, but if that's how someone thinks I come off, that's how I come off to him. Any writing I do is bound to have an underlying sense of "I'm an editor and you're not, so my opinion counts more than yours." But, deep down, (as Howard Mackie can attest) I don't think I'm better than anyone. I just think that I have insights afforded me by my experiences and position here in the comics biz. I'm not the only one with insight — I'm just the guy whose insights are shoved in your face at least three times any given month. (I have this weird fantasy where all my fellow editors are forced to express their opinions to you in this manner in all *their* books — then you readers could see how moderate and reasonable my opinions are compared to some!) Maybe I should spend more time polishing my first-draft prose — sand off some of the hard edges of my crusty writing persona? Nah, I think I'm more honest this way.

So why do I write this column? I guess because I want to be known as someone who likes his job . . . enjoys sharing with his readers . . . someone who talks straight and is willing to tackle the tough subjects. I offer them up to you, my reading public, so that you might learn something — even if what you learn is "This editor is a jerk." Keep letting me know what you think, people, good or bad.

—Mark Gruenwald

## MARK'S REMARKS

This edition of Mark's Remarks I'm writing not as Mark the Comics Editor, nor as Mark the Comics Writer, but as (ta-daa) Mark the Executive Editor of Marvel Comics. The topic: Just what does an Executive Editor of Marvel Comics do anyway? Glad you asked! (Oh, you didn't? Regardless . . . )

The Executive Editor . . . serves as Editor in Chief when the Editor in Chief is absent, handling whatever can't wait till the e-i-c returns . . . coordinates crossovers involving more than two editors' stables of characters . . . arbitrates on questions of proprietorship of characters . . . writes or compiles the Bullpen Bulletin pages . . . consults with the e-i-c on freelancer rates, assignments, and inquiries . . . attends business and sales meetings as the Editor in Chief's aide de camp . . . co-conducts editorial staff meetings and seminars . . . serves as the third party in disputes between the Editor in Chief and line editors or Editor in Chief and freelancers . . . and does whatever the heck the Editor in Chief tells him to do. Other than that, I'm my own man! I might end up doing more than the above, but hey, I've only been at this a little more than eight months by the time you read this.

So I'd hereby like to say that I may no longer be the hardest working editor in the comics industry today (and when I say the industry, I mean the business), but wearing three different creative caps is no picnic in Central Park.

—Mark Gruenwald

## MARK'S REMARKS

Let's talk about superhero origin stories. For most characters, they are something to be gotten out of the way in the character's first appearance and then more or less forgotten unless there's some compelling loose end about the affair. For my money, most origin stories are considerably (shall we say) less satisfying than a hero's subsequent adventures due to all the contrivances needed to set up a hero's powers, costume, motivation for being a hero, methods of operations, etc., all in one story. But because an origin story defines the hero, it necessarily takes on greater significance than most any subsequent adventure, and its details are periodically recounted throughout the hero's published life.

All of which brings us to the headliner of this book, Hawkeye, and SOLO AVENGERS #2's expansion on his origin. (You just knew this was all leading somewhere, didn't you?) About a third of you who wrote in about the story were disturbed by scripter Tom DeFalco's addition to Hawkeye's legend, namely Trickshot, the man who taught him archery. In no prior recounting of Hawk's roots did our bowman mention the guy. Why did we feel obliged to add him? Couldn't we have left well enough alone?

Here was our thinking . . . In previous accounts, it was the Swordsman who was Hawkeye's mentor and presumably his archery coach. When discussing his origin, it struck Tom and me as extremely strange that a master of the broadsword who never evinced any aptitude toward archery in any of his published appearances was able to coach a kid who would grow up to be the world's greatest archer. What did he do, tell Hawk this is the bow, this is the arrow, this is the target, now go teach yourself? Possibly. But why archery? It seemed to us a weakness in Hawkeye's otherwise sound origin. Thus we endeavored to remedy that anomaly, which of course provided grist for our first cycle of Hawkeye stories here, but also brought in a character whose existence would be bothersome to certain readers since not once before did Hawk make any allusions to there being such a figure.

So some of you cried "Foul!" and accused us of playing fast and loose with the facts. I was particularly lambasted in light of my assertion in recent Mark's Remarks in IRON MAN that Marvel was not in the business of revamping its legends since we got them right the first time. What it all boils down to is when do the revisions and amendments to a previous account of a hero's legend qualify as a revamp? (Or, at what point do I deserve to be strung up for making meaningless semantic distinctions?) I assert that *adding* to an origin such as we did here is not the same as *taking away* from a legend and *replacing* it with something different. This replacing process is what I consider revamping, and Marvel for the most part doesn't do this.

Come on now, Mark, Marvel has *never* revamped a hero's origin? Well, ahem, there is the curious case of Captain America's discrepancies to consider. Tell you what, people: now that I've defended what Tom and I did to Hawkeye's back story, join me in this space next month for a discussion of Captain America and the changes his origin account went through over the years.

—Mark Gruenwald

## MARK'S REMARKS

It all began with my controversial assertion that "Marvel doesn't revamp its legends — we got them right the first time." I got a lot of mail about that Mark's Remark — mostly negative — and thought that if I distinguished between a character's legend (origin, motivations, and standard mode of operation) and his/her current status quo (his/her present circumstances, and whatever deviations from his/her long-term status quo), the controversy would subside since every series character (Marvel and elsewhere) undergoes status quo changes from time to time to keep things fresh. But no, I'm not off the hook yet. Some readers pointed to recent revelations in Hawkeye's origin (see SOLO #2) as evidence of sneaky revamping. I replied that enhancement and expansion of murky areas of a character's origin (e.g., how did an expert swordsman with no skills in archery train the kid who'd become the world's greatest archer?) did not a revamp make since it did not substantially negate any element of what was established before. Then I brought up the problematic question of Captain America's origin.

Cap was created in 1940, and his basic origin was chronicled then. When he was revived in 1965 and the origin was retold, a few details were at variance from the original account (e.g., was the scientist who created the Super Soldier formula named Reinstein or Erskine? Where'd these vita-rays come from?). Otherwise, the story was essentially the same. (Later stories accounted for these apparent discrepancies.) But the background of the boy who became Cap was pretty much a blank slate, and fertile ground for exploration. A subsequent CAP writer (not me) filled in a few details — gave his parents names and occupations and gave him a brother who died at Pearl Harbor. Oops — a problem there. Not that Steve Rogers had an older brother we'd not yet heard about, but having his brother dying on December 7, 1941 played hob with prior accounts of when Steve underwent the Super-Soldier treatment. What to do? A still subsequent CAP writer (not me) "explained away" this background story ingeniously as a false set of memories given Cap by the War Department in the event he was captured and interrogated. Do we have revisionist history here? Yes and no. Certain "facts" previously presented as true were indeed falsified in an effort to restore a semblance of consistency to Cap's legend. This process, undertaken for the reasons it was, does not constitute a revamp. To me, it would have been a revamp if essential details were altered with no attempt to account for the alteration. In other words, if it were passed off as the way it was all along. Marvel gums up the details sometimes and has to backtrack to make things jibe, but we *don't* wave our magic editorial wands and say "This new version of the origin was the way it was all along, and if you have any comics that say otherwise, throw them away because they don't really exist." I trust I've now beaten this subject into the ground.

—Mark Gruenwald

## MARK'S REMARKS

What is truth? No, wait, let me amend that question. How does one recognize the truth? Hmmm, let me make it a bit more specific. How can a reader tell if what s/he's reading is what really, actually, truly "happened" or is slightly distorted due to the imperfections of the storytellers (writer and artist), or worse, is a total fabrication that is passed off as truth until a later storyteller sets the record straight? In recent columns, we've been discussing how Marvel doesn't do wholesale revamps of its heroes' legends (origin and history), but does on occasion provide new revelations about old events, and on the rarest of occasions, "explain away" certain details, phenomena, or incidents that are inconsistent with the consensus of past accounts (or aesthetically displeasing to the current storytelling team).

Last month I wrote about how biographical information about Steve Rogers before he became Captain America was revealed and then later revealed to be false. I've got two other famous examples of amended Marvel history. First there's the origin of Quicksilver and the Scarlet Witch. In GIANT-SIZE AVENGERS #1, evidence was presented indicating that the mutant siblings were the progeny of the Golden Age Whizzer and Miss America. This didn't jibe with previous recollections of Quicksilver's of how he was raised by gypsies. In AVENGERS #186, the Whizzer/Miss America theory was "explained away," the gypsy upbringing was accounted for, and the twins' true mother, a Gypsy named Magda, was revealed. (Their father, Magneto, was revealed to the readers but not to them in that month's X-MEN.) The Magneto/Magda parentage is what is believed to be true today.

The second great example of amended past history concerns the Hulk. In the short-lived RAMPAGING HULK black and white magazine, new accounts of the Hulk's activities between the time of the cancellation of his original comic (a 6-issue Limited Series) and his assumption of a regular feature in TALES TO ASTONISH (with issue #60) were given. These new accounts undercut certain classic early Marvel tales by featuring the Hulk's first meetings with such folks as the Avengers and the X-Men prior to the previously known first meetings of said heroes. Furthermore, since these new accounts didn't appear for at least a decade or so after the original accounts did, no mention could be made in the original accounts of recognizing the Hulk from these "continuity-implanted" stories. Then in INCREDIBLE HULK #269, the RAMPAGING HULK material was revealed to have actually been the movies of alien movie-maker Bereet, and thus didn't actually happen at all. (So that's why no one mentioned these prior meetings with the Hulk before!)

So the question is, how do you know if a story's "true" or if it won't be revealed to be somebody's misconception or an alien's movie at some later date? The answer is you don't. But Marvel's writers tend to be a pretty responsible lot — they don't mess with past stories lightly, and when they do there's generally a pretty valid reason. As a general rule, be suspicious of flashbacks (events that are not presented at the time they occurred) because these are subject to the subjectivity of whatever character is having the flashback. Also be leery of stories whose details are inconsistent with the consensus of information in other stories. Beyond that, the bulk of Marvel history is pretty much what it says in print.

—Mark Gruenwald

# *SOLO AVENGERS* SUBSCRIPTION AD

# SURE SHOT SAVINGS!

***Hurry! Offer expires October 31, 1987***

## SUMMER SAVINGS CERTIFICATE

☐ I've enclosed $8.25 per title (14 issues)

Make checks or money orders payable in U.S. currency to Marvel Comics. Canadian and Foreign: Add $2 per title. Allow 10 weeks for delivery. If renewing, enclose your mailing label. If not satisfied, refund guaranteed on all unserved copies.

Mail to: MARVEL Comics-Subscription Dept.
387 Park Avenue South New York, NY 10016

First initial / Last name

NAME

ADDRESS

CITY

STATE

ZIP

KEY: AUG-87

☐ Alpha Flight
☐ Amazing Spider-Man
☐ Avengers
☐ Captain America
☐ Daredevil
☐ Fantastic Four
☐ Incredible Hulk
☐ Iron Man
☐ Marvel Tales
☐ Nam
☐ New Mutants
☐ Peter Parker
☐ Power Pack
☐ Punisher
☐ Silver Surfer
☐ Solo Avengers
☐ Strange Tales
☐ Strikeforce Morituri
☐ Thor
☐ Web of Spider-Man
☐ West Coast Avengers
☐ X-Factor
☐ X-Men
☐ X-Men Classics

SPECIAL PRICES—14 issues

| | | | |
|---|---|---|---|
| ☐ Conan Saga | $18.00 | ☐ G.I. Joe | $10.00 |
| ☐ Savage Sword of Conan | $18.00 | ☐ G.I. Joe Special Missions | $10.00 |
| ☐ Marvel Fanfare | $14.00 | ☐ Groo The Wanderer | $10.00 |
| ☐ Conan the King | $13.00 | ☐ Transformers | $10.00 |
| ☐ Marvel Saga | $11.00 | ☐ Alien Legion (6 issues) | $ 8.00 |
| ☐ Conan | $10.00 | ☐ Marvel Age | $ 6.00 |
| ☐ Elfquest | $10.00 | | |

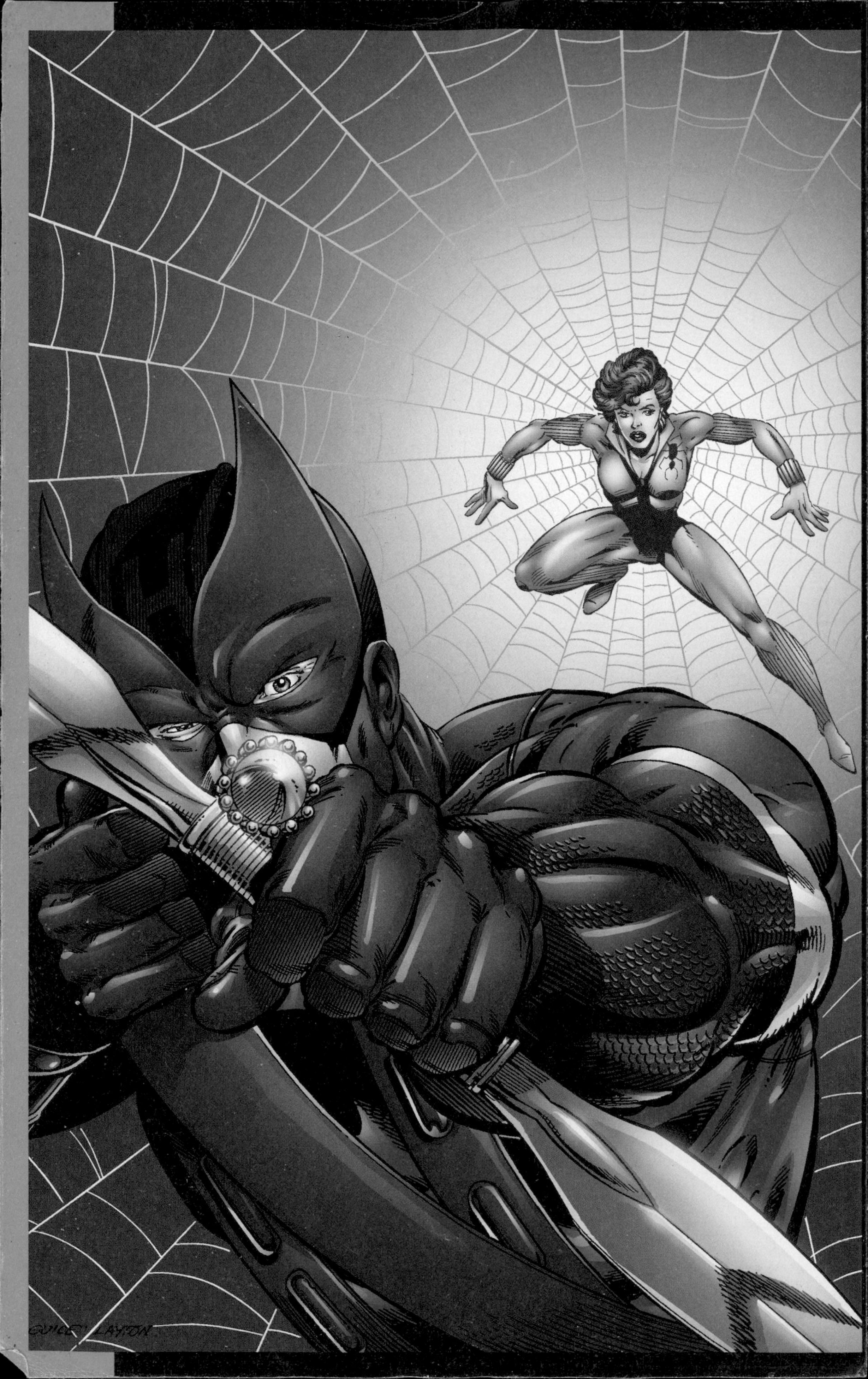
GUICE LAYTON